James Bryce

Transcaucasia and Ararat

Being Notes of a Vacation Tour in the Autumn of 1876. Third Edition

James Bryce

Transcaucasia and Ararat

Being Notes of a Vacation Tour in the Autumn of 1876. Third Edition

ISBN/EAN: 9783744752572

Printed in Europe, USA, Canada, Australia, Japan

Cover: Foto ©Andreas Hilbeck / pixelio.de

More available books at **www.hansebooks.com**

TRANSCAUCASIA

AND

ARARAT

GREAT AND LITTLE ARARAT FROM THE NORTH-EAST.

TRANSCAUCASIA

AND

ARARAT:

BEING

NOTES OF A VACATION TOUR IN THE AUTUMN OF 1876.

By JAMES BRYCE,

AUTHOR OF 'THE HOLY ROMAN EMPIRE.'

.

WITH COLOURED MAP.

THIRD EDITION.

London:

MACMILLAN AND CO.

1878.

PREFACE.

THE following pages contain a record of impressions received during a journey in the autumn of 1876 through Russia, the Caucasian countries, and the Turkish empire. They are first impressions only, for which no value can be claimed except that which belongs to impressions formed on the spot, and (as the author trusts) without a prejudice in favour of either of the states which are now contending in the regions here described. Yet even first impressions, if honestly formed, may sometimes atone for their crudity by their freshness. 'What most readers desire to know about a country is how it strikes a new-comer. A book that tries to give this, to present the general effect, so to speak, of the landscape, may have its function, even though it cannot satisfy the scientific student of geography or politics.

The author, however, did not travel with the intention of writing a book, nor would he, sensible as he is of his imperfect knowledge, have now thought of sending these notes to the press but for two reasons. One is the unexpected importance which the outbreak of war in the countries he visited has given to them.

The other is the urgency of his friends, whose curiosity regarding Mount Ararat has made him think it worth while to print a narrative of what he saw, and who assure him that some account of a mountain which every one has heard of, but about which comparatively little has been written, would be more interesting to English and American readers than he had at first supposed.

He is indebted to his friends Captain J. Buchan Telfer, R.N., Mr. Douglas W. Freshfield, and Professor Judd, of the Royal School of Mines, for information on several points, and returns his thanks to the Editor and proprietors of the 'Cornhill Magazine' for the permission they have given him to reprint the substance of an article which he contributed to that magazine in last May.

The publication of the book has been delayed by a domestic sorrow which has destroyed such pleasure as the composition of it might have given, the loss of one whose companion he had been in mountain expeditions from childhood, and to whom he owes whatever taste he possesses for geographical observation and for the beauties of nature.

LINCOLN'S INN, LONDON :
September 12, 1877.

CONTENTS.

CHAPTER I.

THE VOLGA AND THE STEPPE OF SOUTHERN RUSSIA.

(Pp. 1–41.)

	PAGE
Nijni Novgorod and its Fair ..	2
The Volga steamers and the life on board ..	5
Scenery of the Volga ..	11
Navigation of the river : trade on it ..	13
Kazan ..	15
The Jigoulef Hills ..	19
Saratof ..	22
Resemblances between Russia and the United States ..	23
Railway journey through the steppe to the Sea of Azof ..	30
Character of the steppe : impressions of its scenery ..	31
The Sea of Azof ..	37
From Rostof to the foot of the Caucasus ..	38

CHAPTER II.

THE CAUCASUS.

(Pp. 42–87.)

	PAGE
Structure of the Caucasian chain ..	42
Character of its scenery ..	46
Its historical importance ..	48
Peoples inhabiting the Caucasus ..	51

PAGE

Russian conquest of Daghestan and Circassia 56
Present political condition of the mountain country .. 59
The watering-places : Pjätigorsk 61
Railway to Vladikavkaz 67
Road over the main chain to Tiflis 69
The Dariel Pass : the Caucasian Gates 73
Mount Kazbek 77
Descent into Georgia : arrival at Tiflis 83

CHAPTER III.

TRANSCAUCASIA.

(Pp. 88–130.)

General physical character of Transcaucasia : its mountains and plains 89
Climate and vegetation : scenery 92
Natural productions 95
Inhabitants : Mingrelians ; Imeritians 97
Georgians or Grusinians ; Armenians 100
Tatars : their brigandage 105
Persians ; Russians ; Germans ; the mountain tribes .. 111
Russian government and administration 116
Impressions of the country, social and historical 123
Political future of Transcaucasia 125

CHAPTER IV.

TIFLIS.

(Pp. 131–156.)

Situation and aspect of the city 131
Divisions of the city : the Russian quarter 134
The Eastern town 135
The German colony 138

CONTENTS.

	PAGE
The inhabitants : mixture of races ; aspect of the streets ..	141
History of Tiflis	147
Walks and excursions : the Sololaki Hill : Kajori	151

CHAPTER V.

THROUGH ARMENIA TO ARARAT.

(Pp. 157-197.)

The steppe of the Kur valley ..	159
Alarms of robbers : the Red Bridge ..	162
Valley of the Akstafa : Delijan	165
The Goktcha Lake : Daratchitchak ..	168
Scenery of Armenia : Mount Ala Göz	171
Erivan : aspects of Eastern life	175
The Sardar's palace : the mosque	179
Drive through the Araxes plain	185
The Ford of the Araxes	189
Aralykh at the foot of Ararat ..	190
View of Ararat : ruins of Artaxata	193

CHAPTER VI.

ARARAT.

(Pp. 198-241.)

Various names of the mountain	198
Its identification with the Mountain of the Ark in Genesis	199
Notices of it in mediæval books of travel	204
Legends relating to it ..	208
General structure of the two Ararats	210
Geology : Abich's views stated	214
Volcanic phenomena : absence of central craters ..	217
Meteorology : great height of the snow-line ..	222
Vegetation	227
Animals ..	230

PAGE

General aspect : view of the mountain from the plains .. 231
Political importance of Ararat 233
Belief in its inaccessibility : recorded ascents 235
Great earthquake of 1840 239

CHAPTER VII.

THE ASCENT OF ARARAT.

(Pp. 242–293.)

The start from Aralykh 242
Ascent of the outer slopes 243
The Cossack station and well of Sardarbulakh 247
Kurdish shepherds at the well with their flocks 253
Climb by night from Sardarbulakh to the foot of the cone 258
Ascent of the great cone 264
Cossack and Kurd refuse to ascend further 266
The great snow basin : upper slope of rotten rock .. 273
The Summit 277
View from the summit 279
Descent to Sardarbulakh 285
Reach Aralykh : our Cossack escort 292
Impossibility of ascending Ararat 293

CHAPTER VIII.

ETCHMIADZIN AND THE ARMENIAN PEOPLE.

(Pp. 294–326.)

Road from Erivan to Etchmiadzin 294
Foundation of the Armenian church 297
Monastery of Etchmiadzin : the Cathedral 299
Relics : the hand of St. Gregory 302
The Seminary ; general impressions of the monastery .. 305
Sketch of Armenian history 311
The great Armenian emigration 314

PAGE

Present condition of the Armenians   317
Physical aspect of the Armenians : their language and
    literature   321
Their sufferings under Turkish rule   324

CHAPTER IX.

FROM ERIVAN TO THE BLACK SEA.

(Pp. 327–361.)

The Kurds : their character and history   327
The journey back from Erivan to Tiflis : alarms of robbers   330
Railways in the Caucasus   334
By rail from Tiflis to Gori   335
The rock city of Uphlis Tzikhé   339
Across the watershed into Mingrelia   345
Arrival at Poti : difficulties of embarkation   348
Poti and its inhabitants   351
Crossing the bar of the Phasis   357
View from the sea off Batum   359

CHAPTER X.

FROM POTI TO CONSTANTINOPLE BY THE BLACK SEA.

(Pp. 362–389.)

Batum and its port   362
Trebizond   363
Character of the Pontic coast..   367
Samsun and Sinope   369
The steamer and its passengers : Persians and Turkmans   372
Turks, Greeks, and Armenians   374
Franks ; mixture of languages   377
Condition of Asia Minor : melancholy impression it makes   378
Sail down the Bosphorus   382
Constantinople : first view of the city   384
Picturesqueness of its interior   388

CHAPTER XI.

SOME POLITICAL REFLECTIONS.

(Pp. 390–420.)

PAGE

Remarks on the state of Transcaucasia 390

Religion as a separating influence in the East 392

Difficulties of Russia in working her Asiatic territories .. 394

Annexation injurious to Russia 396

Impressions of Turkey : the Turks an army of occupation 398

The Turkish government is dying 402

Anarchy in the provinces 405

Is it possible to erect an Armenian state ? 406

Can the Turkish administration be reformed ? 408

Colonization 411

British interests : export trade to the Euxine 412

India and the Suez Canal 413

Influence of England in the East 415

Feelings towards England : her true policy 417

C | *K*

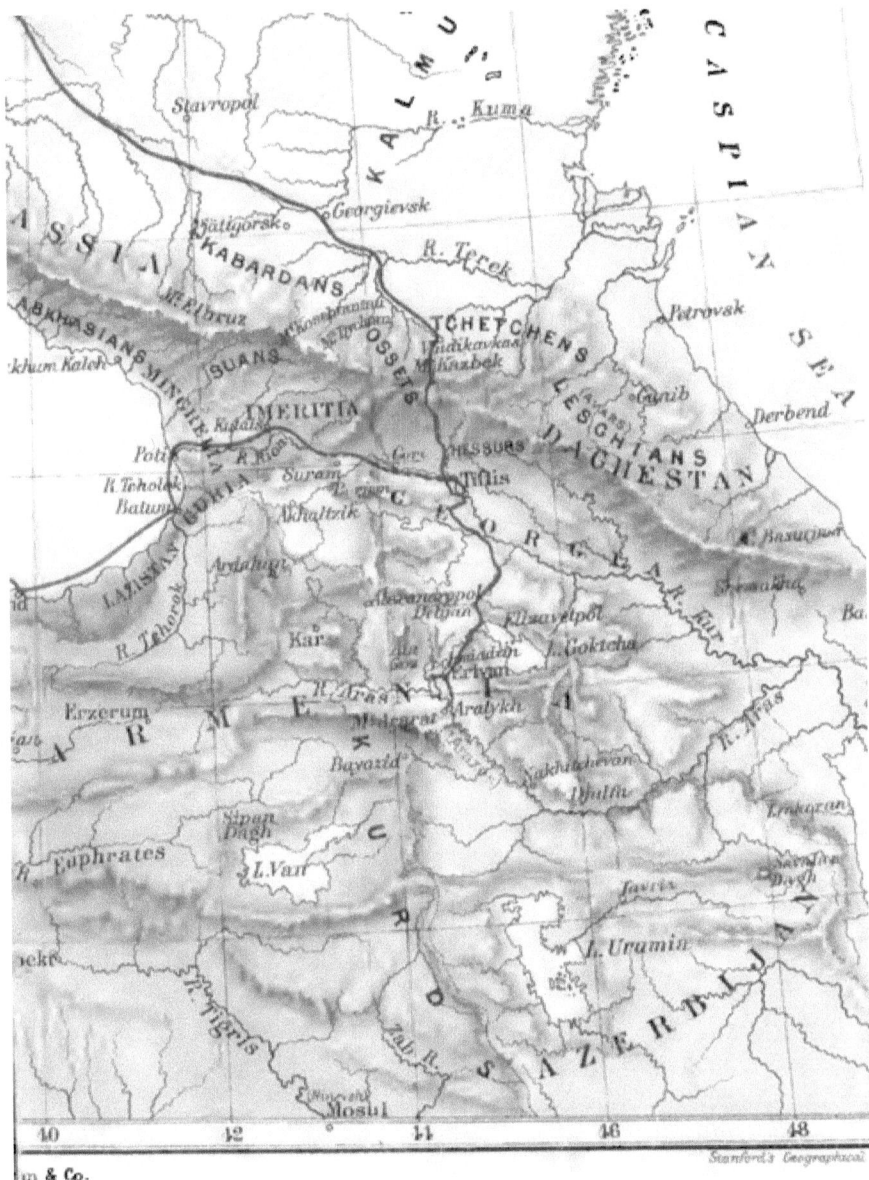

TRANSCAUCASIA AND ARARAT.

CHAPTER I.

NORTH-WESTERN Russia, although it is now pretty
easy of access from Western Europe, and contains
two such wonderfully striking cities as Moscow and
St. Petersburg, is very little visited by travellers.
South-eastern Russia is hardly visited at all. Nijni
Novgorod, whose great fair draws some few sight-
seers as well as men of business from Germany and
the farther west, seems to be the limit of the tourist,
and beyond it, all the way to Tiflis or Constantinople,
one does not see a single stranger travelling for
pleasure, and discovers from the attentions which the
western visitor receives, how rare such a visitor is.
I need, therefore, make no apology for giving some
short account of the Lower Volga, and the great steppe
of Southern Russia, before getting to the Caucasus
and Armenia, for all four are likely to be equally
unfamiliar to English readers. As this does not apply
to the gathering which has made Nijni famous, there
is no occasion to describe it here, especially as a full
account of the fair and its humours may be found in

B

a lively little book of collected letters published three years ago by Mr. Butler Johnstone. One or two observations, however, it is worth while to make by way of advice to future travellers.

People are constantly told that Nijni Fair is Oriental and picturesque, that they will find in it specimens of all the peoples of Eastern Europe and Western Asia, dressed and demeaning themselves each after its several kind—that it is in fact a sort of Eastern ethnological museum. This may have been true twenty years ago; it is not true now. The fair is picturesque, and in a certain way, which I will mention presently, more striking than one expects, but there is no longer any great richness of costume, any great variety of national types observable. Asiatic as well as European Russians have now, except in the peasant class, taken to Western fashions in dress, and so far as the outer man goes it is hard to tell a Siberian of Irkutsk from an Odessa or Riga merchant. The Finnish tribes from both sides of the Ural Mountains, and the various Turkish or Mongol tribes of the steppe, Kirghiz, Bashkirs, Kalmucks, and such like, are not represented, or at any rate not so as to be a noticeable feature; it is only the Persians and the few Turkmans who come from Tashkend or Bokhara that give anything of an Oriental character to the vast crowd, estimated at 100,000 people, that is gathered here every July. Nor, again, are there many beautiful articles to be seen exposed for sale. The display of jewellery was not larger or better than one might see in any two good shops in St. Petersburg; and the other goods shewn—silks and carpets from Tiflis and Persia, furs from Siberia, ornamental work of various kinds from different places in Russia —might have been bought as good, if not as cheap, in the bazaars of Moscow or in Regent Street. The interest of the fair lies deeper, and is matter for the economist or politician rather than for the artist.

Here one stands at the great centre of Russian commerce and influence, the heart which pulsates over Eastern Europe and the half of Asia. The limits of its influence, the remotest points whence people flock to attend it, are Teheran and Bokhara to the south-east, Kiakhta, on the Chinese frontier, to the east, Warsaw and Riga on the west. Over all this area Russia practically commands the markets, and here her manufactured goods, iron, pottery, cotton stuffs, and so forth, are exchanged for the caravan tea which has been brought across Siberia, carpets and silks from Persia, wool from Turkestan. The absence from the stalls of English, French, and German goods makes one realize how successful the Russian protective tariff has been in shutting out foreign competition; while the roughness and tastelessness of the home manufactures, which imitate Western patterns without Western finish, shew how little chance Russian manufacturers would as yet have against their neighbours in a fair field.

Here you have under your eyes, in the substantial form of long islands covered with Siberian or Uralian iron, of fleets laden with fish from Astrakhan, of a whole suburb built with bales of caravan tea, the evi-

dence of those movements and relations of trade
which the imagination usually finds it so hard to
realize, and which are such mighty factors in social as
well as political history. The scene speaks not only
of the vastness of the scale on which this trade goes
on, but also of the rude and undeveloped condition
of the countries that support it, where the mechanism
of exchange and distribution is still so imperfectly
organized that men are obliged to see one another
and to bring their wares to this central spot to be displayed, instead of trusting to agencies and correspond-
ence. This concourse of merchants, and many details
of the business done, which can only be understood
when they are actually seen, do therefore present
enough that is interesting and curious to repay the
trouble of a journey hither. And there is one view,
at least, too striking to be forgotten by any one who
has enjoyed it, I mean the *coup d'œil* over the whole
fair from the Mouravief Tower. To the east, one sees
Nijni town, whose ancient kremlin (citadel) and green-
domed cathedral crowns the lofty southern bank of
the Oka ; in front are the two great tranquil streams—
Volga and Oka—each a quarter of a mile wide,
bearing on their bosoms thousands of vessels from
every part of the vast water system of Russia ; between them lies the Fair itself, long streets of brick
warehouses, booths, and tents, bubbling and throbbing
with the busy crowd, which pours to and fro, on foot
and in carriages, across the bridge of boats that joins
the Fair to the city ; while round all lies a boundless
green plain, along which the straining eye follows the

three shining lines of water till they sink below the far horizon.

We steamed away from Nijni on the morning of August 24th, threading our way through an endless crowd of vessels laden with iron, fish, and wood. As the last masts and domes vanished behind us, we felt as if entering a new world, borne along by the strong majestic stream to the mysterious East—the East which discovery has so spared that it is now less known and more mysterious than the West. One thing, however, remained to remind one forcibly, almost ludicrously, of the West, I mean the steamboat that carried us, which was built exactly on the pattern of those that ply on the Hudson or the Mississippi. Of her three decks, one was almost level with the water, and occupied by the third class passengers ; a second, raised above the last, contained the first and second class saloons ; and a third, which was open, formed the roof of the saloons, and supplied a pleasant promenade. She was a swift as well as light and handsome boat, drawing, when half loaded, only four feet of water, and a jolly old Russian admiral who was on board, and seemed, from the authority he assumed, to be a director of the company that owned her, insisted on showing us over every nook and cranny of her, with an air that seemed to doubt whether England could produce her like. Everything seemed clean and trim and comfortable enough during the day ; the saloon especially, opening immediately on the deck, with windows which commanded a view of both banks, was a better sitting-room than one often finds in an English vessel. But at night we could not help regretting the snug berths of an American steamer. For in Russia there are (speaking generally) only two classes of travellers, those to whom expense incurred for comfort and propriety is nothing, and those to whom comfort and propriety are scarcely known. The former carry their own bedding about with them; the latter do not go to bed at all, but coil themselves up in their sheepskins and go to sleep wherever it may happen. The large and respectable middle class of Germany or France, who want comfort, but cannot afford luxury or lordly independence, do not exist. Hence, in all hotels, except the very best, and everywhere in the steamers, you get no blankets and sheets except by special arrangement, and have always a sort of sense of bivouacking in your rug or great-coat. That was what had to be done here in the little sofa cabins round the saloon.

As regards food there was nothing to complain of. Russia is eminently a land of good cooking ; even the simple *stchi*, or cabbage broth, on which one often has to fall back, is usually tasty and nourishing, and here, with sterlet and sturgeon swimming about him, and cooks who know how to make the most of their materials, an epicure might have been content. The sterlet soup, of which the Russians are so fond of talk- ing, quite answers its reputation, and other dishes whose names I forget are hardly less famous. Our only difficulty about dinner was how to order it, for *table d'hôte* is the rare exception in Russia, and none of the steward's staff spoke anything but Russian or

Tatar.[1] The waiters in Russian inns and steamers are usually Tatars ; most of them come from Riazan or Penza, and are good-looking fellows enough, but some are downright Kalmucks in face. So when six o'clock arrived, we had to hunt up and down the boat for some good-natured passenger who talked French or German, and through him convey our wishes. Fortunately the good-nature of Russians is boundless, and here, where a traveller is so rare, he is an object of special interest and goodwill, who is talked to about the country and its prospects as if he were an ambassador, or even a special correspondent. This friendliness was all the pleasanter because we had hardly expected it. Everyone had said to us in St. Petersburg, "You have come at a bad time. Our people are greatly exasperated against England. They regard you as the abettors of the Turks, as the accomplices in the Bulgarian massacres." (This was just after the great massacres of May had become known in Russia and before the English indignation meetings in September.) "They think that you prefer Mohammedans to Christians, and for your own selfish purposes—heaven knows what they are—are ready to support and justify all the oppressions and cruelties of the Turks. So when you get away from this cosmopolitan town up to Moscow and the interior of our country, you must be prepared to meet with rudeness, perhaps even with insults."

[1] The spelling " Tatar," instead of the old and admittedly erroneous "Tartar," seems to be now sufficiently well established for an unscientific writer to adopt it.

Nothing of the kind. I am bound to say that we never fell into talk with a Russian without being reproached with our sympathy for the Turks. It was always assumed that we, as Englishmen, of course stood over the massacres, and we were asked how we could be so unchristian. Indeed to most people's minds England appeared scarcely less guilty than the Porte, for was it not England that by rejecting the Berlin Memorandum had stopped the joint action of the Six Powers? Was it not the English fleet at Besika Bay and the English envoy at Constantinople that encouraged Turkey to harden her heart? But even the reproaches were made with perfect courtesy. Whether one would have been better treated two years before, I cannot say, but considering the prodigious excitement that reigned—an excitement that pervaded all classes, and which seemed to us to have little to do with Panslavic theories, and still less with schemes of territorial aggression—it was a wonder to me that, being generally recognized as Englishmen, we were treated so well.

Except a few Persians and Turkmans from Bokhara, who performed their devotions towards Mecca with exemplary regularity, the passengers seemed to be all Russian subjects, though several were Germans, natives either of Germany or of the Baltic Provinces. Two or three of the others, as well as the captain, who was an officer in the imperial navy, spoke French or a little English, so that one was not ill off for opportunities of talk. But it is quite a mistake to suppose, as is commonly believed in England, and as the Russians them-

selves are always telling you, that in Russia everybody
in the better classes speaks one or more foreign languages.   The high nobility do, no doubt, speak French
as well as the Parisians themselves, though the growth
of national spirit and of what are called Slavophil
principles makes them use it less than formerly;
many of their daughters, who are often educated by
English governesses, speak English also, while scientific and literary people, professors, engineers, and
such like, must of course know German.   But the
ordinary Russian, not merely the shopkeeper, merchant, and priest or monk, but the officer, civil
servant, or lower noble, is confined to his mother
tongue.   One meets in travelling with enormous
numbers of officers—they are all in uniform and seem
to form half the population of the country—and most
of them shake their heads when you accost them in
either French or German.   In fact I do not believe
that a knowledge of foreign languages is any more
common than in England, or as common as it is in
Germany.   The difference rather is that those who
do speak French or German speak it more fluently
than we.   And the popular notion on the subject
seems to have arisen partly from this fact, partly
because most Englishmen form their impressions from
the high society, or from the commercial society, of
the capital (which is itself quite an exceptional place,
no more typical of Russia than New York is of
America), and partly from the abundance of Germans
scattered all over the country and filling so many
civil and military, educational and scientific posts.   It

is upon these Germans that he who travels without a
courier or a knowledge of Russian has chiefly to rely ;
and it will go hard with him if on a steamer, or at a
railway station, or in a baker's or druggist's shop in one
of the bigger towns, he cannot find such an one willing
to interpret for the nonce. Failing these, he is indeed
badly off. For there are so few words common to the
Slavonic languages with the Teutonic or Romance,
and the alphabet is at first so puzzling, that it is hard
to remember even the common names of things, or to
decipher a railway time-table.

There was an oddly miscellaneous little library on
board, consisting apparently of the leavings of many
travellers, mainly Russian, but with several French
novels and about as many solid German treatises, and
two books in English. One of these last was a record
of spiritual manifestations in America, whose presence
there surprised a Russian acquaintance of ours, for all
spiritualistic writings are strictly prohibited by the
police, and this, instead of lying about on the cabin
table, ought to have been seized at the frontier, and
reserved for the private enjoyment of the censor.
There is a very comprehensive *Index Expurgatorius*
in Russia, and people often told me they found their
best Western books carried off by the custom-house,
never to reappear. But, as every body knows, Alexander Herzen's revolutionary 'Kolokol' found its way
everywhere, and was read by all the officials up to
the Emperor himself; and the same is said to be the
case with the less brilliant socialist writers of to-day.
The other book was 'Scenes of Clerical Life,' whose

pictures of an English country town, with its gossips,
quarrels, and sorrows, lit up by a noble life like that of
Mr. Tryon in 'Janet's Repentance,' had **never seemed
so** vivid as when read in this far-off land, and set side
by side with **the** parallel, yet wonderfully dissimilar,
glimpses of Russian life which were given us in the
pages of a scarcely less wonderful genius, Ivan
Turgenef.

Of all modes of travelling, a river steamboat is
probably the pleasantest. **It is** exhilarating to rush
through the **air** at a pace of eighteen miles an hour,
the swift current adding several miles to what the
strong engines can accomplish. One moves freely
about, reads or writes when so inclined, sits down and
chats with a fellow passenger, enjoys to perfection the
bracing freshness of the air and the changing hues of
sunset. All this is to be had on the Volga steamers,
plus the delightful sense of novelty ; and although the
scenery is not striking, it may be called pleasing, quite
good enough to see once. Mr. Mackenzie Wallace
(whose very interesting book I assume to be known
to any one who reads this one[1]) thinks the Volga
tame, but I cannot help fancying this is because the
Russians, who are eager to make the most of everything their country can shew, had talked too much to
him about it. We, who expected only a muddy stream
between dull, flat banks, were agreeably surprised by
the reality. Of course, it is not so grand as the Danube
is above the Iron Gate, or the Douro between the wine

[1] It may be proper to say that this chapter was written before I had
read more than a very little of Mr. Wallace's book.

country and Oporto, nor comparable in point of beauty
with the richly wooded Upper Mississippi, or the
Rhine, or the Upper Elbe. It is altogether in a less
ambitious style than any of these, so that one is not
even reminded of them. But in its own quiet way it is
enjoyable, and the more so from the contrast between
the two shores. All the way down from Yaroslaf till
near the Caspian the right bank is high, from 120 to
160 or even 200 feet above the stream, generally steep,
often prettily wooded, or cut down by picturesque
little gullies filled with brushwood. On this side one
sees no cultivation, though here and there a village
nestles between the hill and the shore, or crowns the
top of the slope with the green cupola of its church
glittering afar off under the sun ; and might fancy
that one was sailing down through a half-occupied
pastoral land. But up behind, on the table-land of
which this steep bank is the edge, there is a well-
peopled country, full of farms and villages, with a
soil which, away down southward beyond Kazan,
becomes exceedingly fertile. The opposite, the left
or north-eastern bank, is perfectly flat ; first a belt
of sand covered by the stream in the floods of
spring, then willows and alders, then pastures and
cornfields with patches of wood between, and here and
there a low ridge, hardly to be called an eminence,
stretching away farther than the eye can reach. Between this boundless plain and this bold hill the
Volga sweeps along in majestic curves and reaches,
and the contrast between the two, the varying aspects
which the promontories take as one approaches and

recedes from them, give a pleasing variety to the landscape. Except at one point, you cannot call it beautiful, but it is all so green and so peaceful, the air is so exquisitely clear, there is such a sense of expanse in the wide plain and the sky vaulted over it, the stream down which one speeds is so wide, and calm, and strong, that there is a pleasure in the voyage it is easier to feel than describe.

The ship touches but seldom at the banks, for there are few towns, and when she does stop, it is rather for the sake of taking in wood than of passengers or cargo. A gang of women is usually waiting for us at the wharf, who carry on board bundles of chopped wood; while all the spare population of the villages comes down in its sheepskins and stands looking on, munching its cucumbers the while. Sheepskins, with the woolly side turned in, are the usual summer as well as winter wear of the peasants in these parts. As for cucumbers, the national passion for them is something wonderful. They are set down at every meal in hotels and steamers, while the poorer folk seem to live pretty much upon them and bread. If I were asked to characterise the most conspicuous externals of Russia in three words, they should be "sheepskins, cucumbers, emeralds."[1] We meet or overtake plenty of vessels, sometimes making slow way under sail, sometimes towed by a tug, sometimes working themselves up by the primitive contrivance of an anchor and wind-

---

[1] The profusion of fine gems, especially emeralds, rubies, and sapphires, you are shewn in geological and antiquarian collections, sewn on to sacerdotal vestments, stuck on to the gold plates with which the sacred pictures are overlaid, is extraordinary.

lass, the anchor carried up-stream for several hundred yards and dropped, and the ship hauled up to it by winding up the anchor cable with the windlass. But these vessels are nearly all laden either with fish from Astrakhan, to feed the peasantry of the central provinces, or with iron or copper from Siberia and the Ural on its way to the manufacturing district of Tula.

Local traffic there is very little; for the country is peopled only by peasants whose life is simple, and whose wants are few. Many villages are not even Russian, but belong to some of the various Finnish tribes — Tchouvasses, Tcheremisses, Mordvins — who formerly occupied the whole of this region, though most of them have now adopted, or are fast adopting, the religion, customs, and tongue of their Slavonic masters. In another half-century the country will be completely Russian.

But the through traffic, as a railway man would say, is great and still increasing, and for its sake the government have taken some pains with the Volga navigation, which the numerous shoals and sandspits render very troublesome. Buoys are anchored in many dangerous spots, landmarks are placed along the shore, and at night coloured lights are shewn. Although our steamer drew only four feet of water there were so many shoals and sandbanks about, that, instead of holding an even course down the middle of the stream, she was perpetually darting across it from the one shore to the other, so as to keep in the deepest part of the channel. Whenever one of the shallower parts was reached a bell was rung, which brought some of the crew forward, and one of them took his place armed with a long pole, the lower part of which was marked in colours, just like the "stick" in croquet, each foot's length having a different colour. This pole he nimbly plunged into the water just before the bow, till it touched the bottom, and then seeing by the marks on it what the depth was, he sang out, "vosem," "sem," "shest" (eight, seven, six), as the case might be, the vessel still advancing. As the smaller numbers began to be reached, a slight thrill ran through the group that watched, and when "piat" (five) followed, the engines were slowed or stopped in a moment, and we glided softly along over the shoal till "sem," "vosem," "deviat" (nine), following in succession, told .that the risk of grounding was for the moment past.

Watching these manœuvres, and the constantly changing yet singularly uniform landscapes which revealed themselves as we rounded one promontory after another, time wore pleasantly on, till about noon on the second day we saw the towers of the famous city of Kazan rise above the low north-eastern shore, and found that there was just time to drive there and back in a swift droshky, so that to the end of one's life one might talk of having done Kazan. Though in our maps Kazan appears as standing on the Volga, it is really nearly three miles from the summer bed of the stream, on an eminence beyond a flat piece of ground over which the spring floods pour. The country round is so level that the hill, which is covered by its kremlin, seems quite imposing, albeit only some forty feet high. This elevation, with the battlements of the kremlin wall, two or three old towers, and the blue and gilded domes of the churches, gives the city from a distance a somewhat lordly look, not unworthy of the former capital of a great Tatar Khanate. Inside, however, it is disappointing to find scarcely a trace of antiquity. One of the towers of the kremlin, a curious pyramid of brick, is said to come down from the days of independence, but the rest was destroyed and rebuilt by the Czar Ivan the Terrible (a contemporary of Queen Elizabeth), and the town, like most places in Russia, has been so often burnt down that now everything is new. Long straight streets with stuccoed houses, a university with a stiff Corinthian portico (columns also of stucco) and dreary corridors to right and left, official buildings without end, and shops with glass fronts to them, give it an air of respectability and civilization very different from most Russian towns, which are chiefly open spaces of grass or mud, interrupted here and there by brick cottages and wooden shanties. But there is nothing except a few slender minarets in the lower town to betray that Oriental character which we had been wont to associate with its sounding Oriental name. Among the people in the streets, who were few enough, there were some with the black sheepskin hats which the Tatars affect; otherwise there was little to distinguish them from ordinary Russians. However, the truth is that the diversity of blood in all this part of the country gives rise to many types of face, and one finds it hard to say which is the true Russian. In the

centre, between Kief, Moscow, and Petersburg, there
is no doubt a purer Slavonic race; but in these
more easterly governments the Muscovites are only
comparatively recent colonists among Finnish and
Turkish tribes. The Tatars of Kazan, who are no
doubt Turks, retain not only their language and
their religion but their social usages; they rarely or
never intermarry with the Russians, but otherwise live
on good enough terms with them, and do not seem to
complain of the Christian government, which has been
wise enough not to meddle with their faith. Since the
fall of their Khanate three hundred years ago, they
have rarely given any trouble, and now serve in the
army like other subjects of the Czar. They are usually
strong men, lithe and sinewy, of a make more spare
than that of the Russians, and do most of the hard
work both here, in their own country, and at Nijni
and other trading spots along the river. In their
faces is seen a good deal of that grave fixity which
gives a dignity even to the humblest Oriental, and
contrasts so markedly with the mobile features of the
Slav.

Sailing away from Kazan, and seeing its glittering
towers and domes sink slowly from view into the
boundless plain, we inquired from everyone we could
talk to about the ruins of the ancient capital of the
Bulgarians, which are said to exist some few miles
from the river to the east, huge shapeless mounds
which are now the only memorial of a kingdom older
than any of the Russian principalities, a kingdom
which flourished in the sixth and seventh centuries,

C

before the Bulgarian hordes descended into the Danube
valley to vex the Byzantine emperors. But no one
knew anything of the ruins ; indeed I doubt if any one
on board had heard of them before. Archæology,
except perhaps as a branch of hagiology, or in the
learned circles of St. Petersburg and Moscow, has
scarcely begun to exist in Russia ; it is one of the
latest births of time everywhere, and, as one may see
from the fate of so many of our own pre-historic
monuments, does not commend itself to the practical
mind of the agriculturist. The only countries in which
the traveller finds the common people knowing and
revering the monuments and legends of their remote
past are Norway and Iceland, where the sagas read
aloud in the long nights of winter from manuscripts
preserved in lonely farm-houses, have through many
generations fired the imagination and ennobled the
life of the peasant, who knew no other literature and
history than that of his own ancestors.

Below Kazan the scenery of the river remains
much the same for many miles. On the east the
Kama comes in, a majestic stream, about one-third of
a mile wide, bearing on its calm bosom flotillas of
vessels laden with iron from Perm and the Ural, and
tea brought by caravan across Siberia. After the
confluence the Volga is not at first sensibly wider, but
it grows deeper, and the steamer, instead of flitting
like a dragon-fly hither and thither across the current,
holds on an even course down the middle, leaving on
the left a labyrinth of low and generally wooded isles.
Gradually the bank on the right increases in height,
and strata of chalk begin to crop out on its face, till

at last we reach the Jigoulef hills, the most beautiful
piece of scenery on the whole river, and one which
would be beautiful even in a country far more attractive
than Russia. Hills four to six hundred feet high rise
steeply on the right bank of the stream, clothed with
luxuriant wood, beech, hazel, birch, oak, hornbeam,
and other deciduous trees, their autumnal gold and
scarlet mingled here and there with the dark green of
fir clumps, their slopes cut deep by ravines and bushy
little dells, where a patch of sunny greensward is seen
through the boughs beside a sparkling brook. Imagine
this wealth of wood interrupted here and there by a
miniature cliff of blue limestone, crowning the summit
of some jutting promontory, and the whole mirrored
in the glassy flood that pours along, deep and strong,
but smooth and silent as a lake, with ridge after ridge
and bay after bay down the long vista of its banks,
and you have a picture to which all Russia, from the
Euxine to the Frozen Sea, cannot supply the like. The
elements of beauty in it are so simple that one is half
surprised to find the result so beautiful. Perhaps this
is partly because we English are so little accustomed
to great rivers that they make a correspondingly profound impression on us, the sense of their grandeur
and of the tremendous part they play in the development of countries and nations giving them a power
over the imagination which enhances even the visual
perception of their beauty.

All along this range of hills which borders the
stream for more than twenty miles, there is not a
house or sign of life visible; but up behind, on the

level ground stretching out to the south and west, the
land is richly cultivated, and indeed constitutes one of
the largest and best cultivated estates in all Russia,
the property of Count Orloff Davydoff, who owns the
whole country enclosed in that remarkable bend of
the Volga, which may be seen on any map of Europe
between Simbirsk and Saratof. Just at the eastern-
most point of the bend the river turns south, breaking
through the Jigoulef ridge which has bordered it for
twenty miles, and here, at the town of Samara, one
seems suddenly to pass, as if through a gate in the
hills, from Europe into Asia. Up to this point all
has been green, moist, fresh-looking, the air soft
though brilliantly clear, the grass not less juicy than
in England, the wayside flowers and trees very similar
to our own, if not always of the same species. But
once through the hills, and looking away south-east
across the boundless steppe towards Orenburg and
the Ural river, a different climate and scenery reveal
themselves. The air is hot and dry, the parched
earth gapes under the sun, the hills are bare, or
clothed only with withered weeds; plants and shrubs
of unfamiliar aspect appear, the whole landscape has
a tawny torrid look, as if of an African desert.
Henceforth, all the way to the Black Sea, one felt
one's self in the glowing East, and seemed at a glance
to realize the character of the wilderness that stretches
from here all the way, a plain with scarcely a mound
to break its monotony, to the banks of the Oxus and
the foot of the Thian Shan mountains.

Along the first part of this great plain the Russians

were then building a railway, the terminus of which, not quite completed, we saw at Samara. It has now been opened as far as Orenburg, a distance of 280 miles, and they talk of carrying it on from Orenburg to Tashkend, the present capital of their dominions in Turkestan. The distance, however, is so great—over 1200 miles by the present route—and money is so scarce, that this is not likely to be soon accomplished ; although it would immensely strengthen their hold upon Central Asia, enabling troops and supplies to pass from the Volga to the Jaxartes in three days, instead of four or five weeks. As the country is flat, with only one great river, the Ural or Yaik, to be bridged, the construction of the line would not present grave difficulties ; but all the wood for sleepers would have to be carried along as the rails were laid, the steppe being perfectly bare, station-houses must be built, men must be kept to clear the line of snow, and the traffic would not for many years, or perhaps centuries, to come be sufficient to cover the expenses of working. The Russians, who are eager to become a great commercial nation, would no doubt find an easier market for their goods in Central Asia ; but those countries are too thinly peopled, and too likely to remain so, to make even this an object of great consequence. If the railway is made, it will be for military rather than for commercial reasons.

From Samara onwards (a town famous for the "cure" of koumiss or fermented mare's milk, which is said to be so efficacious in consumption and some other complaints) the river scenery becomes less

interesting. On the east, one has always the bare
steppe, stretching farther than eye can reach in an
unbroken flat. On the west, ridges of brown, or red,
or yellow hills run along the river, breaking down to
it in cliffs of limestone, the strata perfectly horizontal
—cliffs not high enough to be fine, with never a wood,
and seldom a village. The stream itself, though wider
than it was above, hardly seems so, on account of the
numerous arms, enclosing low woody islands, into
which it divides itself. Hearing that it was still more
monotonous farther down towards Astrakhan, and
that that city, spite of its high-sounding Oriental
name, was only a second-rate modern Russian town,
full of dried fish and fever, we determined to quit the
steamer at Saratof,[1] and travel thence to the Caucasus by railway, running first west into the heart of
the country, and then south across the great steppe
to the Sea of Azof. By this time nearly all the cabin
passengers had gone, but the lower deck was still
crowded with Armenians and Persians bound for
Astrakhan, whence they were to proceed, by another
steamer of the same company, across the Caspian to
Baku in Transcaucasia, or to Lenkoran on the frontiers of Persia. We took leave with some regret of
these picturesque groups and of the majestic stream,
which we never expected to see again ; and, landing
at Saratof, climbed the high brown hills that rise above
it to take a last look over the solemn eastern steppe,
still for the most part left to the rude tribes of Kirghiz
and Bashkirs that wander over it with their flocks and

---

[1] Pronounced Sarātof.

their tents of felt, but destined, such is the fertility of its soil, to wave one day from end to end with luxuriant harvests.

Travellers are fond of talking of the Oriental character of Russia ; and though the smart saying about scratching Russians and finding Tatars is pretty well exploded (nobody can be essentially less like a Tatar than the Russian is), there are, no doubt, certain points, mostly mere externals, in which Russian towns, or Russian usages, recall those of the East. For instance, the cupolas of churches are covered outside with tiles or iron plates of gay colours, and in the interior the most honourable places are the corners, in which, therefore, czars, patriarchs, and other great folk, are buried. The houses (except in the greatest cities) are low, buying and selling goes on chiefly in the bazaars, the horses carry loud jangling bells, people prostrate themselves at worship, instead of merely bowing or kneeling ; and when you ask for water, they do not give you a basin, but they pour water on your hands. Such resemblances as these are only natural ; the wonder is, considering that Russia had for many centuries closer relations with the East than with the West, that there are not many more of them. What is far more curious is to find on the Volga so many things and ways in Russia which remind one of America ; points of resemblance between nations apparently as far removed from one another in manners, religion, history, and government, as they are in space. I amused myself in noting down some of these points of resemblance—those which are merely

external and accidental, as well as those which really
have a meaning—and give the list for what it is worth.

Both are big countries. Their extent is immense,
and everything in them is on a vast scale—rivers,
forests, lakes, distances. One thinks little of a journey
of a thousand miles. Land, being so abundant, is of
little value ; hence, partly, it is that in both a town
covers so great an area, with its wide streets, its
gardens, its unutilized open spaces. Hence we find in
the middle of settled districts ground that has never
been touched by plough, or spade, or axe. Hence
agriculture is apt to be wasteful, because, when the
soil grows less productive, he who tills it can move
elsewhere.

Both are new countries. Although the Russian
race and kingdom are old enough, they have occupied
most of their present territory no longer than our
colonists America, while they have been learning the
arts of civilization only since the days of Peter the
Great, and have acquired them very imperfectly even
now. Material development is therefore still incom-
plete, and is the first thing in every one's thoughts,
the thing to which the energies of the people are
mainly devoted. Literature and science have struck
root, but have not yet had time to grow high or spread
their branches. Things are still pretty much in the
rough,—have what we should call a colonial air about
them ; streets are ill-paved, public buildings are unfinished, there is a mixture of magnificent designs
with imperfect accomplishment. It is chiefly raw
material that the country produces, timber, corn, and

cattle ; the finer kinds of manufacture are still backward, and so, on the whole, is art.   The general want
of settledness is seen in the ease with which the population move from place to place.   Single workmen
wander over the whole country ; a peasant family
thinks little of migrating from the central provinces to
the steppes of the far south.

Both are countries whose interest lies in the future
rather than in the past.   Indeed Russia has less of a
past than America, seeing that the latter has the past
of England, whereas Russian history is a very twilight
sort of business till the great Polish war of the six-
teenth century.   Names of czars and patriarchs can be
given, and a few famous battles fixed, but in the main
it is an uncertain as well as dreary record of family
quarrels between savage princes and incessant border
warfare with the Tatar hordes.   Russia has comparatively few great characters or great historic scenes to
look back to ; all the more, therefore, must she look
forward and scan the new horizon that rises towards
her.   Like America, she sees a prodigious territory,
much of it wonderfully fertile, magnificent stores of
minerals, undeveloped regions lying beyond the limits
of her present settlements ; and she cannot but indulge
in many schemes and fancies for the future.   An educated Russian, like an American, is penetrated by a
sense of the great destiny reserved for his country,
and is apt to carry the sort of sanguine temperament
which this feeling breeds into his private concerns.
People venture boldly, live expensively, enjoy and
indulge the moment, confident that things will some-

how come right in the long run. No nations are so
fond of speculating, writing and talking about themselves[1]; readers of Turgenef need only be reminded
of what goes on among the Russians at Baden-Baden,
in his famous novel 'Smoke,' which gave so much
offence at home. Not unconnected with this is their
tendency to sudden impressions and waves of feeling.
Naturally a susceptible, perhaps an inconstant, certainly an impatient, people, the Russians are apt to be
intoxicated by the last new idea or doctrine ; and
their lively sympathy makes a feeling, belief, enthu-
siasm, that has once been started, spread like wild-fire
through the whole educated, sometimes even down
into the uneducated, class. This is less the case in
America, but several of the political and social movements we can remember there, like Know-nothingism
and (in a somewhat different way) the women's whisky
war, seem to illustrate the same kind of temper.

Being new, and feeling themselves new, both are
extremely sensitive to the opinion of older countries,
and anxious sometimes to compel, more often to con-
ciliate, the admiration of their neighbours. In Russia,
as in America, the first question put to the stranger is,
"What do you think of our country ?" and an appre-
ciative answer is received with a thrill of pleasure
which a German or an English breast would never
experience on the like occasion. With all their
patriotic self-confidence, they have a consciousness of
having but just entered the circle of civilization, and
are pleased to be re-assured. They are, therefore, like

[1] This, however, has very much diminished in America of late years.

the Americans, eager to learn what foreigners think of them, they do everything they can to set off the good points of the country, both physical and social ; and they are apt to be unduly annoyed at hostile criticism, even when it proceeds from foolish or ignorant people. It is partly perhaps for the same reason, as well as from the dominant officialism, that they are more particular in some small points of social etiquette (the wearing a black coat, for instance, or the use of appropriate titles in addressing a comparative stranger) than people are in countries where the rules of etiquette are so old that every educated man may be assumed to know them. It does not satisfy them that their material greatness should be fully admitted ; they wish to be recognized as the equals of Western Europe in social and intellectual progress, and insist, as many American writers used to do, on their mission to diffuse new economical and social principles.

Among minor points of similarity that strike one, may be named the mysterious element that underlies their politics—here, as in America, one hears a great deal of talk about secret societies, and cannot quite make out what these societies amount to (I do not believe they are really dangerous to the Government) ; the attitude of women, who are here more aspiring, independent, and, in the slang sense of the term, "advanced," than anywhere else in Europe ; the development of strange sects, such as the Duchobortz and Molokans, and semi-religious, semi-socialist communities ; the forwardness of children, who are much more seen and indulged than in France or Germany ; the costliness of inns, of living, of manufactured

goods, indeed of almost everything except locomo-
tion ; the corruption of officials (or at least the general
belief in such corruption, for whether it really exists
I do not venture to pronounce) ; even the structure
of railway cars and steamboats, which seems to have
been borrowed from America, and is certainly preferable to what one finds in the rest of Europe ;
and, lastly, the general good-nature and easy-going
friendly ways of the people, who, like the Americans,
are far more willing to make friends with and do
their best for a stranger, if only he will shew some
little politeness and some little interest in the country,
than are either the French, or the Germans, or ourselves.

Of course I am not insensible to the many striking
contrasts between the two nations, the most striking
of which is that in Russia there is, speaking broadly,
no middle class, but only an upper and a lower, and
that lower almost entirely uneducated and politically
powerless. In America there is nothing but middle-
class, a middle-class which is well-taught, intelligent,
political to the marrow of its bones. Any one can
draw out for himself all the differences which flow
from this one, and from the singular unlikeness of
religions. But the curious thing is to find in the face
of these differences so many points of resemblance.

Saratof is one of the largest towns in Russia—that
is to say, it has a population of 80,000 people, scattered over a space of some four or five miles square,
the meanest streets being as wide as Regent Street, and
the main ones twice as wide. It lies high above the
Volga in a shelf-like recess among the bare hills, burnt

up in August to a dismal brown, and so dry that a dust-
cloud raised by the least wind is perpetually hanging
over the town, just as smoke-clouds do over Sheffield
or Manchester. Like most towns in Russia, it has
absolutely nothing in the way of a sight, not even a
provincial museum or an old church; everything is
modern, common-place, and uninteresting, and life
itself, one would think, must partake of the same
character. The only thing to remember it by, besides
its splendid situation, looking out over the Volga and
the great steppe, was the more than usually large
proportion of Germans among the people, a lucky
thing for the traveller asking his way, and one which
gave to many of the houses an appearance of snug
neatness distinctly Teutonic; for though your Slav
is sometimes magnificent, he is rarely comfortable.
All this part of Russia, down the river as far as
Tzaritsyn, is full of German colonies, planted by
Catherine II. in the hope that they would teach
cleanliness, neatness, and comfort, and, above all,
good methods of agriculture, to their Russian neighbours—a hope which has not been realized, for they
have remained for the most part quite distinct, living
in their own villages, not intermarrying with the
Muscovites, often remaining ignorant of their language. By far the most prosperous of these colonies
belong to the Mennonite or Moravian persuasions,
who thrive as the Quaker colonists throve in America.
But now one hears that they are mostly leaving Russia
altogether, fearing the enforcement of the new law of
universal conscription. To them, who hold war a

sin, service in the army is a more serious evil than emigration to Canada; and they appeal to the promise Catherine made that they should never be so required to violate their conscientious scruples. The government is perplexed: it does not wish to break faith, but, like all governments, it hates making exceptions, especially invidious exceptions in favour of people who do not hold the national faith.

At Saratof we took the railway which carried us with only two changes of carriage all the way to the foot of the Caucasus, a journey of 1100 miles, which occupied from Sunday afternoon to Wednesday afternoon. We had intended to descend the Volga as far as Tzaritsyn, cross over to the Don at Kalatch, and descend the Don by steamer; but finding that there was only one, or at most two steamers a week on the Don, that the steamer would probably have started from Kalatch just before we arrived there, that the duration of her voyage could not even be guessed at, since most of the time was spent in getting her off the sandbanks on which she was constantly grounding, and finally that the only way of escaping the voracious crowds of mosquitoes was to fling oneself into the river, which, however, was too shallow to afford the relief of drowning, we abandoned this idea, and preferred even the fatigue of seventy continuous hours in a railway car. Fortunately that fatigue turned out a great deal less than we had expected. In no country, except America, is railway travelling so easy, I might almost say enjoyable, as in Russia, if only you are not in a

hurry to get over the ground. The cars have a passage down the middle, and a little platform at each
end where you may stand when the dust is not too
distressing. The seats, even in the second class, are
wide, low, and comfortable, and they can be pulled
out in such a way as to form an excellent couch, where
one can sleep soundly all night long. In the first
class there are luxurious couches, both for night and
day. The pace never exceeds, and seldom reaches,
twenty miles an hour, so that one is not much shaken,
and can read without injury to the eyes. Excellent
refreshment-rooms are provided at intervals of three
or four hours, at all of which the passengers dismount
and take a hearty meal, washed down by vodka or
by countless glasses of lemon-flavoured tea, weak no
doubt, but of a flavour such as one never gets in an
English hotel. One has ample time, not only to eat
at these stations, but to get out and walk up and down
at most of the others. Except upon such lines as that
from St. Petersburg to Moscow, or Moscow to Nijni
Novgorod, the number of passengers is not so great
as to crowd the carriage, and you can generally find
somebody who talks French or German (most probably a German himself), and is pleased at the opportunity of airing his knowledge. Partly from these
facilities for moving about, partly from the interest
of seeing a new bit of country, we stepped out of the
train after three nights and three days less tired
than one usually is by a journey from London to
Edinburgh.

The scenery of this vast region, which the Don and

its tributaries drain, is intensely monotonous, so
monotonous that its uniformity almost rises to grandeur.   From Saratof the railway climbs the slope of
the hills that border the Volga, whose bed is here
little above the ocean (the Caspian being, as everybody knows, some eighty feet below the Black Sea),
and comes out on a wide slightly rolling upland, not
wholly unlike the country round Newmarket, only
that it is more bare of wood.   Then it passes through
a land most of which is cultivated, and which is, indeed,
of extraordinary fertility, for here we are in the famous
black soil region, but where scarcely a sign of human
life is visible.   The villages are few, and a solitary
farmhouse is almost unheard of ; the Russian peasant
is gregarious, and apparently does not mind having to
walk a good many miles to his work.   The fields are
not divided, or rather there are no fields at all, but
one vast open space, in which the different crops run
in long parallel patches, corn and buckwheat predo-
minating. The greenness of Northern Russia is utterly
gone : everything is dry, bare, dusty ; a stream seldom
appears, and when it does, is muddy and sluggish.
The houses of the peasantry, which further north
towards the forest country are always of wood, are
here mostly of clay, strengthened possibly by a few
bricks or wattles. They are wretched enough, yet not
so much worse than those of our agricultural labourers
on backward estates.   Sometimes one sees on the
skirts of a village a pretty large farm standing not
without evidences of wealth, but there is mostly an
untidy look about it—haystacks tumbling over, fences

ill-kept, nothing trim or finished. The bucolic Russian has no gift for neatness, any more than his urban brother has for comfort.

As the line runs farther west, past Tambof, famous for its horses, Kozlof,[1] a junction for a line from the north, and Griazi, a still greater junction, where the train from Moscow to the Caucasus joins us, the country grows flatter and also somewhat better wooded. Between Griazi and Voronej, the next considerable place, one runs through an unbroken forest of beech for eight or ten miles, a forest, however, as is mostly the case in Russia, whose trees do not exceed twenty-five or thirty feet in height, and which has therefore nothing of forest gloom or forest grandeur about it ; it is only land covered with trees. After Voronej, a handsome-looking town which runs along the steep westerly bank of the Don—here, too, as on the Volga, the right bank is the steep one—the woods finally disappear, and one enters the true steppe, that strange, solitary, dreary region, whose few features it is so easy to describe in words, but the general impression of which I do not know how to convey. Our train traversed it during an entire afternoon, night, and day, from Voronej to Rostof, at the mouth of the Don, so

---

[1] *A propos* of Kozlof, a story is told in Russia to illustrate the dominance of the Germans, and the supposed dislike to them of the present heir to the throne, which is as follows. At a review a great number of officers were being presented to the Czarevitch. One after another comes forward bearing a German name, till at length the name of a certain Lieutenant Kozlof is called out. "At last a Russian," cried the heir to the throne. "Lieutenant Kozlof, I wish you success in your career."

the impression had time to sink in. The northern
half of it is perfectly flat, as flat as a table or a pan-
cake, and is mostly all cultivated, being, indeed, as
rich a bit of soil as there is in Europe. The corn had
all been reaped when we passed, but even from
the stubble one could partly judge how heavy the
harvest had been, and where the plough was at work
could admire the deep black friable loam which has
gone on till now, and will go on for many a year
to come, producing noble crops without the aid of
manure. Further south the country rises into a
great waving table-land, not unlike some parts of
the Sussex downs or the moors of Western York-
shire, traversed by long broad-backed ridges between
which lie wide shallow hollows. Here, except in the
river bottoms, the land is mostly untouched by cultivation, some of it roamed over by sheep and oxen,
much of it altogether desolate, all of it open and un-
enclosed. It is fertile in the main, and would support
a population almost as large again as that of Russia is
now. Whatever Russia may want, she does not want
land, and has no occasion to annex Bulgaria or
Armenia, or any other country to provide an outlet
for her superfluous children. No rock appears, except
here and there a tiny chalk cliff, and farther south
beds of sandstone and shale in the railway cuttings;
no tree, except willows and poplars along the streams,
and occasionally some bushes round one of the few
villages that nestle in the hollows; no detached houses
anywhere. Hour after hour the train journeys on
through a silent wilderness of brown scorched grass

and withered weeds,[1] climbing or descending in long
sweeps the swelling downs, now catching sight of a
herd of cattle in the distance, now caught by a dust
storm which the strong wind drives careering over the
expanse, but with the same unchanging horizon all
round, the same sense of motion without progress,
which those who have crossed the ocean know so
well. Even now, with a bright sun overhead, the
dreariness and loneliness were almost terrible ; what
must they be in winter, when north-eastern gales
howl over the waste of snow ? Yet even in this
dreariness there is a certain strange charm. Looking
from one of these billowy ridge-tops across the vast
expanse, with the wide blue sky vaulted over it, full
of that intense luminous clearness which marks the
East, glowing at sunrise and sunset with the richest
hues, you come to feel that there is a beauty of
the plain not less solemn and inspiring than that
of the mountain.

Traversing this steppe for two whole days enables
one to understand the kind of impression that Scythia
made on the imagination of the Greeks : how all
sorts of wonders and horrors, like those Herodotus
relates, were credible about the peoples that roamed
over these wilds ; how terrible to their neighbours, how
inaccessible and unconquerable themselves, they must
have seemed to the natives of the sunny shores of the

---

[1] The plants appeared, so far as one could make them out from the
train, to be still mostly of British genera. There were several *Polygonaceae*
and *Labiatae*, an *Artemisia*, a pretty purplish *Statice*, a small-flowered,
much-branching *Dianthus*, and everywhere *Achillaea millefolium*, which
seems to be the commonest of all weeds in Russia.

Ægean.   One realizes also how emphatically this is
the undefended side of Europe, the open space through
which all the Asiatic hordes, Huns, Alans, Avars,
Bulgarians, Mongols entered, their cavalry darting
over the steppe in search of enemies or booty, their
waggons following with their families and cattle, un-
checked, except now and then by some great river,
which, if it were too deep to ford, they crossed upon
inflated skins.   One understands what was the
nature of the warfare that raged for so many
centuries here between the Russians of Moscow
and Kief, gradually pushing forward to the south
and east, and the nomad tribes, whom they slowly
subdued or dispossessed—Khazars, Polovtzi, Petch-
enegs, Komans, Tatars of various names, who were
wont to scour across these plains on horseback plundering and burning every outlying settlement, and
returning to the banks of the Volga or the Lower Don
before the Russians had gathered to resist them.
And turning from the past to the future, one specu-
lates on the aspect which this vast and fertile territory
will present a century or two hence when it has been
all brought under cultivation, when populous towns
will have arisen, when coal mines will have been
opened, and yellow harvests be waving all over
these now lonely downs.   If Russia is then still
Russia, a nation one in sentiment and faith, swayed
by a single will, she may have become a tremendous
power in the world.   But, meantime, colonization
goes on slowly; the future of the Russian government and people is out of all prediction, and Europe

itself may have changed in some way that would
make our present calculations vain. One need not
be too sanguine or too apprehensive of the future
when it is remembered that about the future there
is only one thing that can be positively asserted, to
wit, that it will turn out not in the least like what
the shrewdest observers expect. Of all the prophe-
cies that philosophers or statesmen have made, from
Aristotle to De Tocqueville, how many have come
true? It is hard enough to say what ought to be
done next year ; and next century may surely be left
to take care of itself. Moral and social causes are so
much more powerful than physical ones, or, to speak
more exactly, so often turn physical causes in an unexpected direction, that there is really no reason why
an Englishman or a German should look on the
material growth of Russia with alarm.

As one approaches the Sea of Azof, the steppe
descends pretty steeply towards the south, and near
the low ground forms some little cliffs which may
perhaps be the origin of the name Κρήμνοι (the
Crags) which Herodotus gives to the emporium of
the Greek traders in Scythia, at the north-east corner
of the Maeotis. Here, at the modern town of Rostof,
the Don comes down, a broad muddy stream that
dawdles along through a mesh of sandbanks to that
wretched Sea of Azof which the ancients, considering
its shallowness, and the fact that its water is almost
quite fresh, more appropriately called a marsh. It
is even shallower now than it was then, and grows
shallower every year, not only by the action of the

Don pouring in mud, but also by that of the sea captains who sail up to Taganrog or Rostof for corn. Having no cargo to fetch with them, they mostly come "in ballast," and this ballast they fling overboard somewhere between the Straits of Kertch and Taganrog, thus forming shoals all along the track of navigation, on which the next comer runs aground. The government has threatened penalties on those who are detected, but detection is no easy matter. The trade from the Don is not only in corn, shipped here in vast quantities, but also in wine, which is pretty largely grown along the lower course of the stream, and is very tolerable drinking. It is consumed almost entirely by the Russians, who are especially fond of the effervescing sort which they call Don champagne. Nowhere in European Russia, except here and in the Crimea, some of whose wines are excellent, does the grape seem to be regularly cultivated.

A dense haze filled the air as we crossed the Don, caused either by the dust-storms which the wind raised, or by the smoke of steppe-fires, and cut off such view towards the sea as the flatness of the ground would have permitted. Soon we were again in the grassy wilderness, hundreds of miles wide, that lies between the Don and the Caucasus. Fires were blazing all over the steppe, whether accidental or lit for the sake of improving the pasture, I do not know; the effect, at any rate, was extremely fine when night came on, though the grass was too short to give either the volume of blaze or the swift progress

which makes a prairie fire so splendid and terrible.
I say "grass" from habit, but in reality it is rather
weeds than a carpet of herbage that are to be found
on the steppe, at least in autumn ; weeds whose
flowers, especially one of a clear light yellow which
reminded me of a small hollyhock, pleasantly diversify
the plain, but which seldom rise over two feet from
the ground.   However, as they have gone on living
and dying and burying themselves for myriads of
years on this soil, they must have accumulated a
considerable depth of vegetable mould, of which the
settler now reaps the benefit.   All this country is now
beginning to be settled, not indeed at an American
pace, but sufficiently for a visitor who returns every
fifth or sixth year to notice the difference.   There are
so few villages visible that one finds it hard to know
where the settlers live ; however, the sight of haycocks
right and left of the line, and less frequently of stubble
fields whence the corn has just been lifted, proves
well enough that inhabitants there must be somewhere.   Though every ten or fifteen miles there is a
station, a station does not in Russia imply that there
is any likelihood of passengers ; it is a place for the
train to stop, for tumblers of tea to be consumed, for
people to stretch themselves, for the station-master to
exchange remarks with the engine-driver.   There is
but one train in the day ; so its arrival is something
of an event in the neighbourhood, and not to be
treated lightly.   Few of these stations had villages
attached.   All through this region, as elsewhere in
Russia, one never sees a solitary house, or even a

group of houses, and unless a village happens to be
in sight, the country seems, according to the season,
a green or a brown wilderness, unbroken by tree or
hedge.   Hereabouts there is not even the chance of
seeing a wandering horde of Kalmucks, for that interesting race, who are nearly all Buddhists, and, as
most ethnologists hold, of Mongol stock, dislike the
neighbourhood of Russian colonists, and keep more
to the east along the Lower Volga, and by the shores
of the Caspian, where the steppe is mostly salt, and
therefore less fit for agriculture.   It was a disappointment not to meet with this last remnant of the hosts
of Zinghis Khan, dwelling in felt tents, and worshipping the Dalai Lama ; but the world is large, and
one cannot see everything in it.

As we get southward, the country grows rather
more uneven, and long smooth ridges, mostly of gravel,
but sometimes shewing sections of sandstone or limestone strata, where a gully, the bed of some winter
stream, has cut through them, run across the plain.
There are few rivers, but a good many muddy ponds,
in which cattle are trying to find refuge from the
scorching air.   Who they belong to does not appear,
for the long straggling villages of mud-built rudely-
thatched houses come at intervals of many miles.
Hitherto there had been no sign of the proximity of
the Caucasus, except the sight of the strong flood
of the Kuban, whose muddy white, ugly in itself,
but lovely to the eyes of a mountaineer, proclaimed it
glacier-born.   But now, some eighteen hours after
we had left Rostof, several sharp craggy hills of

limestone rose on the southern horizon, and behind
them, dimly seen under brooding clouds, appeared a
huge mass of high land, stretching east and west
further than the eye could follow. It was the Caucasus,
and all the weariness of the steppe and the railway
was forgotten in a moment, when, after the two thousand miles of plain we had traversed from the Gulf of
Bothnia hither, we saw the majestic chain unroll itself
before us.

CHAPTER II.

THE CAUCASUS.

IN the days of the Crimean War, when the Caucasus first drew the attention of the Western world, Englishmen mostly thought of it as a chain of snowy mountains running from the Straits of Kertch to the Caspian Sea, inhabited by a race of patriotic heroes and beautiful women, called Circassians, who maintained perpetual strife against the encroaching Muscovite. Since then travellers have begun to penetrate it, and some of our own countrymen have even scaled its loftiest summits. But our conceptions are still so vague that there will be no harm in making some general remarks on the range before I describe what I saw in traversing it.

It is really a chain, that is to say, a long and comparatively narrow strip of high land sloping steeply both ways from its central axis ; whereas many of our so-called mountain ranges are rather, like the Himalayas, the edges of plateaux, or, like the Andes, themselves a vast plateau with isolated eruptive masses scattered over its surface. It is, however, by no means, as the old maps represent it, a uniform chain, but rather consists of three sufficiently well marked

divisions. **First,** we **have the** western section, **lying**
along **the** Black **Sea coast,** where it is comparatively
low, indeed, in the north-west little more **than a** line
of insignificant hills, and mostly covered **with** wood.
The first considerable heights begin about the fort of
Gagri, fifty miles west-north-west of Sukhum Kaleh,
where one peak reaches 9000 feet. Next comes the
central section, from the neighbourhood of Sukhum
Kaleh, a well-known Black Sea port, eastward **as far**
as Mount Kazbek and the Dariel Pass. This is **the**
loftiest and grandest part, having many summits that
rise far above the line of perpetual snow, and at least
seven exceeding 15,000 feet, deep and gloriously
wooded valleys ; ample seas of ice surrounding the
great peaks. Lastly, there is the eastern section, which
is almost conterminous with (and which I shall therefore call by the name of) Daghestan, the " **Mountain
Land,"** extending **from** the Dariel Pass to the Caspian
Sea.   Here the heights are not quite so great, though
three or four peaks exceed 13,000 feet, and one, the
extinct volcano of Basarjusi, reaches 14,722 feet.
There is of course, therefore, much less snow and ice.
The range splits, throwing out, some forty miles east
of the **Dariel road,** a great spur to the north-east,
crowned **by** several lofty glacier peaks, while the main
axis runs south-east at a uniform elevation of **10,000**
or 11,000 feet, till it rises for the last time in the summit
of Basarjusi.   In the angle between the above men-
tioned spur and the main chain lies Daghestan, a
wide table-land, intersected by profound gorges, itself
mostly bare of wood, but throwing off **to** the north a

sort of buttress of hilly country, which sinks gradually
into the great Kalmuck Steppe. Approaching the
Caspian, the declivities become gentler, the summits
lower, the country altogether more open ; so that here
the people dwelling to the south found it necessary to
protect themselves from the irruptions of the bar-
barous tribes of the northern steppe by the erection
of a mighty rampart, the so-called Caucasian Wall,
remains of which may still be seen near the port of
Derbend, on the Caspian coast.

The length of the whole mountain country, from
Taman, on the Sea of Azov, to the peninsula of
Apsheron, on the Caspian, is about 800 miles ; its
greatest width, in Daghestan, about 120.

Orographically, the most remarkable features of
the Caucasus are the simplicity of its structure, the
steepness of its declivities, and its great persistent
altitude through the central and eastern sections.
Unlike the Alps and the Rocky Mountains, it does
not throw out, or rather split up into, any long secondary ranges parallel to one another ; I mean such
ranges as the Bernese Alps or the great Vorarlberg
ridge to the north of the Inn. Nearly all the higher
branch chains, and by consequence nearly all the
valleys, are at right angles to the main axis, and are
therefore comparatively short. All the loftiest summits are on or close to the watershed, which may be
taken as being in the Caucasus generally coincident
with the axis of elevation. One may conclude from
this that the elevating forces acted (again speaking
generally, for there are exceptions) along one or two

lines only,[1] and acted there with an intensity which is
fairly represented by the prodigious height of the
great summits. Several of these, and notably Elbruz
and Kazbek, are volcanic, both composed of trachyte,
and Elbruz—according to Mr. Freshfield, who, with
Messrs. Tucker and Moore, first ascended it—showing
traces of a crater at the top. The other great peaks
of the central section, such as Koschtantau, are believed to be mostly granitic; while in Daghestan it is
asserted that limestone rocks are found to form nearly
all the loftiest summits. Every one knows that the
height of the peaks of a mountain chain is quite a
different thing from the average height of its watershed. In the Pyrenees, for instance, the average of
the watershed is higher than in the Alps, though the
tops are very much lower. In the Caucasus this persistency of elevation is even more remarkable. For
some two hundred miles east from Sukhum Kaleh,
there is no point where the range sinks below 8000
feet, and very few where it is nearly as low; whereas
in the Alps one has a good many passes across the
main chain between 4000 and 5000 feet high. The
consequence of this is that there are only two passes
across the Caucasus which are practically used by
travellers, those of the Dariel and the Mamisson (a
little farther west than the Dariel), and only one, the

---

[1] The geological structure of the chain is still imperfectly known;
but there seems reason to believe that in the central section there are
two parallel axes of upheaval not far apart from one another, the
northernmost of which is also, in the western part of that section, the
watershed, while farther east the southern axis divides the stream
heads.

Dariel, which is traversed by a road practicable for wheeled carriages.

These physical features naturally impress a peculiar character upon the scenery of the Caucasus. First of all, they give it a certain want of variety. You do not, as in the Alps, see, when you reach a lofty point of outlook, snow mountains lying all around you in different ranges or knots; as, from the Aeggischhorn, one sees the Finsteraarhorn and Jungfrau group to the north, and the icy giants of Zermatt to the south, or as, from the Sasso di Pelmo or Marmolata in the Venetian Alps, with snow-capped summits rising on either hand, you can trace the vast arc of Noric and Rhaetian snows from the Tauern of Gastein to the far-off crags of the Ortler. There is not the same richness of re-grouping among the great mountains, discerned from different points, as one has among the numerous parallel chains of the Alps. Then, secondly, there is a complete want of lakes, which usually occur where a ridge more or less parallel to the axis turns the course of a valley, or at any rate where the general declivity is not very abrupt. No tarn bigger than Buttermere or Loch Achray seems to have been discovered in the whole length of the Caucasus. This defect the rivers do not atone for, since in the central section they are muddy glacier torrents, and in the eastern the dryness of the climate and want of glacier reservoirs leaves them insignificant. And with this there is in many parts a want of the gentler elements of picturesque beauty which act as a foil to the severe grandeur of snow landscapes and inner gorges of the mountains, relieve the mind from their gloom and terror, and enable it to return with fresh enjoyment to scenery that taxes all its powers.

Against these drawbacks there are to be set the magnificent scale on which the Caucasus is built, and the extraordinary boldness of its lines. On the north, especially, it rises in some places like a wall, the snowy tops seeming to run down with a steeply falling, unbroken ridge into the dead flat of the steppe. The gorges are deeper and more savage, the summits mount with a more imposing steepness, than one sees elsewhere in Europe; and in some of the southern valleys, especially those of the Ingur and Kodor, to the south-west of Elbruz, the forests have a tropical luxuriance, for which no parallel can be found nearer than India or South America. What Dr. Hooker, in his 'Himalayan Journals' (most delightful among books of scientific travel), says of the Himalayas as compared with the Alps is true of the Caucasus also, though in a less degree. They are not so beautiful as the Alps, but they are more majestic. One is less charmed, but more awed. And this impression of awe is heightened by the fact, that in the Caucasus there is so much less of human life and history than in the Alps. Instead of groups of cheerful *châlets*, surrounded by herds of cattle browsing on the lofty pastures up to the very edge of the glacier, one finds either solitude or at most a dingy stone or log-built hut. Few corn-fields are seen waving in the valleys, such as the climber descries from the summit of the

Jungfrau or the Tödi. There are no passes that have
echoed to the tramp of armies; no towns, *congesta
manu praeruptis oppida saxis*, that have been the
strongholds of ancient freedom or the bulwarks of
hostile empires. Nature alone speaks to the traveller,
and speaks in her sternest accents.

Nevertheless, the Caucasus has a profound historical
importance, and that importance depends in a remarkable manner on the peculiar physical character which
I have endeavoured to describe. It is just because
the chain is so steep and with an axis so uninter-
ruptedly lofty that it has formed in all ages an im-
passable barrier between the nomad peoples who
roamed over the northern steppes and the more
civilized and settled races dwelling to the south, in
the valleys of the Kur and Aras, the Phasis and the
Euphrates. From the beginning of history the
Caucasus is to the civilized nations, both Greek and
Oriental, the boundary of geographical knowledge—
indeed, the boundary of the world itself. Beyond it
all is fable and mystery, not only to Herodotus, but
even to Strabo and Ptolemy. Pompey, in the last
Mithridatic war, led the Roman legions as far as its
southern foot, defeating the Iberians in a battle near
the spot where the Dariel road emerges from the
mountains above Tiflis. Some centuries later, the
armies of Justinian repeatedly disputed with those of
Chosroes Nushirvan the possession of Imeritia, and
sometimes advanced their outposts far up into the
gorges of the hills above Gori and Suram. But
neither Roman nor Persian ever crossed to the north,

or endeavoured to hold any part of the mountain country in permanent subjection. So, too, the waves of barbarian conquest that successively descended from the Ural and the Altai across the plains of the Caspian fretted and foamed in vain against this gigantic wall, and were forced to seek their ingress to the southern countries either to the east of the Caspian into Iran, or round the northern shores of the Black Sea towards the Danube valley. In this respect there is a singular contrast between the case of the Alps and that of the Caucasus. Since the days when the Rhaetians saw Drusus, "like the bird that bears Jove's thunderbolt," carrying war into the valleys of the Inn and Drave, there has never been a time (save during the seventh and eighth centuries), down till the cession of Venetia in 1866, when regions on both sides of the Alps have not, either practically or nominally, formed parts of the same empire—Roman, or Romano-Germanic, or Austrian ; whereas the countries immediately to the north and south of the Caucasus have never obeyed the same ruler (except, perhaps, in the lifetime of Zinghis Khan), until Russia established herself in Georgia at the beginning of this century. So, too, while commerce has in all ages gone on pretty briskly across the Alps, there has been none, so far as can be made out, over the few and difficult passes which the Caucasus presents. Greek traders from the colonies on the Pontic coast penetrated to the foot of the mountains long before the Christian era, as Genoese traders did in the middle ages ; but we hear of no one crossing them or ex-

E

ploring their recesses. What little trade there was crept up by Derbend, between the Caspian and the hills, from Persia to the north. In them, as in the other mysterious boundary of the ancient world, the Pillars of Hercules, the Greeks laid the scene of mythological exploits and marvels. Colchis, to which the Argo sailed, lay under their shadow; Prometheus was chained to one of their towering rocks; near them dwelt the man-hating Amazons; beyond them gold-guarding griffins and one-eyed Arimaspians carried on perpetual war. So it remained for many centuries, down to the days of Marco Polo and Mandeville, in the east as well as in the west. Readers of the Arabian Nights will remember that there Mount Kaf is the limit of the world, and the usual threat of a magician to an obstinate sultan is, "I will transport thy city beyond Mount Kaf, and transform all the people in it into stones."

It is true, no doubt, that this complete absence, down till quite recent times, of knowledge about the Caucasus, and of attempts to carry trade or conquest into it from the south, is partly due to the uninviting nature of the countries beyond, and to the fact that, so far as trade was concerned, even the stormy Euxine provided an easier route to Scythia. But a good deal must be ascribed to the peculiarly difficult and impracticable character of the chain itself, which not only stopped armies and caravans, but kept the inhabitants in a state of isolation and barbarism. One of the most remarkable characteristics of the Caucasus is that, while it has acted as a barrier be-

tween the north and the south, stopping and turning
aside the movements of population, it has also preserved within its sheltered recesses fragments of the
different peoples who from time to time have passed
by it, or who have been driven by conquest into it
from the lower country. Thus it is a kind of ethnological museum, where specimens may be found of
countless races and languages, some of which probably belong to the early ages of the world; races
that seem to have little affinity with their present
neighbours, and of whose history we know nothing
except what comparative philology can reveal. Even
before the Christian era it was famous for the variety
of its peoples. Herodotus says :—

"Along the west side of the Caspian Sea stretches
the Caucasus, which is of all mountains both the
greatest in extent and the loftiest in height. It contains many and various nations, living mostly on the
fruits of wild trees."

Strabo describes the Caucasus as inhabited by an
immense number of different tribes, speaking different
tongues, and many of them very savage. He reports
the story that seventy such tribes resort, chiefly to buy
salt, to the Greek trading station of Dioscurias, on the
Euxine coast, of whom the bravest and most powerful
are the ferocious Soanes, and tells how in summer the
natives climb the mountains shod with shoes of ox-
hide, their soles full of spikes to give them a hold upon
the ice. Many of them are troglodytes, he adds, who,
owing to the cold, dwell in holes. Some use poisoned
arrows. Another writer says that some are cannibals

—there is at any rate a consensus as to their ferocity. And Procopius, writing under Justinian, when the region might have been comparatively well known, declares that on the top of the mountains there never falls either snow or rain, because they are above the highest clouds.

No more inappropriate ethnological name was ever propounded than that of Caucasian for a fancied division of the human family, the cream of mankind, from which the civilized peoples of Europe are supposed to have sprung. For the Caucasus is to-day as it was in Strabo's time, full of races differing in religion, language, aspect, manners, character ; races so numerous and still so little known that I shall not attempt to do more than mention some of the most important.

In Daghestan, the "mountain land" *par excellence,* the most numerous race, and one of the finest races anywhere, is the Lesghian, whose number, including minor allied tribes, is estimated at 560,000. They are all Sunni Mohammedans, and devout Mohammedans, a people profoundly religious, among whom Shamyl found his chief support, and whom he ruled chiefly through their zeal for that enthusiastic form of their faith which went by the name of Muridism, a sort of revived Islamism, not unlike that of the Wahabis in Arabia. It began with the preaching of a certain Kazi Mollah, about the year 1823. The word Murid is said to mean "teaching disciple." Shamyl himself was by birth of a tribe apparently akin to the Lesghian stock, named Avars, whom one may fancy to be a branch, left behind in its old dwelling-place, of the great nomad nation which held Pannonia (Hungary) from the sixth to the eighth century, and which, after being for some generations the terror of the Greeks, Franks, and Italians, was finally subdued or extinguished by Charlemagne. These Avars are said, alone among these peoples, to have a regular literary language, which, however, is written in Persian characters. Here in Daghestan many of the tribes occupy only one or two valleys, yet remain distinct in language and customs from their neighbours, and may probably remain so for centuries to come, an inexhaustible field for the ethnologist. North-west of the Lesghians, towards Vladikavkaz, is the large Mohammedan tribe Tchetchens, and beyond them the Ingushes, while south-west of Lesghistan, towards the Dariel Pass, dwell the Hessurs, or Chewsurs, a small people, who still array themselves in helmets and chain armour, carry shields and spears, and declare themselves descended from the Crusaders, though how Crusaders should have come there they do not explain. The truth seems to be that they wear, being nominally Christians, small crosses of red or black cloth sewed upon their clothes, and that some one, having been struck by the similarity of this to the Crusaders' usage, set the tale a-going.

On both sides of the chain to the west of the Dariel road, are the Ossets, a people partly Christian, partly Mohammedan, partly pagan, speaking an Indo-European tongue, in which some traveller discovered a strong resemblance to German, but which is now generally held to belong to the Iranian group. They

call themselves Ir, or Iron, and number about 30,000.[1]
They have been well disposed to the Russians almost
from the first, though indulging in occasional robberies, and their position, close to the great line of
communication, made their friendship valuable. On
the northern slopes of the mountains, between Vladikavkaz and Pjätigorsk, lies the territory of Kabarda,
inhabited by Mohammedans speaking a tongue which
is generally held to be a branch of the Tcherkess
or Circassian,[2] a manly and vigorous race, who have
mostly been on good terms with Russia, and some of
whose nobles have risen to high places in her army.
Still farther west, between the watershed and the
Kuban, stretching far to the north-west of Elbruz
lay Circassia, inhabited by tribes who called themselves Adighé, and whom the Russians knew as Tcherkesses. They were nearly all Mohammedans, though
of rather a loose kind, admirable horsemen and marks-
men, living by war and pillage, and leaving to their
women such tillage as the character of the country
permitted. South of them, in the upper valley of the
Ingur, and amid the grandest scenery of the whole
Caucasus, dwell the Suans or Svanny, the Soanes of
Strabo; and still farther west, on the wooded mountains that border the Euxine all along by Sukhum
Kaleh, are the Abhasians, a people supposed to be

[1] Other estimates raise the number of the Ossets to 60,000. The
numbers given here are taken from a Russian statistical publication of
some reputation, but I dare say they are only rough estimates.

[2] The Kabardans are sometimes, but apparently on insufficient grounds,
classed as Circassians. Distinct from both seems to be the small tribe
of Tatars who inhabit the upper valley of the Baksan, at the foot of
Elbruz.

allied to the Tcherkesses, and sometimes included
with them under the Circassian name, but speaking
a distinct language. They were converted to Christianity by Justinian, but have since relapsed, some into
a loose sort of Mohammedanism, some into paganism.
They are the most unmitigated rogues and thieves in
the whole Caucasus, whose only occupation, since
they were first heard of, has been kidnapping children
to sell for slaves, formerly into the Roman and, since
its fall, into the Turkish empire. In their country the
Turks have lately, in May 1877, effected a landing,
and are reported to have been joined by 10,000
mountaineers. As the whole Abhasian population
probably does not exceed 70,000, this story must be
received with more than distrust. They are, no doubt,
disaffected to Russia now, as they were to Turkey
formerly, and would be to anybody who should try
to check their misdeeds. But they are too wild and
unstable to be of the least use in a campaign.

The Muslim peoples of the Caucasus are held by
most travellers to be superior in energy and upright-
ness to the Christians. I saw too little to judge
whether this is so, but enough to be sure that the
Christianity of the mountain tribes is the merest
name. Some, like the Hessurs and the cognate tribes
of Pshaws and Tushins, are really polytheists, and
worship, besides what they call the Christ-God, a god
of war, and gods or " angels " of the earth, the oak, the
mountain, and so forth. In fact, their Christianity
consists in kissing the cross, in feasting and idling on
certain holidays, fasting on others, and in worshipping

deities, some of whom go by the names of Christian saints. Such ceremonies as they have bear traces of Georgian origin; so it is likely enough that the Georgian princes, whose suzerainty they used to acknowledge, were the instruments of their conversion. The Suans worship the Georgian queen Tamara to this day, along with St. George : and the priest—they seem to have a hereditary and illiterate priesthood—repeats fragments of prayers and psalms, and receives a gift for his pains. Bitter blood feuds rage among them, for they are a fierce and passionate race, and seldom rich enough to pay the heavy compensation in cattle which ancient custom entitles the relatives of a slain man to require ; hence murders go on from generation to generation exactly as in Corsica till lately, or in Iceland in the days of the old republic.

To write the history of Russian conquest in the Caucasus would lead me too far afield, and would require various geographical elucidations which I have no space for. One remark, however, is worth making, to remove a misconception which was current in England at the time of the Crimean War, when some enterprising spirits proposed that we should use the mountaineers as allies against the Czar Nicholas. There never was any general war in the Caucasus, nor any concerted action among the tribes who defended their independence. We used to talk of the Circassians as a people inhabiting the whole chain, and carrying on war against the Russians, whereas in reality they were only one among many races, the majority of whom were neutral or favourable to

Russia. Although outbursts and disturbances occasionally happened in other places, the struggle was in the main confined to two districts : Daghestan, in the east, where Shamyl, at the head of the Lesghians, and one or two minor cognate tribes, maintained a religious war ; and Circassia proper, the country of the Adighé or Tcherkesses, who occupied what I have called the western and lowest section of the chain, and the hilly country lying to the north of it and drained by the Kuban. The intermediate tribes, Tatars of the Baksan valley, and Kabardans, both of whom are Mohammedans, as well as the semi-Christian Ossets, Ingushes, and Suans, were generally quiet, and prevented that co-operation against the Russians which Shamyl more than once tried to bring about. The Tchetchens, who number about 115,000, had given the Czar some trouble, but were mostly reduced to a sullen submission before 1854, being inferior in martial qualities to both Lesghians and Kabardans. Shamyl himself was a great man, crafty and cruel, no doubt, but with a daring, a tenacity, and a fertility of resource that remind one of Abd-el-Kader, and able to raise to a marvellous height the fanaticism of his followers.[1] He was wonderfully eloquent, and added to his reputation for sanctity that of bearing a charmed life, for he had, like Abd-el-Kader, repeatedly escaped when he was believed to have been

[1] A prophet is not an uncommon phenomenon among these peoples. There have been some of late years in Persia ; and a quite remarkable one appeared among the Tcherkesses at the end of last century, by name Bey Mansur, who roused his countrymen against the Russians and was captured by them at Anapa in 1790.

killed, and reappeared unhurt in some distant spot.
Though he never commanded more than a few thousand warriors, and in his later days only a few hundreds, the physical character of Daghestan, a country
of plateaux intersected by profound and narrow gorges,
made all the efforts of the Russians fruitless, until they
abandoned the plan of regular expeditions against
him, and set themselves to hem him in by constructing military roads, and erecting forts which commanded the gorges, and drew a narrowing cordon
around him.   When his last stronghold, the rock fortress of Gunib, was stormed by the army of Prince
Bariatinski, in August 1859, he came down and surrendered like Vercingetorix to Caesar, happily to meet
a milder fate, for, after an honourable exile of a few
years near Moscow, he was allowed to proceed to
Mecca, and died there not long ago.

A little later, in 1864, the Tcherkesses of the west
finally submitted.   The Russian government, who
knew by experience that their marauding propensities
were incurable, adopted a plan which was no doubt
stern, but may have been necessary.   They offered
them their choice of quitting the mountains, where
they were uncontrollable, and settling in the low
country along the Kuban, or else of emigrating into
Turkish territory.   Numerous envoys from Turkey
came among them, and urged the latter course, which
was accordingly chosen by the bulk of the nation.
Four hundred thousand are said to have come down
to the ports whither the Sultan had promised to send
vessels to receive them.   The vessels, however, like

everything else Turkish, were late in coming, diseases
broke out, and a large part of the Tcherkesses died
before the embarkation took place. Of those who
sailed, the majority were settled in Lazistan, or in
Turkish Armenia, north of Erzerum. Of these last,
some have been since transferred to Europe, and have
played their part in the Bulgarian massacres of 1876.
Others are now fighting the Russians, or rather taking
the opportunity which the war gives them, of murdering the natives in Armenia. The fate of a nation
driven from its ancestral seats cannot but move our
sympathy. But there was nothing else in the character or history of the Circassians to justify that
sympathy. Their supposed chivalry, like most chival-
ries, disappeared upon close examination. They lived
upon robbery and the sale of their children, and of
the ferocity which accompanies their robberies they
have given us hideous examples in Bulgaria, and still
more recently in the Armenian campaign.

The Tcherkess country is now for the most part uninhabited, though some few of the old inhabitants linger
in the valleys or in the Russian towns of the steppe.
Its lower parts, along the tributaries of the Kuban, are
being colonized by the Russians, but the fevers that
infest these wooded valleys have proved very fatal to
the new-comers, and the inner hollows of the mountains remain abandoned to the wild bull, largest of
European quadrupeds, who ranges unpursued through
these vast solitudes. Last autumn all was quiet
through the Caucasus from end to end, and a traveller
with a couple of Cossacks was safe even among the

warlike Lesghians, many of whom have taken service as irregular cavalry under the Russian flag.[1] The only exception is to be found among the independent Suans before mentioned, who, singularly ill-conditioned fellows as they are, are nevertheless in some ways the most interesting of all the Caucasian races, having preserved many curious primitive customs and forms of ritual. They have resisted several attempts of the Russians to collect taxes from them, and one one of their villages was last summer in a state of armed resistance to the feebly led attacks of a detachment of troops sent against them. Being only some 10,000 in number, they will, of course, be reduced without difficulty as soon as a military road is made into their country, and all the more readily as they live in a state of perpetual feud with one another, village against village, and family against family. There is no political organization. Each man, like the Cyclopes in Homer, rules over his wife and children, and cares nothing for his neighbour.[2]

[1] Since the above was written, an insurrection is reported to have broken out not only in Abhasia, where the Turks have landed, but among the Tchetchens and the Lesghians in Daghestan. It is hard to make out what has really happened; but apparently the rising has not been important there, and will be easily suppressed. So long as the Dariel road is not threatened, Russia need not much care about Daghestan, whose tribes are too far from the Euxine to co-operate with the Turks. The Tcherkesses are all gone from Circassia, and the Abhasians are too fickle and cowardly to constitute any real danger. Indeed, the Turkish troops are now (July 1877) being withdrawn from their country altogether.

[2] For further details regarding these Suans, the curious reader may be referred to 'Central Caucasus' of Mr. Freshfield, whose party was almost the first in recent times to visit their country, and were exposed to some danger from them; to Captain Telfer's 'Crimea and Transcaucasia,' vol. ii. and appendix; and to a work by Dr. Radde, the eminent botanist, entitled 'Die drei Langenhochthäler Imeritiens.'

So far, therefore, as safety to life is concerned, the explorer of the Caucasus has little to fear. But of course there are absolutely no facilities for travelling such as we find in the Alps or even in the Carpathians, no inns, no roads, no guides, and in some regions no beasts of burden. Except that the risk of being eaten or pierced by poisoned arrows is gone, the mountains are much in the same state as they were in the time of Herodotus and Strabo. The Dariel military road, of which more anon, crosses the chain near its centre, and there is, as I have said, a network of roads in one part of Daghestan; otherwise nothing passable by wheels. Here and there a village or a shepherd's hut will shelter the traveller, but often he must depend upon his tent, and, like Virgil's Libyan herdsman, carry all that he wants with him, food, bedding, and weapons; and to do this, he needs a little army of porters, whom it is often troublesome enough to manage.

There is only one part of the Caucasus that has been, as the French say, "utilised" for the purposes of tourists or pleasure seekers, and even that part is not in the Caucasus at all, but in the steppe at the foot of it. This is the mineral water region lying to the south-west of the town of Stavropol, and due north of Mount Elbruz or Minghi Tau,[1] the highest summit of the whole chain. Here four or five little

---

[1] Minghi Tau (*tau=dagh*=mountain) is the true local name, the Tatar name, of this monarch of European mountains (it lies entirely in Europe, north of the watershed). Elbruz is said to be Persian, and is certainly the usual Persian name for the Caucasus and for a mountain chain in general; it is given to the lofty chain which runs round the south and south-east extremity of the Caspian.

bathing-places lie pretty near to one another, the chief
of which, Pjätigorsk, is entitled to a few words of
description.

To reach Pjätigorsk, one leaves the railway from
Rostof to Vladikavkaz at a station called (by inter-
pretation) Mineral Waters, a wooden erection planted
right down in the middle of the desolate steppe, and
finds some twenty two-horse droshkys drawn up outside, whose drivers are shouting, gesticulating, and
jostling one another like so many Irish carmen. It is
a long business making a bargain with one of them,
for though there is plenty of competition, there is also
a trade-union feeling that prices must be kept up in
the common interest; and in Russia the driver is
generally pretty resolute, and, though he asks at first
a great deal more than he expects to get, can never
be brought below the minimum he has originally resolved upon. Our experience was that, when the bargain has once been made, he will abide by it, and not
try to spring fresh demands upon you. When at last
a driver had got us, and embarked our baggage, he
set off at full speed over what seemed to be the open
steppe, though after a while we discovered from the
wheel tracks on it that it was the regular and only
road to the most frequented of all the watering-
places in the Russian empire. Here, where the
neighbouring mountains make the climate moister,
the grass was pretty thick and not so utterly brown
as farther north. Of flowers, the commonest is a
species of *Statice*, growing in large patches, which
light up the rolling steppe with a purple glow that

reminded one of the heather bloom on the moors of
Scotland in August. Mounting gradually towards a
gap in the group of limestone hills which here projects
into the plain, and culminates in the bold peak of
Beschtau, 7000 feet above the sea-level, we entered a
low wood of beech and oak, the first we had seen
since Voronej, 700 miles back, and, on emerging from
it, to the south-west, saw Pjätigorsk at our feet, and
the outer slopes of the Caucasus rising behind it.
Alas! the southern sky was thick, and where the
glittering snows of Elbruz and Dykhtau ought to have
appeared, there were only clouds and darkness.

Pjätigorsk, which takes its name (Five Mountains)
from the five summits of the picturesque mountain
group just mentioned, has been resorted to for its
sulphurous waters, which are drunk as well as bathed
in, for nearly one hundred years. Its progress was
slow so long as the Tcherkesses were accustomed to
swoop down from the hills to the south-west and
carry off the unlucky patients as prisoners. In those
days Russian magnates came with a train of two or
three hundred servants, and encamped by the springs
for two months at a time. Afterwards a military post
was established, to keep off the marauders, a
bath-house was erected, and now, since the railway
has come within three hours' drive, new streets are
rising in all directions, and the number of visitors will
no doubt increase rapidly. Far as the Caucasus is from
St. Petersburg, the bathing-places of the Rhine or
Bohemia are still farther, and as Southern Russia fills
up, the population which forms the special *clientèle* of

Pjätigorsk grows larger and wealthier. One great advantage which it possesses is that, in addition to its
own sulphurous waters, there are three other springs
not far off, round each of which a bathing village has
grown up, one of them chalybeate, a second alkaline,
with iodides and bromides, and a third, the Narsan
spring at Kislovodsk, strongly impregnated with carbonic acid as well as iron. This last discharges 190,000
cubic feet of gas in twenty-four hours, and is often
resorted to as a sort of tonic by people who have gone
through the regular course of sulphurous or alkaline
waters. Like the famous spring of Bórszek, in Tran-
sylvania, which is used in the same way as an " after
cure," it is quite cold (56° F.) ; and the physical pleasure
of a plunge into its glittering waters, filled with carbonic acid gas rising and breaking in great bubbles,
is one of the most intense that can be conceived. It
is like bathing in iced champagne.

Watering-places in all countries are pretty much like
one another ; I suppose because they are all new, and
all designed for the same class of persons. There is
therefore not much that is distinctive about Pjätigorsk,
except the contrast, so frequent in Russia, of civilization, even a rather pretentious civilization in the town,
with a primitive rudeness all round it. It is as if Ems
or Luchon were to be set down in the middle of a
Western prairie, where everything is as nature made
it. To the east and west there is the open steppe, all
pasture land ; to the north, a hill called Mashukha,
rising boldly some 1600 feet above the town and 3500
feet above the sea ; to the south, an upland, which

mounts slowly into great grassy downs that stretch
backwards towards the main chain of the Caucasus,
whose summits shew above it much as the giants of the
Bernese Oberland do from the Jura between Basle and
Olten. There can be few finer panoramic mountain
views in the world than that from the top of Mashukha
in clear weather, with this long line of icy pinnacles
on one side, and the boundless steppe on the other.
I climbed the hill before breakfast, in the hopes
of enjoying this prospect, but jealous clouds still
brooded over Elbruz and his brethren, and the only
glimpse I got of him was long afterwards from the
sea between Poti and Batum. One was well repaid,
however, by the view over Pjätigorsk itself, and the
two other villages which lie near to, though quite
distinct from, it : one of them, the Scotch colony,
planted here in the time of Alexander I. by mis-
sionaries sent to convert the Tcherkesses ; the other
a German colony, of somewhat later origin ; all three
laid out in straight lines, with trees running down
their streets, and roads being made to connect them.
They bore an almost ludicrous resemblance to those
bird's-eye views of suburban estates or rising watering-places which one sees on the advertisement boards
of our railway stations, and suggested how little
variety there is in the world after all. Here at the
foot of Mount Kaf one is reminded of Saltburn-by-
the-Sea, or the Holland Park Estate. The advantage,
on the whole, was on the side of Pjätigorsk, which is
not only a pretty little place, but has that look of

F

what the Germans call *Freundlichkeit*, a cosy cheerfulness, which is not common in watering-places, and rare everywhere in Russia. What amuses one most is that, in so apparently peaceful a place, everybody goes about fully armed. Nearly all the male visitors are in uniform. After you leave Rostof, all the guards on the train, the porters at the stations, the waiters at the hotels, seem in a state of constant preparation to resist a Circassian foray. The very boy who brings up your boots in the morning comes with daggers rattling in his belt, and a string of cartridge holders sewed to the breast of his coat. So it is all through the Caucasian countries. In fact, arms are as necessary a part of a man's dress as a hat; you are remarked, and in the wilder places, despised, if you do not wear them. Inside the town there is not much to notice. There is an hotel with a handsome façade, a highly ornate coffee-room, and sleeping accommodation little better than that of a Russian steamer. There is a sort of boulevard in a hollow of the hill, where officers on sick leave, all in uniform, and a few ladies saunter up and down under the rows of trees between the bath-houses and the long wooden gallery where the waters are drunk. The drinking arrangements are agreeably simple. A glass tumbler is let down by a string into a deep well and pulled up with the water, whose taste, to be sulphurous, is not very disagreeable. Nobody has anything to do except play cards and smoke, the ladies joining freely in both amusements. The immediate neighbourhood is too bare to supply inviting drives, and as for the Caucasus, a Russian would as soon think of starting to scale those rosy-tinted peaks as a Scarborough dandy of chartering a smack to cross to Holland. English travellers are a puzzle altogether to the Muscovite mind; but when it comes to alpine boots and ice-axes, they give the problem up.

We had intended to break into the Caucasus here, and make our way past Elbruz into Suanetia, where the grandest scenery in the chain is to be found, and thence to Kutais or Suram. But partly the difficulty of finding a courier or interpreter, partly the disturbances among the Suans, and, most of all, want of time, made it necessary to abandon this plan, and be content with travelling by railway to Vladikavkaz, and thence by the Dariel road to Tiflis, a journey which, though it is by no means so grand as the other, is still rich enough in beauty and interest to be worth coming for all the way from England. Accordingly we returned to the station at which we had left the railway to reach Pjätigorsk, and, catching the same train—there is but one in the day—reached Vladikavkaz after a journey of about six hours. The line runs along the open steppe, which is intersected by many low ridges, and occasionally by deep gullies, traversed by whitish torrents, the offspring of the glaciers which in this part of the chain descend from the great snow mountains. A remarkable feature of this steppe is the great number of tumuli which lie scattered over its surface, and which are supposed to be the burial

mounds of primitive races. They are commonly
called Kurgans, and are found associated with rudely
hewn wooden figures exceeding life size. Nothing is
known of the purpose of these last, though probably
they were idols, nor of their origin, except that it
must lie in very remote times, since they are mentioned by ancient Greek writers as then existing in
Scythia.

To the south the great chain rises with extraordinary abruptness, its snowy tops seeming to run straight
down into the plain, so that one almost fancies it possible to reach one of these tops by following a single
ridge right upwards without descending into any inter-
vening valley. What with the gloomy weather and
the gathering shades of night, we could distinguish
nothing more than patches of white under the clouds,
but the lower declivities seemed to be thickly wooded
almost down to the level of the steppe. The line
comes to an end at Vladikavkaz, more than a thousand miles from Moscow, and now a place of much
consequence, not only as the chief fortress of this
part of the country, commanding the entrance to the
Dariel military road, but also as a trade centre from
which the goods brought hither by the railway are
forwarded by road to Tiflis or distributed through
the surrounding country. Its name means Controller,
or Key, of the Caucasus. It is a large, straggling sort
of place, with the usual wide streets and low houses,
improved, however, by the rows of trees that have
been planted down some of them, and by the variety
of uniforms and picturesque Caucasian dresses which

its mixed population displays. The inn is highly primitive; but as we had arranged to start next day with the dawn, that was neither here nor there; the mountain fever had seized us on finding ourselves at last under the shadow of this mysterious chain, and made us reckless of discomforts. At five next morning the sky was clear and bright, and, to our amazement, a snow-peak was looking in at the window, seeming to hang over the town. We were in the steppe, outside the mountains altogether, and here was an icy pinnacle, soaring into the air 14,000 feet above us, no farther off than Pilatus looks from Luzern. It was Kazbek, the mountain where Prometheus hung in chains. Hither the ocean nymphs came to console him; over this desert to the north Io wandered, driven by the gadfly of Hera.

Up to this point we had managed to get on pretty well in hotels, railways, and steamers with German and French and a few words of Russian. Now, however, that it became necessary to take to the road, and enter upon those interminable wranglings with postmasters at post stations which every preceding traveller has described in such repulsive colours, the real difficulties of the way seemed to begin. We therefore thought ourselves fortunate in falling in with two Russian ladies bound for Tiflis, whose acquaintance we made in the train, and who, after a preliminary skirmish about English sympathy with Turkish cruelties, had proposed we should make up a party to hire a vehicle to carry us over the 126 miles of road to the southern capital. Afterwards they

picked up, rather to our disgust, a fifth partner, a Circassian gentleman, also making for Tiflis.   We had of
course conceived of a Tcherkess as a gigantic warrior,
armed to the teeth with helmet and shield and the
unerring rifle, hating the Russian intruder, and ready
to die for Islam.   This Circassian, however, turned
out to be an advocate practising at Stavropol, and
graduate of the university of Moscow — a short,
swarthy man, who was, I believe, a Mohammedan,
but never turned to Mecca all the time we were with
him, and in other ways shewed small regard for the
precepts of the Prophet.   Our vehicle went by the
name of an omnibus, but was what we should call a
covered waggonette, with a leather roof and leather
curtains made to draw round the sides, no useless
protection against the dust and sun.   It held four, or,
at a pinch, six, inside, and one outside beside the
driver and conductor, and seems to be the kind of
carriage most used by travellers of the richer sort on
this frequented piece of road.   We made our bargain
with the conductor for the whole way, but changed
horses and driver at each post station.   There are in
all eleven stations on the road, at intervals of from
eight to sixteen miles, better supplied with horses,
and altogether better appointed, than probably anywhere else in Russia, as is natural when one considers
the importance of the route, and the great number of
military and civil officials who are constantly traversing it.   These stations, however, are not necessarily or properly inns.   At most of them it is a
mere chance if you find anything to eat beyond

bread, and possibly eggs. The room or rooms in which the traveller halts while horses are being changed contains no furniture, except a table, two wooden chairs, and either an ancient sofa or two wooden frames—they cannot be called bedsteads—on which a luxurious traveller may lay his mattress and pillows, if he can spare the time for sleep, and does not mind being disturbed by the irruptions of other wayfarers at all hours during the night. In point of fact, few travellers do stop. The rule in Russia is to go straight ahead, by night as well as by day, eating at odd times, and dozing in your carriage when you can. One soon gets accustomed to that way of life, fresh air and excitement keeping any one who is in good health right enough so long as the journey lasts. The drawback is that you may happen to be uncontrollably drowsy just when you are passing through the finest bit of scenery.

Vladikavkaz lies sufficiently clear of the mountains to enjoy a noble view, looking westward along their northern slope, which is capped by several snowy summits; among them, and almost farthest to the west, the magnificent Dykhtau (16,925 feet). All this, however, is soon lost, for the road runs straight south into the hills, keeping the bottom of the valley, and in eight or nine miles enters a superb gorge among the limestone mountains which here, as in the Alps, form the outer heights of the chain. Clothed, wherever there is room for a root to hold, with the richest deciduous wood, they rise in wonderful precipices 5000 or 6000 feet above the valley, ledge

over ledge, and crag above crag, while at the bottom
they press the river so close that at some points
the road has been cut out in the overhanging cliff
face, and the streamlets from above break in spray
over it.   The scenery is like that of parts of the
Bavarian Alps, only on a far grander scale.   After
a time the glen widens a little, and its character
changes, for we leave the limestone, and come between
mountains of slate or schist.   Here the slopes are
scarcely less steep, but more uniform.   They rise so
abruptly that one hardly understands how wood can
grow on them, and are seamed by deep torrent beds,
dry at this season, but shewing by the piles of stone
and gravel on each side of them with what tremendous force the winter waters must descend.   Behind
them bare, rocky tops occasionally stand out, rising
far above the region of trees, and here and there,
where a lateral glen comes down, and the declivity
is less abrupt, Osset villages are seen, clusters of huts
more like beehives than human dwellings, with small,
rude square towers, perched on eminences for refuge
against a sudden attack.   The population of the
valley is chiefly Osset ; to the east, behind the savage
ridges which guard it on that side, lies the country,
first, of the mainly pagan Ingushes, and then of the
Mohammedan Tchetchens, a powerful group of tribes
quite distinct from the Ossets and Ingushes in blood
and speech.

Hitherto the valley bottom has scarcely risen above
the level of the steppe, and several of the characteristic steppe plants have held their ground, mixed with

the alpine flora of saxifrages, gentians, and so forth,
which is beginning to appear.[1] But now, about sixteen miles from Vladikavkaz, the valley seems suddenly to come to an end, and the track to vanish
among the tremendous crags out of which the river
descends in a succession of cataracts. The road
crosses to its eastern bank, and mounts rapidly along
a shelf cut out of the mountain-side. At the bottom
of the gorge there is the furious torrent; on each side
walls of granite rising (vertically, one would think,
though I suppose they cannot be quite vertical)
4000 feet above it; behind are still loftier ranges of
sharp, red pinnacles, broken, jagged, and terrible,
their topmost summits flecked with snow, not a bush,
or flower, or blade of green to relieve their bare stern-
ness. This is the famous Dariel Pass, a scene whose
grandeur is all the more striking because one comes
so suddenly upon it after the exquisite beauty of the
wooded limestone mountains farther down; a scene
worthy of the historical associations which invest it,
alone of all Caucasian glens, with an atmosphere of
ancient romance. Virgil is renowned for nothing more
than the singular felicity of the epithets with which
he conveys a picture or a story in a single word; and
the phrase, "*duris cautibus horrens Caucasus*," seemed
so exactly to describe this spot that I was tempted
to fancy he had in his mind, when he used it, some
account by a Greek traveller who had wandered thus
far. The mighty masses that hem in this ravine do

---

[1] Among the commonest plants up the valley are our pretty little
English ferns *Cistopteris fragilis* and *Asplenium septentrionale.*

literally bristle with sharp crags in a way that one
does not see even in the *aiguille* ranges of Mont
Blanc. The scene is more absolutely savage, if not
more majestic, than any of the famous passes of the
Alps or Norway. It is not merely the prodigious
height and steepness of the mountains; it is their
utter bareness and the fantastic wildness of their
riven summits, towering 7000 or 8000 feet above
the glen, that fill one with such a sense of terror
and desolation. A stronger military post can hardly
be imagined. Approaching it either way, the precipices seem to bar all further progress, and the
eye seeks in vain to follow the road, which in one
place passes by a tunnel behind a projecting mass of
rock. For about a quarter of a mile the bottom of
the gorge is filled by the foaming stream, so that it is
only along the road that an army could advance.
Half-a-dozen cannon could command the road, and
a single explosion destroy it. At the upper end,
where the ravine widens a little, and gives space for
buildings, the Russians have erected a fort, and
keep a small garrison. Behind, on a great rock
mass, that rises some 300 feet in the middle of the
glen, are the ruins of a far more ancient fortress,
where, according to the Georgian legend, Queen
Tamara dwelt, and caused all those of her suitors
who did not please her (they were more numerous
than Penelope's) to be flung into the torrent below.
Some of the foundations looked so like Roman work
that we wondered whether they might not be the
remains of the fortress which tradition attributes

sometimes to Darius, son of Hystaspes, sometimes
to Alexander the Great, which Pliny describes, and
which was offered by a Hunnish prince to the Roman
emperor Anastasius, and, when he hesitated, seized
by the Persian king Kobad. His son Chosroes, the
great enemy of Rome, held the pass to prevent the
irruption of the nomads of the northern steppe, and,
in the treaties he made with Justinian, stipulated that
the latter should pay his share of the expenses incurred for a common benefit. Certain it is that this
pass is the farthest point to which the dominion of
Rome can ever have stretched on this side; and to
think that we were re-entering here, after traversing
such huge spaces of Scandinavia and Scythia, the
former territories of the same empire which we had
quitted at Hull, conveyed to us a lively idea of the
vastness of that empire. It is hard, however, to
believe that there can ever have been much danger
of invasion through such a gorge as this; and I
cannot but think that the Scythians who ravaged
Upper Asia in the seventh century B.C., and the other
nomad tribes which have from time to time penetrated from the north, must have come along the
Caspian shore by Derbend. Nimble mountaineers
might conceivably have effected a passage, when
there was nothing but the rude track which can be
just discerned here and there on the western bank
of the Terek (the present road is on the east bank,
high above the stream); but that a whole people
should have brought through their waggons and their
flocks seems well-nigh impossible. Be that as it

may, this is beyond question the site of the famous
Caucasian or Iberian Gates.[1]

Above the gorge the valley widens a little, and its
sides, though not less lofty, are somewhat less precipitous. To avoid the floods which have covered the bottom
with gravel, the road mounts the western slope, along
which prodigious masses of alluvium are heaped up,
the remains, one would think, of some ancient moraine.
Such traces of glacial action abound in the glen
through its entire length. Towards Vladikavkaz they
take the form of well-marked terraces; here they are
less regular, but quite as huge, and where some side
ravine comes in, its stream often cuts through a hard
mass of rounded blocks and gravel for a depth of
several hundred feet. The walls of the Dariel gorge
itself are of grey, large-grained granite; but one sees
many other igneous rocks in the cliffs—porphyries,

---

[1] See Strabo, xi. 3, 5; Tac. Ann. vi. 33; Pliny, Nat. Hist. vi. 5, 112 and
xiv. (who gives the fullest description both of the Caucasian and Caspian
Gates, which he distinguishes carefully, evidently intending the Dariel
by his Caucasian Gates); and Procopius, Pers. i. 10, and Goth. iv. 3.
I wish some university or other learned body would offer a prize for an
essay on the Caucasian and Caspian Gates, for there is hardly a subject
in ancient or mediæval geography more perplexing than the use of those
names. There were three passes between which boundless confusion has
arisen: first, the Dariel, sometimes called the Caucasian, sometimes the
Caspian, sometimes the Iberian Gates; second, the pass between the
mountains and the sea near Derbend, where is the wall of Gog and
Magog, called sometimes the Caucasian, sometimes the Caspian, sometimes the Albanian Gates; third, a pass somewhere on the south coast
of the Caspian, called the Caspian Gates, which was really visited and
fortified by Alexander the Great, who never came near our Caucasus
at all. Pliny (loc. cit.) talks of a gate and fortress: "Fores obditae
ferratis trabibus subter medias amne diri odoris fluente, citraque in
rupe castello quod vocatur Cumania, communito ad arcendas transitu
gentes innumeras, ibi loci terrarum orbe portis discluso."

syenites, and basalts ; about four miles above the
fort a beautiful range of basaltic columns, much like
those of the Giant's Causeway, runs along the steep
mountain-side for some distance. After this the
metamorphic schists reappear, and prevail, with occasional patches of interjected igneous rocks, until,
far down in the southern spurs of the chain, one
comes again upon the limestones which have been
thrown off upon both flanks of the central crystalline
mass.

Some ten miles above the Dariel, and about twenty-
seven from Vladikavkaz, the road, descending to the
river, suddenly rounds a corner of rock, and with a
start the traveller finds himself full in face of the
magnificent Kazbek, a steep dome of snow breaking
down on the east in a grand black precipice. The
top is 16,533 feet above the sea, and 11,000 feet
above the little alpine plain or circular hollow in
the mountains where stands the *aoul* (village) of
Kazbek, inhabited by Georgians. The post-house
here is one of the best on the road, and actually fur-
nishes two or three beds—European beds with sheets
and a dirty blanket ; so, wishing to have a little time
to take in the wonderful scenery, we proposed to make
a halt for the night. This, however, our companions,
who were anxious to reach Tiflis, would by no means
agree to ; and all we could obtain by way of concession was an hour and a half to climb to a little church
which stands perched on a height 1400 feet above the
glen, and commands a noble view of Kazbek with his
attendant peaks. The building interested us as the

first specimen we had seen of Georgian or Armenian
architecture ; it was, indeed still is, a much visited place
of pilgrimage, and seemed to date from the twelfth or
thirteenth century.   When we reached it, the clouds
which each morning gather round the great summits
as soon as the day grows hot, about nine or ten o'clock,
still kept the top of Kazbek hid ; but after waiting
ten minutes, we were rewarded, about 4.30 P.M., by
seeing them disperse under the strong breeze, and his
glorious snowy crest came out against the intense blue
of a sky whose clearness seemed to surpass even that
of the Alps.   North of it a savage glen shewed where
lay the great glacier of Devdorak, by which the
summit is ascended ; on the other side, a line of un-
trodden snows runs south-west into the heart of the
chain ; in the middle stood up the perfectly isolated
dome, all snow-covered, except where on the eastern
face stands out the great black precipice to which
Prometheus was chained.[1]   Kazbek is a mass of
trachyte, probably an ancient volcano, with its two
snow sides looking so steep that we did not wonder
that all travellers had pronounced them inaccessible
till they yielded to the courage and skill of our
countrymen, Messrs. Freshfield, Moore, and Tucker,
in 1868. The climbers incurred some danger, especially in the latter part of the ascent ; but the easier
route they discovered in descending has been taken

---

[1] According to the generally accepted legend, which probably took
its origin from some Greek traveller passing this way.   But Aeschylus
does not conceive of Prometheus as chained in the Caucasus.   In his
drama the rock hangs over the sea and the plain of Scythia, and the
Caucasus is spoken of as being at some considerable distance away.

once or twice since ; and by it the ascent is not really difficult, and involves, if the climber has proper appliances, no serious risk. We longed to try our fortune, but having nothing in the shape of a guide, nor any chance of procuring one, and no other mountaineering apparatus, there was little use thinking further of it.

Below us, on the opposite side from Kazbek, lay the little green plain with its patches of rye and oats, its fields divided by low stone walls and tiny, flat-roofed cottages ; beyond it, again, the eastern wall of the valley rose with terrific steepness to a height of 11,000 or 12,000 feet, with slopes too abrupt to bear snow, which only lay in sheltered northward hollows. The elements of the view were the same as we had seen many a time before, but somehow the view had a character of its own quite unlike anything European. Whether it was that one missed the cheerful pastures dotted over with herds and *châlets*, or that there was no wood below, and comparatively little snow above, or simply that the mountain lines were more ruthlessly stern and jagged, it was hard to tell ; but, anyhow, the impression was quite new. The Caucasus, though its latitude is but little farther south than that of the Alps, is not a mere repetition of the Alps on a larger scale, any more than the Russian steppe is a repetition of the Hungarian plain ; its character, the impression which its scenery makes, is wholly different.

We returned to the post-house punctually at the appointed hour, but were met by reproachful faces.

"There are now no horses to be had; in your absence other travellers came up, and, being ready to start, called for all that were in the stable; we could not retain them. There will be none fit for work now before to-morrow morning." Although secretly rejoiced to have a few more hours under the shadow of Kazbek, still, as politeness required, we dissembled our satisfaction, were forgiven, and prepared to spend the night at the uninviting post-house. There still wanted an hour to sunset; so we rambled up to an Osset *aoul*, which stands on the western bank of the Terek, and examined the quaint little corn-mills that have been planted along the courses of the descending brooks, rude buildings of loose stone about four feet high, with a horizontal wheel inside a foot and a half in diameter, and two bits of millstones scarcely larger than those of the old Irish quern or hand-mill. Civilization in the Caucasian countries has not got so far as a windmill: at any rate, we never saw one. On the flat, earthen roofs of the houses the people were treading or thrashing out their rye; the interiors were dark, windowless, and apparently without furniture; the walls of unmortared stone. Pretty, fair-haired children followed us about, offering crystals for sale, or begging in an unknown tongue.

The Georgian village on the opposite side of the river, where the post-house stands, is more civilized; its houses are arranged in something like lanes; it has a church which from the style I took to be ancient, but found to date from the beginning of this century only, a curious instance of that steadfast adhesion to

old architectural models which is the rule in Georgia
and Russia, and makes it difficult to tell the age of
a building from its style, as one can generally do in
Western Europe; though, to be sure, our descendants
may not find it so simple a matter to fix the churches
of the nineteenth century, which imitate every earlier
fashion.   In this village several of the houses had singular square towers, erected, no doubt, for purposes of
defence in the unquiet times, before the coming of the
Russians, when some neighbouring tribe might swoop
down at any moment on the peasant.   Such towers
are common among most of the Caucasian peoples;
the finest, one hears, are to be found among the independent Suans in the Ingur valley.   While we were
wandering round the church, we asked some question
about it of a gentleman leaning over the second floor
verandah of an adjoining house, the biggest in the
village, and were desired, in French, to come up the
ladder.   Complying, we were welcomed by a young
man with those soft handsome features which are so
common among the Georgians, who turned out to be
the Prince of Kazbek, a Georgian noble, who owns this
part of the valley.   He was entertaining two or three
government *employés* sent from Tiflis to examine the
glacier of Devdorak, which has several times formed
a *debâcle*, behind which water accumulated in a lake,
which, breaking out at last, devastated the Terek
valley.   Among them was a young engineer from the
Baltic provinces, speaking German, and an accomplished Armenian official, speaking both German and
French, with whom we talked about the Caucasus to

G

our heart's content, over endless glasses of lemon tea,
while the great mountain glittered before us in the
clear cold starlight.   It was late when we parted
from our genial host at the door of the post-house;
and before light next morning we had mounted the
omnibus again, and were pursuing our drowsy way
up the valley.   It is comparatively open up here, perfectly bare of wood, and uninhabited, except for an
occasional village surrounding two or three grim old
square towers.   The scenery is more savage than
beautiful; but if we had not seen the Dariel defile
lower down, we should have thought it magnificent,
for Kazbek occasionally shewed his snows, blushing
rosy under the first sunlight, to the west, while the
great eastern range rose more imposing than ever as
we approached the axis of the chain.   The last station
on the north side of the watershed is Kobi, where we
breakfasted (as usual off the alone attainable eggs and
tea), and where is a curious Osset altar, adorned all
round with the horns of the great wild goat, *Capra
caucasica*, at which sacrifices, half Christian, half
pagan, are offered.   Here the Terek comes down
from a wild glen running deep into pathless mountains to the west, and the road turns up the short
valley of a lesser stream, remarkable from the great
number of mineral springs that gush out from its
sides.   One which we drank of sparkles with bubbles
of carbonic acid gas, and had a pleasant sweetish taste;
but all, as we were afterwards told, contain, along with
their iron and other valuable ingredients, too much
chalk to make them serviceable for medicinal pur-

poses. The summit level of the road, about twenty miles from Kazbek station and forty-one from Vladikavkaz, is 8015 feet above the sea, a green, slightly undulating level, from which no distant view can be obtained, except straight south, for on both sides it is enclosed by mountains rising about 1400 feet above it, while other summits farther back reach 11,000 or 12,000 feet. The Russians call this *col* or pass Krestovaya Gora, or Cross Mountain, from a cross planted on it. The name, " Pass of Dariel," belongs properly only to the gorge below Kazbek station, where the fort stands; but as this gorge is the most remarkable feature of the whole route, and the most important military position, geographers and foreigners generally extend its name to the whole road from Vladikavkaz to Tiflis. There is no fortification at the top, or anywhere, save at the Dariel gorge; nor did I see any military posts along the road. During the war with Shamyl, however, it was strongly guarded, and was indeed of the utmost importance to Russia; since by holding it they not only kept open their communications with Georgia, but prevented a junction between the hero of Daghestan and the tribes that were in arms to the west. Needless to say that it is also of the greatest consequence to her in the present struggle, since across it all her troops and munitions of war are sent to Armenia.

From the open green pastures of the watershed the road descends an almost precipitous mountain face in a series of long zigzags, cut with admirable skill, and at their foot reaches the pretty little Georgian village

of Mleti. Nothing can be more beautiful than the view
in descending.   To the north-east you look up into a
wilderness of stern red mountains, their hollows filled
with snow or ice, their sides strewed with huge loose
blocks.   Round Mleti itself woods begin to hang upon
the hills, and fields of rye diversify the pastures, while
down the long vista that opens to the south dense
forests enclose the narrow ravine through which the
river Aragva finds its way to the low country.   The
pastoral beauty of the scene is all the more felt because
you have come straight from a land of desolation ;
there is a sense of southern luxuriance about the landscape like that which greets the traveller who drops
into Italy from the Alps of Switzerland.   Down from
Mleti the road follows the Aragva (the Aragon of
Strabo) through its deep, richly wooded valley, adorned
here and there with ruined towers, perched upon projecting points, as far as the little town of Ananaur,
where the Caucasus proper may be said to subside into
the hilly rather than mountainous country of Georgia.
These woods are really splendid, composed almost
entirely of deciduous trees, beech, oak, hazel, birch,
and such like, and so close as to look perfectly im-
penetrable.   The scenery is something like that of
Killiecrankie, in Perthshire, only on a far vaster scale ;
but the river is scanty and whitish from its parent
glaciers, every way inferior to the Scottish stream.
Ananaur has a grand old castle, commanding the road
and valley, within whose walls stand two ancient
churches, elaborately adorned outside in the Georgian
style with the figures of lions and other creatures

elegantly carved in relief, and surrounded with ara-
besques. From here the road, which first mounts over
a ridge of hills, and then descends past the quaint
little town of Dushet towards the Kur, is pretty
enough, but less interesting, and I relieved its tedium
by a long talk with the ladies, who, it appeared, had
done us the honour to take us for poets, because we
seemed to admire the scenery, and I had been gathering plants. As we are both lawyers, and considered
by our friends to be rather plain matter-of-fact people,
this unexpected compliment flattered us not a little,
and on the strength of it I indited a sonnet to the
younger lady's cigarette, which was however, like its
subject, of so evanescent a nature that it need not be
reproduced here. Asking them about the writers of
modern Russia, we found what had already surprised
us, that Turgenef does not hold among his own country
folk so transcendently conspicuous a place as Western
readers would allot him. They appear to put others,
whose works have not been translated into French or
German, or, when translated, have made little impression, on a level with him. Perhaps this is because he
has been so keen a critic of Russian weaknesses : if
so, it is another instance of that sensitiveness one so
often remarks among them.

About 11 P.M. our omnibus drew up in the famous
city of Mtzkhet, once the capital of the Georgian kingdom, and seat of their patriarch, and now a wretched
village of some hundred and fifty people, dwelling in the
shadow of two noble old churches and a large ruined
castle. The position is a fine one, for it occupies the

middle of and commands the narrow valley by which the Kur descends from its upper basin into the lower basin of Tiflis, and is defended on one side by the Kur itself, on the other by the Aragva, which here mingle their waters. From very early times the site has been inhabited, witness the numerous cave dwellings hewn out in the soft limestone rock of the cliffs along the Kur; and it was not far off that Pompey, in his famous march to the Caucasus, defeated the Iberian armies. Two centuries after the introduction of Christianity, a Georgian king forsook it for Tiflis, and now its chief importance lies in being the point where the military road to Vladikavkaz strikes the railway from Tiflis to the Black Sea. Anxious to examine it, and still more anxious to lie down and sleep, on the ground, in a post-house, anywhere, we heard with pleasure the conventional postmaster declare that no horses could be had before nine o'clock next morning; it was impossible, not a hoof in his stable, nor in any of the peasants' either. However, our companions, and especially the Circassian, who, I fancy, had a law-suit in Tiflis, were unwearied and inexorable. In vain we dwelt on the antiquarian interest of Mtzkhet, and proposed to give them a sketch of its early history, beginning from its founder, the great-grandson of Japhet; in vain on the advantage of entering Tiflis by daylight, and the unlikelihood of getting a bed there in the small hours. In vain we even condescended to put in a word for the postmaster, insisting on the duty of travellers not to press too hardly on these poor men and their hard-worked horses. " Let

us get at once to the journey's end," they replied;
"we have been travelling only forty hours. Surely
that has not tired you" (dear energetic ladies). "As
for Mtzkhet and its churches, the world is a big world,
and you cannot see everything in it." At last, relying
on the obstinacy of the postmaster, we agreed to go
on if horses could be found ; whereupon the Circassian
barrister bullied him with so much vigour that horses
were found forthwith, and in two hours more we were
rattling over the stones of the capital of Transcaucasia, and on our first night in Asia were received
by the drowsy but friendly servants of the Hôtel de
l'Europe.

CHAPTER III.

TRANSCAUCASIA.

IN this chapter I shall attempt to give a sort of general sketch of the Russian territories lying to the south of the Caucasus, the richest, and, for the present at least, geographically the most important of all the Asiatic dominions of the Czar. It is, like the rest of this book, a record of first impressions only, but of impressions formed, as I venture to believe, without any pre-existing bias, and to a considerable extent tested by comparison with the conclusions which other travellers have reached. And even for first impressions there is this much to be said, that the risk of errors of observation and of hasty generalization has some compensation in the freshness with which things present themselves to a new-comer. Occasionally he is struck by aspects of society or politics which are really true and important, but which one who has lived long in a country finds so familiar that they have ceased to stimulate his curiosity, and would perhaps be omitted from his descriptions. This may supply some justification for the apparent presumption of a traveller who admits that he had to see, and now has to write, more hastily than he could have wished. What I have got to say of particular parts of the country, such as Tiflis, the capital, and Armenia, is reserved for later chapters.

Transcaucasia is a convenient general name for the countries lying between the Black Sea, the Caspian, and the Caucasus, which make up the dominions of the Czar in Western Asia. It is not, however, an official Russian name, for although for some purposes they distinguish Ciscaucasia and Transcaucasia, the administrative district or lieutenancy of the empire which they call the Caucasus (Kavkaz) includes not only the regions south of the mountains, but also several governments lying to the north, in what the geographers call Europe. Nor does it denote any similarity or common character in these countries, the chief of which are Georgia, which lies along the upper course of the Kur, south of the Caucasus; Armenia, farther south, on the Araxes, between Georgia, Persia, and Turkey; Imeritia, west of Georgia; and Mingrelia, west of Imeritia, along the eastern coast of the Black Sea. However, it is a convenient name, and before speaking of each of these countries by itself, something may be said of the general physical features of Transcaucasia as a whole. It may be broadly described as consisting of two mountain regions and two plains. First, all along the north, there are the slopes of the Caucasus, which on this side (at least in its western half, for towards the east the main chain sinks quite abruptly into the levels of Kakhitia) sends off several lateral ranges descending far from the axis, and at last subsiding into a

fertile and well-peopled hilly country. Secondly, on
the south, over against the Caucasus, there is another
mountain land, less elevated, but wider in extent,
consisting of the chain which under various local
names (some geographers have called it the Anti-
Caucasus) runs from Lazistan at the south-east angle
of the Black Sea away to the east and south-east
till it meets the ranges of Persia. Towards the
south, this chain ramifies all over Armenia, and here
attains its greatest height in the volcanic summits of
Ala Göz, 13,460 feet above the sea, while northward
its spurs form a hilly country stretching to Tiflis.
These two mountain masses are connected by a ridge
which, branching off from the Caucasus between
Elbruz and Kazbek, the two best known of all the
summits of that chain, divides the waters of the Kur
from those of the Rion (Phasis), and is crossed by the
great road and railway from Tiflis to the Black Sea
near the town of Suram. Although of no great height
—it is only about 3600 feet at Suram—this ridge has
a most important influence (to be referred to presently) both on the climate and on the ethnology
of the country. It is that which Strabo speaks of
as inhabited by the Moschici,[1] and is sometimes, therefore, called by modern geographers the Meschic ridge.

The two plains I have spoken of are of very unequal size. The eastern extends all along the Caspian, from the southern foot of the Caucasus to the

---

[1] Interpreters, from the time of Josephus downwards (who places
them more towards Cappadocia), have sought to identify these Moschici
or Meschi (as Procopius calls them, Goth. iv. 3) with the Mesech of
the Bible (Gen. x. 2 ; Ps. cxx. 5).

Persian frontier, and runs up the valley of the Kur, gradually rising, to within a few miles of Tiflis. It is open, bare, and dry; is, in fact, what the Russians call steppe country, or the Americans prairie, through nearly its whole extent, and though the soil is fertile, much of it, especially towards the Caspian, is but thinly peopled or cultivated. The western plain, on the other hand, lying along the lower course of the Rion, between the Caucasus, the Anti-Caucasus, and the Black Sea, is moist and densely wooded, parts of it little better than a forest swamp, but the whole, where dry enough for tillage, extremely rich. It has all the appearance of having been, at no distant period, a bay of the Euxine, which may gradually have got filled up by the alluvium brought down by the Rion and other Caucasian streams. When this bay existed, and when the Caspian, which we know to have greatly shrunk, even in comparatively recent times, extended far up the valley of the Kur, and was joined to the Euxine north of the Caucasus, between the mouths of the Kuban and Terek, the Caucasus itself formed an immense mountain peninsula, joined to the highlands of Western Asia by an isthmus consisting of the Suram ridge already referred to and the elevated country east of it. And as at this time the Caspian was also, no doubt, connected with the Sea of Aral (which is only some 160 feet above the present level of the Caspian, and about 80 above the ocean), one may say that the Mediterranean then extended through this chain of inland seas, far into Central Asia, perhaps to the sites of those cities, Khiva, Tashkend, Bokhara, of which we have lately heard so much.

The climates of these two plains are strangely contrasted, and the ridge of Suram marks the boundary between them. On the Black Sea coast the winters are mild (mean winter temperature about 44° F., mean annual temperature 58°), snow falls, perhaps, but hardly lies, all sorts of southern plants thrive in the open air, and the rainfall is so abundant that vegetation is everywhere, even up in the mountains, marvellously profuse. At Poti, the seaport at the mouth of the Rion which every traveller from the West is condemned to pass through, the most fever-smitten den in all Asia, one feels in a perpetual vapour bath, and soon becomes too enervated to take the most obvious precautions against the prevailing malady. Higher up, in the deep valleys of the Ingur and Kodor, rivers which descend from the great chain, the forests are positively tropical (though the vegetation itself is European) in the splendour of the trees and the rank luxuriance of the underwood. If there were a few roads and any enterprise, this country might drive a magnificent trade in wood and all sorts of natural productions.

This is the general character of the Black Sea coast. But when you cross the Meschic watershed at Suram, and enter the basin of the Kur, drawing towards the Caspian, everything changes. The streams are few, the grass is withered on the hillside, by degrees even the beechwoods begin to disappear; and as one gets farther and farther to the east, beyond Tiflis, there is

in autumn hardly a trace of vegetation either on plain
or hills, except along the courses of the shrunken
rivers and on the northern slopes of the mountains
that divide the basins of the Kur and Aras. In these
regions the winter is very severe, and the summer
heats are tremendous. At Lenkoran, on the Caspian,
in latitude 38° N., the sea is often blocked with ice
for two miles from the shore, and the average winter
temperature is the same as that of Maestricht, in latitude 51°, or Reykjavik (in Iceland), in latitude 64°.
The rainfall, which near Poti reaches 63 inches in
the year, is at Baku only 13·7, and in some parts of
the Aras valley only 5 inches. The explanation, of
course, is that, while the moist westerly winds are
arrested by the ridge at Suram, the eastern steppe lies
open to the parching and bitter blasts which descend
from Siberia and the frozen plains of Turkestan, while
the scorching summers are not moderated by the influence of a neighbouring sea, the Caspian being too
small to make any great difference in the climate.

In Armenia the same causes operate, with the addition that, as a good deal of the country stands at a
great height above the sea-level, the winters are in
those parts long and terrible. At Alexandropol, for
instance, the great Russian fortress over against Kars,
where a large part of her army is always stationed,
snow lies till the middle of April, spring lasts only
about a fortnight, and during summer the country is
parched like any desert.[1]

[1] The mean winter temperature of Alexandropol is 16° F. ; its annual
rainfall 14·68 inches.

A result of this remarkable dryness of the climate, away from the Black Sea and its influences, is that the landscapes of Eastern Transcaucasia are bare, brown, and generally dreary. If there was ever wood on the lower grounds, it has been long since cut away, and probably could hardly be made to grow if now re-planted. There is a certain impressiveness in the wide views of bare brown open plains and stern red mountains which are so often before one in these countries, and, I fancy, in Persia also; the effects both of light and shade, and of colour, are broad, deep, solemn. These are the merits of Eastern land-scape generally, which an eye accustomed to the minuter prettiness of such a country as our own perhaps underrates. Admitting them, however, I must still remark that there is not much in Transcaucasia to attract the lover of natural beauty, except in two regions, the spurs of the Caucasus and the part of Armenia which lies round and commands a prospect of Mount Ararat. These are certainly considerable exceptions, for the scenery of each is quite unlike anything to be found in Europe. The luxuriant vegetation of the deep western valleys of the chain and the noble views of its tremendous snowy sum-mits, streaming with glaciers, present pictures sur-passing even those of the Italian valleys of the Alps —pictures that one must go to the Himalaya to find a parallel for. Ararat, again, an isolated volcanic cone rising 17,000 feet above the sea and 14,400 feet above the plain at its own base, is a phenomenon the like of which hardly exists in the world.

Whether beautiful or the reverse, however, the country is nearly everywhere rich, and might do wonders if it were filled by a larger, more energetic, and better educated population. There are only three millions of people in it now; it could easily support twenty. The steppe soil is generally extremely fertile, needing nothing but irrigation to produce heavy crops of grain. In some parts, especially along the Araxes, cotton is raised. The warm valleys of Mingrelia and Imeritia produce maize, rice, and other southern cereals; corn grows up to a height of 5000 or 7000 feet, and the tea shrub thrives on the hills. The olive is not common, and, though the vine will grow almost everywhere, the wine is generally inferior. Some of that which is made in Armenia is tolerable, but by far the best is that of Kakhitia, a delightfully pretty region lying immediately under the great wall of the Eastern Caucasus, north-east of Tiflis. Its wine is sound and wholesome, albeit a little acid. The natives are very proud of it, and incessantly vaunt its merits as a specific against fever and otherwise; they certainly all follow the prescription, and the Georgians in particular, a race of jovial topers, are apt to carry their appreciation a little too far. If it would bear travelling, it would be a valuable article of export; and possibly, when better methods of making it than the present very primitive ones are introduced, and when it is put in casks instead of buffalo hides smeared with naphtha, it may rival the wines of the Don and the Crimea in the markets of Southern Russia. Of

the wealth of the western forests in box, walnut, and
woods of all sorts, suited for furniture as well as
shipbuilding, it is needless to speak ; of the minerals,
it is rather difficult, for although everyone believes
that there is abundance in the mountains, and there
is constant talk of getting up companies to work
them, very little has been done to determine their
precise amount or quality. Coal certainly exists in
the west, among the mountains of Imeritia, north-east
of Kutais, but the abundance of wood has made people
remiss in availing themselves of it.   Iron and copper
have been discovered in many places ; the best copper
mines hitherto opened lie in the northern declivity of
the Karabagh Mountains, to the south-west of Elizavetpol, and are worked by Messrs. Siemens Brothers.
Salt is abundant in Armenia, especially near Kulpi, on
the Upper Aras ; and the Mingrelians, who really have
silver mines, appeal to the instance of the Golden
Fleece as proof that the precious metals exist among
them.   There is no doubt that grains of gold are
found in the detritus brought down by the Phasis and
other streams, but whether it is true, as geographers
and travellers have gone on repeating ever since
Strabo set the story going, that the natives place
fleeces in the current to catch the passing particles,
I have not been able to ascertain.   Sulphur has been
got in Daghestan, and was used by Shamyl to make
gunpowder when he could get none from Persia.
Perhaps the most remarkable mineral product is
naphtha, which bursts forth in many places, but most
profusely near Baku, on the coast of the Caspian, in

strong springs, some of which are said to be always burning, while others, lying close to or even below the sea, will sometimes, in calm weather, discharge the spirit over the water, so that, when a light is applied, the sea takes fire, and blue flames flicker for miles over the surface. The place was greatly revered of old by the fire-worshippers, and after they were extirpated from Persia by the Mohammedans, who hate them bitterly, some few occasionally slunk here on pilgrimage. Now, under the more tolerant sway of the Czar, a solitary priest of fire is maintained by the Parsee community of Bombay, who inhabits a small temple built over one of the springs, and, like a vestal, tends the sacred flame by day and night.

If it is hard to give a general idea of a country so various in its physical aspects, it is even more so to describe its strangely mixed population. From the beginning of history, all sorts of tribes and races have lived in this isthmus between the Euxine and the Caspian, and though some of them may have now disappeared or been absorbed by others, new elements have pressed in from the north and east. Strabo, writing under Augustus, mentions four peoples as dwelling south of the Caucasus : the Colchians, along the Black Sea; the Iberians, farther to the east, beyond the cross ridge of Suram (which he calls an ἄγκων of the Caucasus) ; the Albanians, still farther eastward, in the plains along the Caspian Sea ; and the Armenians, to the south of all these, in the country we still call Armenia. To the north of the three former, the wooded valleys of the Caucasus were occupied by

H

many wild tribes, more akin, says he, to the Sarmatians, but speaking many different languages ; one of the wildest are the Soanes, the name still borne by an extremely disagreeable race, who inhabit the grandest part of the whole Caucasus, immediately to the south of Elbruz and Koschtantau, and of whom I have spoken in the preceding chapter. While these Soanes have been protected by their inaccessibility in the pathless recesses of the mountains, all trace of Colchians, Iberians, and Albanians,[1] has long since passed away, and though Mingrelians now live where Jason found the Colchians, there is nothing to show that any of the blood of Aeëtes and Medea flows in their degenerate veins. Russian ethnologists talk of a Karthalinian stock, to which Mingrelians, Imeritians, and Georgians, as well as some of the mountain tribes, are declared to belong. But, without discussing problems of ethnology for whose solution sufficient materials have not yet been collected, I will shortly describe the chief races that now occupy the country.

Beginning from the west, we find the Mingrelians along the Black Sea coast, from the Turkish border to Sukhum Kaleh. They are the ne'er-do-wells of the Caucasian family. All their neighbours, however contemptible a Western may think them, have a bad word and a kick for the still more contemptible Mingrelian. To believe them, he is lazy, sensual, treacherous, and stupid, a liar and a thief. The strain

---

[1] Those who build ethnological theories on similarities of name may be asked whether they can establish any relationship between these Albanians and the Albanians of Epirus and the Scottish Alban, or between these Iberians and the Iberians of Spain.

in which the Russians and Armenians talk of them reminded me of the description one gets from the Transylvanian Saxons and Magyars of the Roumans who live among them. You ask what kind of people the Wallachs are. " A dirty people," they answer, "a treacherous people, a lazy people, a superstitious people, a cruel people, a gluttonous people. Otherwise not such a bad kind of people." (" *Sonst ist es kein schlechtes Volk.*") Lazy the Mingrelian certainly is, but in other respects I doubt if he is worse than his neighbours ; and he lives in so damp and warm a climate that violent exercise must be disagreeable. He is a well-made, good-looking fellow, but with a dull and heavy expression which is sensual so far as it goes. And he is certainly backward in agriculture and trade, making very little of a singularly rich country. South of Mingrelia lies Guria, on the slopes and ridges of the Anti-Caucasus, a land where the people are more vigorous and upright, and where, as they have been less affected by conquest and immigration, the picturesque old costumes have best maintained themselves. West of the Mingrelians, in the hilly regions of the Upper Rion and its tributaries, live the Imeritians, a race speaking a dialect of Georgian, who may generally be distinguished by their bushy hair. My personal knowledge of them is confined to three waiters at three several inns, rather a narrow basis for induction, but quite as wide as many travellers have had for some very sweeping conclusions. They have a better name than the Mingrelians,

I

both for industry and honesty, and these three waiters were pleasant, civil fellows, though not particularly bright.

Still farther east, and occupying the centre of Transcaucasia, are the Georgians, called by the Russians Grusinians or Grusians, who may be con-considered the principal and, till the arrival of the Muscovite, the dominant race of the country. They call themselves Karthli, deducing their origin from a patriarch Karthlos (who was brother of Haik, the patriarch of the Armenian nation, and of Legis, the ancestor of the Lesghians), a grandson, or, as others hold, great-grandson of Gomer, son of Japhet. According to their own legends, they worshipped the sun and the moon and the five planets, and swore by the grave of Karthlos until converted to Christianity by St. Nina, in the fourth century of our era. For several centuries their kingdom extended almost to the Black Sea in one direction and the Caspian in another, and maintained itself with some credit against the hostility of Turks and Persians, though often wasted by Persian armies, and for long periods obliged to admit the suzerainty of the Shah. Its heroic age was the time of Queen Tamara, who flourished in the twelfth century, and is still honoured by pictures all over the country, in which she appears as a beautiful Amazon, not unlike the fancy portraits of Joan of Arc. To her is ascribed the foundation of every ancient church or monastery, just as all the strongholds are said to have been built by the robber

Kir Oghlu,[1] and as in Scotland there is hardly an
old mansion but shows Wallace's sword and Queen
Mary's apartment. Somewhat later the kingdom became divided into three, Kakhitia, Karthli or Georgia
proper, on the Upper Kur, and Imeritia ; and in the
period of weakness that followed it began to look for
help to Russia. As early as 1492, a king of Kakhitia
invoked the Czar Ivan III., and in 1638 the king of
Imeritia swore fealty to Alexis Mihailovitch. The
famous treaty of Kainardji in 1774 (about which we
have had so many lively discussions) placed Georgia,
Imeritia, and Mingrelia, under the protection of Russia.[2]
However, the *coup de grâce* was given by the invasion
of the Persians, under Aga Mohammed Khan, in
1795, which reduced Georgia to such wretchedness
that the reigning king George made over his dominions
to Alexander I. in 1799, and the country was finally
occupied by Russian troops in 1802.[3] One sees traces
of a sort of feudal period in the numerous castles ;
most of them mere square towers, such as we see on
the coast of Scotland and the north of Ireland, which

[1] Stories of Kir (or Kara = Black) Oghlu are told all about the country.
One, localised in Armenia, represents him as meeting a party of travellers,
and among them one with pistols (then lately invented) stuck in his
belt. He asks what those things are, and, when their use is explained
to him, exclaims, "Farewell, Kir Oghlu, your occupation is gone,"
rides off into the mountains, and is never more seen.

[2] See this treaty in the appendix to Mr. Hollands' 'Lecture on the
Treaty Relations of Russia and Turkey.'

[3] Russia, however, did not acquire Imeritia till 1810, the Mingrelian
coast till 1829 (by the treaty of Adrianople), the Caspian coast south o
the mouth of the Kur till 1813, and the valley of the Middle Araxes till
1828. She had already obtained from Persia in 1797 Daghestan and
Shirvan as far as the Kur mouth.

lie scattered all over Georgia and Imeritia ; and the
organization of society was feudal till quite lately, the
peasantry serfs, the upper class landowning nobles and
their dependants.   It is a joke among the Russians
that every Georgian is a noble ; and as the only title of
nobility is Prince, the effect to an English ear of hearing all sorts of obscure people, country postmasters,
droshky drivers, sometimes even servants, described
as being Prince So-and-so, is at first grotesque.   This
at least may be said for the numerous nobility, that,
although it is both vain and frivolous, it does not
despise all honest occupations.

Everyone has heard of the Georgian beauties, who
in the estimation of Turkish importers rivalled or sur-
passed those of Circassia itself.   Among them a great
many handsome and even some beautiful faces may
certainly be seen, regular and finely chiselled features,
a clear complexion, large and liquid eyes, an erect
carriage, in which there is a good deal of dignity as
well as of voluptuousness.   To a taste, however,
formed upon Western models, mere beauty of features
and figure, without expression, is not very interesting ;
and these faces have seldom any expression.   They
want even that vivacity which, in the parallel case of
the women of Andalusia, partly redeems the absence
of intelligence.   Admirable as pieces of Nature's
handiwork, they are not charming.   A Turk may
think them perfection, but it may be doubted whether
anyone who had seen the ladies of Cork or Baltimore
would take much pleasure in their society.   However,
this is a point on which people will disagree to the

end of time ; and those who hold that it is enough to
look at a beauty without feeling inclined to talk to
her need not go beyond Georgia to find all they can
wish. It must be remembered, however, that this
loveliness is rather fleeting. Towards middle life the
complexion is apt to become sallow, and the nose and
chin rather too prominent, while the vacuity of look
remains. One is told that they are, as indeed the
whole nation is, almost uneducated, with nothing but
the pettiest personal interests to fill their thoughts
or animate their lives.

The men are sufficiently good-looking and pleasing
in manner, with, perhaps, a shade of effeminacy in
their countenances, at least in those of the lowland.
They do not strike one as a strong race, either physically or otherwise, with any future before it, nor have
they ever produced a great man, or done anything
considerable in history, although they have had
civilization and Christianity, after a sort, ever since
the third century of our era, and have maintained
their religion and national existence with great tenacity
against both Turks and Persians. So early as the
sixth century, Procopius compliments the Iberians
(who are doubtless the ancestors of our Georgians) on
their resolute adherence to Christian rites in spite of
the attacks of the Persian fire-worshippers,[1] who, it may
be remarked in passing, seem to have been the first to

---

[1] Kobad, the reigning king of Persia, whose supremacy the Iberians
then owned, had tried to force them over to his faith, and began by
ordering them to desist from burying their dead, and to adopt the
Persian practice of exposing the dead body to the birds and beasts.
They refused, and sought help from the Romans (Procop. Pers. i. 12).

set the example of religious persecution. The Muslims say that the Christianity of the Georgians is owing to their fondness for wine and for pork, both which good things, as everybody knows, the Prophet has forbidden to true believers. They belong, of course, to the Orthodox Eastern Church, and are now in full communion with the Church of Russia, of which indeed they may be said to have become a branch, though their liturgy differs a little in some points. During the earlier middle ages I suspect that they were more influenced by heterodox Armenia than by Constantinople, though they separated from the Armenian Church in the end of the sixth century, when the latter finally anathematized the Council of Chalcedon. Their ecclesiastical alphabet, for they have two, is taken from the Armenian. Of their number it is difficult to form an estimate ; it can hardly exceed 500,000 souls, and may be considerably less.[1]

Scattered through Upper Georgia, and to be found among the peasantry as well as in the towns, there is a considerable Armenian population, who probably settled here when their national kingdom was destroyed by the Seljukian conquerors, Alp Arslan and Malek Shah, in the eleventh century. Farther south, in Armenia proper, they constitute the bulk of the population in the country districts, Kurds being mixed with them in the mountains, Tatars in the plains, and Persians in the towns. As I shall have something to say of them in a later chapter, it is unnecessary to

---

[1] The total number of the Grusinian race, including Imeritians and Mingrelians, is estimated by a recent Russian statistician of authority at 850,000.

describe them at present, further than to remark that they are the most vigorous and intelligent of the Transcaucasian races, with a gift for trade which has enabled them to get most of the larger business of the country into their hands. Their total number in these countries is estimated at 550,000.

Going down the Kur from Tiflis towards the Caspian, one finds the Georgians give place to a people whom the Russians call Tatars, and who are unquestionably a branch of the great Turkic family. When or how they settled here, no one can precisely tell, but it seems likely the earliest immigration was from the north, along the Caspian coast. There is no doubt that the Emperor Heraclius, in his long war with Persia in the middle of the seventh century, called in to his aid the Khazars, a Scythian tribe, from the Caspian steppe north of Derbend. Probably these Khazars were the first Turks who settled on this side the mountains ; but many others must have come in afterwards from the south-east at the time of the great Seljukian conquests in the eleventh century. Veritable Turks these fellows certainly are, quite unlike the mongrel race who go by the name of the Turks in Europe, and much more resembling, in face, figure, and character, the pure undiluted Turkman of Khiva and the steppes of the Jaxartes. Being in some districts a settled and industrious race, they are, however, less wild-looking than the Turkmans, and remind one more of the grave and respectable Tatar of Kazan or the Crimea. Their villages, often mere burrows in the dry soil, are scattered all over the steppe eastward to the Caspian, and southward as far as the Persian frontier. Many are agricultural, many more live by their sheep and cattle, which in summer are driven up towards the Armenian mountains and in winter return to the steppe ; and some of them, settled in the larger towns, practise various handicrafts, and among others weave those rich carpets and other woollen fabrics which pass in the markets of Europe under the name of Persian, but really come from the south-west shores of the Caspian.

The Tatars are also the general carriers of the country. On the few roads, or oftener upon the open steppe, one sees their endless trains of carts, and more rarely their strings of camels, fetching goods from Shemakha, or Baku, or Tavriz, to Tiflis, thence to be despatched over the Dariel into Southern Russia, or by railway to Poti and Western Europe. The last of their occupations, the one in which they most excel, and which they have almost to themselves, is brigand-age. To what extent it prevails, I cannot attempt to say, for, as every traveller knows, there is no subject, not even court scandal, on which one hears such an immense number of stories, some of them obviously exaggerated, many of them honestly related, most of them absolutely impossible to test. If we had believed a quarter part of what the quidnuncs of Tiflis told us, we should have thought the country seriously dis-turbed, and travelling, especially by night, full of peril. If we had gone by our own experience, we should have pronounced the steppes of the Kur a great deal safer than Blackheath Common. Stories

were always being brought into the city, and even
appearing in the papers, of robberies, sometimes of
murders, committed on the roads to Elizavetpol and
Erivan ; and along the latter road, we found the folk
at the post stations with imaginations ready to see a
Tatar behind every bush. Even the Russian officials
at Tiflis, who of course desired to make little of anything that reflects on the vigilance of the government,
advised us to be careful where we halted, and how we
displayed any valuables. I cannot help believing, therefore, that robberies do sometimes occur, and no doubt
it is the Tatars, or at least bands led by a Tatar chief,
who perpetrate them. But the substantial danger is
not really more than sufficient to give a little piquancy
to travelling, and make you fondle your pistols with
the air of a man who feels himself prepared for an
emergency. In a dull country, far removed from the
interests and movements of the Western world, the
pleasure of life is sensibly increased when people have
got the exploits of robbers to talk about. It is a
subject level with the meanest imagination ; the idle
Georgian noble and the ignorant peasant enjoy it as
heartily as Walter Scott himself.

Some of the tales related about these robbers remind one of the legends of Robin Hood and other
high-minded outlaws, who relieved the rich in order
to relieve the poor. It is told, for instance, of Dali
Agha, who seems to be at this moment the most
famous of these brigand chiefs, that, being in love
with the daughter of a man of substance, her father
refused to give her to him except for a large sum of

money. Dali was poor, but brave and sanguine ; he demanded two years time to collect it, and when the father promised to wait for so long, he took to the road to collect the sum by robbery ; and though the faithless father had married the girl to another suitor before the appointed time, he liked the profession so well that he has not quitted it.[1] He is at the head of a large band, and directs them to use all possible courtesy towards their victims, who are never killed except in case of necessity. Out of his plunder he gives freely to the poor, and is so much beloved that no one will betray him ; once, while Cossacks were scouring the country after him, he was living quietly in Erivan under the governor's nose. A physician in government employment was travelling towards Elizavetpol to inspect the hospitals of his district, when he saw two suspicious persons on horseback a little way off, and drove faster on. As he turned the corner of a hill, three more appeared, and then a band, whose leader rode forward and wished him good evening. "Good evening," replied the doctor, who recognised the bandit. "I perceive you are in want of money ; well, I haven't got much, only some hundred roubles ; here they are in my trunk."—"I see you are a good man," says Dali ; "on what business are you travelling ?" The doctor explains that he is going to visit a hospital, and needs some little money to reach it, so begs Dali to let him have a couple of roubles, which will pay for the post-horses thither. "You shall

---

[1] A similar tale was told of the robber Arsen many years ago ; so I dare say it is a stock incident, applied to every famous robber in turn, and may (who knows ?) be a form of the Sun and Dawn myth.

have fifty," Dali answered, and, taking them from his followers, who had opened the trunk, "here they are for you. And on your way back, stop at this place; my men will meet you and bring you to me; you shall be my guest for the night."

Another time, some of the band seized a poor priest, who was travelling home with twenty-five roubles, which he had scraped together as a dowry for his daughter. Fearing for his life, he gives them the money, and is led to Dali, whom he finds in a thick wood, seated on a carpet-spread divan. Dali, seeing him to be a priest, receives him with respect— there is a good feeling between Mohammedans and Christians in some parts of these countries—makes him sit down, offers him coffee, sweetmeats, and a pipe, and hears the story of the dowry for the daughter's marriage. He apologizes for the conduct of his men, and, pointing to the bales of precious stuffs that lie around, bids the captive take out of them the worth of twenty-five roubles. The priest does so, and, finding that the robbers are not watching him, he pockets a good deal more, thinking, I suppose, that he was spoiling the Egyptians, and makes off with his booty. However, he is pursued and caught by some of the band, who had not understood that he was to be favourably treated. Brought back before Dali, he is in terror lest they should discover how much he has taken, and flings himself down to beg for his life. Dali interrupts him, repeats that he is sorry anything was taken from so poor a man. "It was an unfortunate mistake, but mistakes will sometimes occur, and you must pardon it. Here, however, are twenty-five roubles; it is my gift to your daughter for her marriage portion; give them to her from Dali Agha and go in peace."

Whatever truth there is in such stories as these, they show the way in which the country people regard the robbers, and explain why brigandage still holds its ground against the efforts of the government. Some people give another reason, and say that the inferior officials do not care to put it down, but take a share of the spoils, and sometimes, when they have caught a notable robber, release him for a good round ransom which his friends will always pay. This I believe to be a calumny, though of course such a thing may have occurred once and again; the chief difficulty in the way of putting down brigandage is the vicinity of the Persian and Turkish dominions, into which marauders can easily escape, and whence the bands are constantly recruited by all sorts of adventurous spirits, who have lived under a government so bad that lawlessness seems justified. Take them all in all, these brigands, if they are not, as one of my informants said, "fine fellows who mean no harm," are evidently much better fellows than the members of their profession in Sicily or Greece, and deserve to be ranked with Dick Turpin or Claude Duval. Very different are the Turkman robbers who infest the road from the Caspian to Teheran, or those still fiercer tribes, described by Vámbéry, in the deserts of Khorassan and Bokhara, who carry off into cruel slavery all whom they do not kill on the spot.

Besides these four nations, and the Armenians who live scattered among them, there are plenty of Persians in Transcaucasia, especially towards the south-west angle of the Caspian, and on the Aras, beyond Erivan, a region which Russia acquired from Persia only in 1828. They are singularly unlike the Tatars, whose enemies they have been ever since the mythic times of Sohrab and Rustum, and have an even deeper cause of hatred than this old one of race, for while some of the Tatars, like the Osmanli Turks and the Turkmans, are Sunni Mohammedans, the Persians are Shiahs, who reject and abominate the three first Khalifs and honour Ali almost as much as the Prophet himself. Here, however, they live peaceably enough together. The Tatar is mostly tall and robust, with a round face, rather prominent cheekbones, a short nose, and small eyes. The Persian is slim, lithe, stealthy and cat-like in his movements; his face is long, of a clear yellowish tint, his eyes dark and rather large, nose aquiline, eyebrows delicately arched. The Tatar is inclined to be open; he is faithful to his word, and more inclined to force than to fraud; the Persian has the name of being the greatest liar in the East. "In Iran no man believes another" has become in these countries almost a proverb. With these moral disadvantages, the Persians are no doubt in many ways a superior race, industrious and polished even in the dregs of their civilization, after centuries of tyranny and misgovernment. In their time they produced great men, rulers such as Kai Khosru (the just Nushirvan) and Shah Abbas the Great; poets like Firdusi and Omar Khayyám; metaphysicians whose names are hardly known in the West. Their carpets and silks and metal work are still full of exquisite taste and finish. But modern Persia, from all that one can hear, is more execrably misgoverned than Turkey itself. The duty of the governor of a province or town is simply to squeeze as much money as he can out of the inhabitants; his methods are the bastinado, impalement, crucifixion, burying up to the neck in the ground, and similar tortures.

Besides these aboriginal races, Georgians, Imeritians, and Armenians, and the incomers of old standing, such as Tatars and Persians,[1] there is what may be called a top-dressing of recent immigrants from Europe, mostly Russians and Germans. The Russians, with one exception, consist of the officials, who generally consider Russia as their home, almost as our Indian civilians consider England, and intend to return to it when their work is over. The exception is formed by the various sects of dissenters whom the government, fearing their disturbing political and social influence, has banished, or at least transferred, to these remote seats. They are mostly industrious, well-disposed people, morally, if not intellectually, above the level of the rest of the peasantry, who live in large villages, exactly like those of Central Russia, and keep themselves quite apart from the surrounding native population. Still more distinct are the Germans, of whom there are several colonies,

[1] A recent Russian statistical estimate gives the number of Turks and Persians in Transcaucasia at 790,000, that of the Steppe-Tatars at 90,000.

the largest, established in Tiflis, numbering some four or five thousand souls. They came hither from Würtemberg about sixty years ago, driven out by an obnoxious hymn-book. In respect of education and intelligence, they are of course far above any of the natives, while their Protestantism prevents them from intermarrying with, and therefore from sensibly affecting, their Russian neighbours. They have lost, if they ever possessed, the impulse of progress; their own farms are the best in the country, and their handicraftsmen in Tiflis superior to the Georgians or Persians; but they are content to go on in their old ways, not spreading out from the community, not teaching or in any way stimulating the rest of the population.

All these races live together, not merely within the limits of the same country, a country politically and physically one, but to a great extent actually on the same soil, mixed up with and crossing one another. In one part Georgians, in another Armenians, in a third Tatars, predominate; but there are large districts where Armenians and Georgians, or Armenians, Georgians, and Tatars, or Tatars and Persians, or Persians, Tatars, and Armenians, are so equally represented in point of numbers that it is hard to say which element predominates. This phenomenon—so strange to one who knows only the homogeneous population of West European countries, or of a country like America, where all sorts of elements are day by day being flung into the melting-pot, and lose their identity almost at once—comes

out most noticeably in the capital of Transcaucasia,
the city of Tiflis.   Here six nations dwell together in
a town smaller than Brighton, and six languages are
constantly, three or four more occasionally, to be heard
in the streets.   Varieties of dress, religion, manners,
and physical aspect correspond to these diversities of
race.

The traveller's or interpreter's *lingua franca* of
Eastern and Southern Transcaucasia and the Caucasus generally is what the Russians call Tartar (or
rather Tatar), but what we should call Turkish, as it
differs from the Osmanli of Constantinople only in
being somewhat rougher, and having adopted fewer
foreign words.   The official language, and that which
in a civilized city like Tiflis is usually the general
means of intercourse between persons of different
nationalities, is Russian, which, in spite of its difficulty,
is learnt and spoken by a great many Armenians and
Persians, and by most of the German colonists.   In
Georgia itself and the region farther west, Imeritia
and Mingrelia, Georgian carries one pretty well
through, the dialects of these peoples apparently
belonging to the same parent stock.

These peoples inhabit the more or less level country
south of the Caucasus.   Besides them, there is a multitude of mountain tribes of whom I have said something in the last preceding chapter, but who are far
too numerous and too diverse in their character to be
described at length.   Probably nowhere else in the
world can so great a variety of stocks, languages, and
religions be found huddled together in so narrow an

area as in the Caucasian chain between the Euxine and the Caspian. It is as if every nation that passed from north to south, or west to east, had left some specimens of its people here behind to found a kind of ethnological museum. Of many of these tribes especially of those inhabiting Daghestan and the Eastern Caucasus generally, hardly anything is known, that is, scientifically known: I doubt if an enumeration of them exists in any book.

All these tribes and regions, both of the mountain and of the plain, have now accepted the rule of Russia. The country is quiet from sea to sea. Save for an occasional outbreak among the Suans when the tax-gatherer or land-surveyor makes his appearance, one may travel unharmed through mountain and plain with a small escort, or perhaps unescorted altogether. It is surprising enough when one remembers how unsafe places nearer home are, and how long it took to suppress private war and brigandage in civilized Europe. The Russian military organization deserves part of the credit, but even more is to be attributed to the sort of simplicity of manners which many of these tribes retain, to the absence of travellers to be plundered, to the isolation in which they live, separated from the world and one another by prodigious mountain masses. Some of them are pagans to this day, and others who, like the Suans, call themselves Christians, have preserved nothing of it but the internal arrangements of a church and one or two ceremonies whose meaning has been long since forgotten. Often they mix it with paganism, much in

K

the fashion of the Tcheremiss of whom Mr. Wallace tells the story that he sacrificed a foal to the Virgin Mary.   There is a wonderful deal to be done in investigating the customs and beliefs, as well as the languages, of these people, and it is surprising to find that so few of those assiduous Germans who explore every corner of human knowledge should have been at work here.

That Russian influence, bringing science and civilization in its train, should not have penetrated the hidden nooks of these mountains, may well be understood.   One is less prepared to find how little it has changed the accessible regions of Georgia and Mingrelia, where, although the capital is a little Paris in its way, the country parts remain much what they were a century ago.   The reason, however, soon discloses itself to a traveller, that Russian government is before all things military.   The first object thought of is the movement of troops, the organization of the army, the planting of fortresses and barracks.   This was natural and necessary while the war in the Caucasus lasted, but since 1864, when the Tcherkesses of the west submitted, the same system seems to have been maintained.   Such roads as have been made, and they are few, were made almost wholly for military purposes, and a sort of military atmosphere still pervades all Transcaucasia.   While the Dariel military road cost £4,000,000, and Daghestan is traversed by two or three beautiful lines of road with iron bridges over the torrents, many fertile parts of European Russia are almost without any means of internal communication.   An enormous army, something like

150,000 men, is kept in these provinces always on a war footing. Upon this force the government has had to spend vast sums, and consequently there has been neither the money nor the thought and care that are needed to bestow upon the material development of the land and the intellectual development of the people. Nor is this a process for which the Russians have yet proved themselves to have a gift. They have a wonderfully elaborate system of government, but the machinery is so complicated that the force is spent in making it move at all, and hardly reaches the material to be acted upon. The effect, therefore, considered as a means of improvement, is small in proportion to the cost (poorly as the *employés* are paid) and to the number of officials at work. And the civil service loses that sense of initiative which is so precious in half civilized countries. They go on working their bureaux among these Asiatics much as if they were in Novgorod or Riga, forgetting that what is wanted is not to maintain the existing state of things, but to improve it, to enlighten and stimulate these backward races.

For some time past the whole Caucasus (i.e. both Transcaucasia and the governments immediately north of the mountains) has formed a separate administrative division of the Russian empire, governed by a lieutenant who is directly responsible to the Czar.[1] The present lieutenant is the Grand Duke

---

[1] Transcaucasia and Daghestan consist of the following six governments, whose respective populations I append :—Tiflis, 650,000 ; Erivan, 436,000 ; Elizavetpol, 503,000 ; Baku, 486,000 ; Kutais, 650,000 ; Daghestan, 450,000.

Michael, a brother of Alexander II., who succeeded
in 1867 to Prince Bariatinski, the conqueror of Shamyl.
Like all, or nearly all, of the imperial family, he is per-
sonally courteous and popular, and is said to discharge
his official duties well. The higher offices, both military and civil, are of course filled by Russians, many
of them, as everywhere in the empire, of German ex-
traction, or else by Armenians. All subjects, however,
are admissible to office ; this has been long a tradition
of Russian administration, and it is no doubt one
reason of its success in conciliating the good-will of
its subjects, wherever there has not been, as in the
dismal case of Poland, a vehement race and religious
hatred to begin with between conquerors and conquered. The sort of good-nature and susceptibility
to impressions which is so marked a feature in the
Russian character makes them get on far better with
strange races than either we, or the Dutch, or the
Spaniards, have ever been able to do. It is not occasional acts of cruelty, it is not even a permanently
repressive system, that makes conquerors hated nearly
so much as coldness, hauteur, contempt, an incapacity
to appreciate or sympathize with a different set of
customs and ideas. Doubtless the English govern
India far better than the Russians do their Asiatic
dominions. That is to say, we do more to promote
the welfare of the people and administer a pure justice,
and we hold ourselves far more impartial in religious
matters. For though Russia does not interfere with
Islam, and has the prudence to respect the Armenian
Church, she is hostile to both Roman Catholic and

Protestant missions, and does her best to advance her own church in every way. Nevertheless there does not seem to be either in the Caucasian countries or in the south and east of European Russia, where so many strange races live beneath the sceptre of the Czar, nearly so much bitterness of feeling among the subjects as there is towards ourselves in India, or to the French in Algiers now, and in the West Indies formerly. Perhaps this is partly because the Russians leave their subjects more to themselves, while we try to improve them : and the fact that in Georgia there is no distinction of faith or of colour between the two races has something to do with it. The Tatar Mohammedans, however, do not seem to have anything to complain of, either here or at Kazan on the Volga, where so many of them live, and one never hears that they are disaffected to the Czar, in spite of the long strife of the middle ages and the fanaticism of the Russian peasantry. So that, after all, there seems to be a good deal in the difference of manner with which we and they behave to inferior races. With us, every word and look betray a sense of immeasurable superiority. Sometimes we are brusque, sometimes we are politely condescending, but we are always at bottom contemptuous, and contempt makes deeper wounds than violence. In India and China the fault naturally reaches its climax, but the whole continent of Europe can hardly be wrong in accusing us of a milder form of it ; indeed, every Englishman who is honest with himself must admit that whenever he travels in a foreign country, aye

even in France or Italy, he is conscious of some
stirrings of this haughty insular spirit.   The Spaniards
are more offensive in this regard than ourselves ;
among the Romans there must have been plenty of
it in their era of conquest ; the Americans, with all
their self-complacency, are comparatively free from it.
But the Russians have really very little of it.   Perhaps
they would be stronger if they had more ; but at any
rate its absence largely covers or atones for some of
their defects as a conquering and governing power.

The upshot of this digression is that Transcaucasia
is on the whole a fairly contented and peaceable part
of the Czar's dominions, and that this is due partly to
the apathy of the Russians, partly to their good-
nature, partly to their being in religious matters in
sympathy with the faith of so large a part of their
subjects.   Last autumn, when war with Turkey was
daily expected, no one seemed to have any fear of an
insurrection even among the Lesghians, though it is
only some twenty years since they used to swoop
down from the mountains and carry off landowners
from their country-houses a few stages out of Tiflis.
Since Shamyl's surrender in 1859, there has been but
one attempt at a rising in Daghestan, and that speedily
ended by the head of the leader being sent by his own
people to the Russians at Tiflis.   As I write these
lines, news comes of a disturbance among the Mohammedan Tchetchens, who live to the north of the Caucasus, south-east of Vladikavkaz.   It is hardly likely
to prove serious ; and the idea which some people in
Europe seem to entertain of its spreading westward

to the Black Sea, where the Turks are said to have
effected a landing, and of a general rising among the
Caucasian tribes, is too wild to deserve refutation.
The Circassians, whom the Turks are supposed to be
endeavouring to excite, hardly exist in this country;
they perished or emigrated in 1864; the Abhasians,
who are left along the coast about Sukhum, are few
and inert; the Imeritians, Mingrelians, and Gurians
towards Batum, are Christians, a people not much
inclined to fight for anybody, and certainly not against
the Czar; among the remaining tribes there is no
community in race, language, or religion which could
enable them to co-operate were they ever so disaffected. The only thing that could make an insurrection among any of them dangerous to Russian
movements would be a seizure of the Dariel military
road, and of that there is no likelihood.

The same laws, the same mechanism of courts,
the same educational system, omitting diversities
of detail, obtain in these provinces as in European
Russia. The great emancipation of the serfs, which
here took place on the 1st of December, 1866, was
carried out much upon the same lines as elsewhere;
the peasantry of Georgia and Mingrelia, where serfdom prevailed from the middle ages downwards,
are now all free, and the ancient, semi-feudal jurisdictions of the Mingrelian and Imeritian nobles have
been replaced by the new-modelled Russian courts.
Practically, indeed, education is still more backward
than it is in Europe. There are comparatively few
elementary schools; the upper schools are said to

be poor, and are much hampered by difficulties of language, for the school-books in every subject are Russian, though Russian is a foreign tongue to the immense majority of the pupils. There is no university nearer than Kharkof or Odessa ; the necessity for one in Tiflis is admitted, but the money is not forthcoming, since considerable salaries would be needed to tempt learned men so far from home, and all the money that can be got is wanted for the army and railways. Of literature, one of course expects to find very little, and except in the capital there is no public to care for it. Agriculture is much what it may have been five centuries ago, witness the implements used. The plough is a ruder contrivance than that which Hesiod describes ; no wonder that a large team is needed to drag it through the hard dry earth. Just outside the houses of Tiflis I have seen no less than sixteen oxen yoked to a single plough. The want of a market discourages improvements in tillage, as well as trade generally, for although there is a railway to the Black Sea, with steamers thence to Odessa and Constantinople, as well as one or two great roads through the country, such as that to Erivan, there are no roads of the second order to bring produce to the railway from places lying even a few miles away. The manufactures, as already remarked, are mostly of what we should call Persian goods, or of arms, which the Georgians chase most tastefully, and other articles in metal, silver flagons, belts, daggers, and so forth. Things needed for ordinary life, such as cutlery, crockery, glass, paper, cotton goods, are mostly brought from European Russia. What export trade there is—and it is not, considering the resources to be drawn upon, of any great consequence—is mostly in carpets and silks, made in the Tatar country towards the Caspian or among the Persians of Lenkoran, naphtha from Baku, and woods, especially box-wood and walnut roots, from Mingrelia and the south-west slopes of the Caucasus. Nature has made the country rich, but the course of events has not brought to it that which a country needs to develop its riches, capital and enterprise. Both must come from without, and at present Russia can spare neither. Her capital is all wanted at home; her peasants, except some sects of dissenters who have been deported hither by the Czars, have not crossed the mountains to colonize, nor are they the sort of colonists that change the face of a country as Americans do. They are uneducated, attached to their old ways, unreceptive of new ideas even in a new land.

If it is hard to convey an impression of the general character of Transcaucasia, the reason possibly is that it has not one general character, but two or three. It is like a mixed tissue, whose colour seems to vary according as the light falls this way or that upon it. There is no place in Europe except Constantinople, and probably few places in the world, where one feels in the middle, so to speak, of so many cross-currents, so many diverse associations of the past and possibilities for the future. Perhaps this puzzling, pleasing complexity, creating a desire to predict as well as to explain, and a sense of the difficulty of prediction, is

the thing which·makes the country so full of interest.
It is Eastern—Eastern not only in the dry, bare glowing landscape (I speak chiefly of the Caspian basin),
but in the look of the villages, the bazaars, the agriculture, the sense of immobility. Yet many Oriental
features are wanting. It is Christian, to begin with.
The ruined castles of the nobility, with peasants'
dwellings clustering beneath them, have an air of
Western feudalism. In the large towns, and along the
great roads, one feels the influence of Russia, and the
influence of Russia, superficially at least, suggests the
influence of France. The streets are filled with men
in uniform ; the hotels, where the town is big enough
to have more than a wretched *duchan*, or public-house,
are kept by Frenchmen. You have intelligence and
polish in the towns, and in the country the blankest
ignorance and the most primitive rudeness. The
telegraphic wire runs along a road on each side of
which there lie regions almost unexplored, whose inhabitants worship unknown deities and speak unknown
tongues. This contrast gives all the idea of a new
country, like Western America or one of our colonies ;
yet here one feels at every step that the country is old,
with a civilization which, though it never blossomed,
never quite withered up, a civilization older than our
own. Seeing the ancient churches and castles, most
of which have some legend attached to them (though
such legends are as seldom poetical as they are trustworthy), one has an odd sort of sense of being in a
country which has had a history, but a history that
never emerged from twilight, which nobody knows,

and which is perhaps hardly worth the knowing. In Eastern Russia and Siberia you acquiesce in the fact that there never was any history; the past is a blank, and must remain so. In Asia Minor, on the other hand, you are within the circle of Greek and Roman civilization; everybody, from Herodotus downwards, has something to tell of its cities and peoples. But Georgia, and the regions immediately round it, have been always the frontier land of light and darkness, a battlefield of hostile empires and religions; first of the Roman empire and the Persians, then of Christianity and fire-worship, then of Christianity and Islam, then of Persians and Turks, lastly of Russia against both the Sultan and the Shah. One finds traces in the buildings and the art of the people of all these influences—of the Greek traders who frequented the markets of the Euxine; of the Byzantine emperors, who held sometimes more, sometimes less of the country, Justinian having pushed forward his garrisons as far as the Upper Kur and Heraclius as far down as Tavriz; of the Genoese, who monopolized the Black Sea trade in the later days of Byzantine rule, and had their settlements all round its coasts; of the Persians and Armenians, who came as conquerors or immigrants. There is a wonderful harvest awaiting the archæologist here, and the labourers are still few.

With this curious sense of a complex and almost unexplored past, the traveller has a still stranger feeling of perplexity as to the future. Transcaucasia is so rich by nature, so important by position, that nobody can doubt it has a considerable part to play in history. What will that part be? Are commerce and culture likely to advance? Can Russia maintain her hold on these peoples? Will they themselves be melted down into one nation, and if so, what is the element, out of the many now contending, that will ultimately prevail?

So far, little or no assimilation among the various races of the country has taken place. In the towns they get somewhat more mixed together as trade grows and communications are opened up. But they are not fused, and with one insignificant exception they do not seem on the way to become fused. For this there are several obvious causes. The chief races are in point of numbers pretty equally balanced, so that no one of them is able to absorb the other. Neither is any one sufficiently superior in intellect and force of character to take the lead and impress its type upon the whole mass. The Russians, as being the rulers and the most civilized, might be expected to be able to effect this, but it must be remembered that they are not very numerous, consisting only of the upper officials, of the soldiers, who are a transitory element in the population, and of some isolated settlements of dissenting peasants. Moreover, they are not thoroughly civilized themselves, and cannot impart what they have not got. Civilization in Russia is like a coat of paint over unseasoned wood; you may not at first detect the unsoundness of the material, but test it, and it fails. A further obstacle is to be found in the differences of language and manners between the various Transcaucasian

peoples, differences **greater than those that separate**
Frenchmen from Spaniards or even **from Englishmen ;**
differences which **might of course yield to** the influences of commerce and a common participation in the
working of free institutions, but which prolong **them-**
selves from **generation to generation under a** bureaucratic despotism **which treats the people merely as**
taxpayers **to be kept in order,** which does something
for them, but nothing by or through **them.** General
compulsory **service in the** army, which **has not yet**
been introduced here, might **in time diminish this sense**
of separation ; **nothing** else seems **likely to do so.**

Finally, and this is the chief **cause of the mutual**
repulsion of the atoms, there **is** the religious difficulty.
It is of course greatest between the Tatars, **the Les-**
ghians, Tchetchens, and other Caucasian peoples, **and**
the Persians, **all** of whom are Mohammedans of **the**
Sunni or Shiah persuasion, and the Christians. So far
as one can see, **there is not** much active Mohammedan
fanaticism in these countries ; even among **the Les-**
ghians it has **very** much cooled down **from the**
heat of Shamyl's days. No one in Tiflis **seemed last**
autumn to fear that the Czar might be embarrassed in
any war with **Turkey by** the disaffection of his own
Muslem subjects. **The Persians hate all Turks worse**
than they hate Christians, and **may even, to the**
extent of **their** very limited **power, side with** Russia
in the quarrel. The Tatars are a **simple folk** of shepherds, carriers, highwaymen, **with no** sense of the
"solidarity **of the Turkish race,"** and no desire to
draw the sword against the infidel. **But** since religion

is the main influence that governs the lives of these peoples, is indeed the only intellectual life they have, and makes itself felt in all their customs and sympathies, it erects a barrier hardly to be crossed between them and the Christians. The Armenian peasantry of the Araxes valley seem to live much in the same way as their Tatar neighbours; their villages are little better, nor are they less illiterate. But one never hears of intermarriages nor any sort of *rapprochement* between them. Among the Christians themselves, the separate existence and strongly national character of the Armenian Church keeps its children apart not only from Protestant Germans, but from those who own the Orthodox Eastern faith. And it is really only where such a religious repulsion does not exist, as, for instance, between Russians and Georgians, that any social amalgamation goes on.

An able traveller who visited these countries several years ago, and has written some interesting remarks upon them,[1] suggests the probability of their growing into a Transcaucasian state independent of Russia. Admitting that the army and the administration of the Caucasus have already a certain amount of distinctive character, the facts above stated seem to oppose themselves to such a prospect. To an observer in Tiflis now there seems hardly more likelihood of a Russian hero, however able or ambitious, making himself the sovereign of a kingdom of the Caucasus than there is of a Viceroy of India revolting from the English Queen.

[1] Mr. Ashton Dilke, in the 'Fortnightly Review,' some years ago.

There is no unity among these races, no common
national feeling to appeal to, nothing on which a
national kingdom could be based. Nothing, in fact,
keeps them together but the Russian army and administration, and the loyalty of both these to the Czar
is that which keeps Russia herself together, rising as
it does almost to the dignity of a national worship.
A very extraordinary concurrence of circumstances
must be imagined to make the rebellion of a Russian
general have any prospect of success, while a peaceable separation of these provinces, so valuable in a
strategical point of view, is even less likely. Moreover, they are every day being brought nearer and
nearer to the heart of the empire. Since the completion of the railway from Rostof on the Don to Vladikavkaz at the north foot of the Caucasus, the post
which leaves Moscow on Sunday night can reach
Tiflis on the Friday morning, having to traverse only
126 miles of road from the terminus to Tiflis itself.
The project of a railway over the mountains to super-
sede even this piece of road travelling, and to enable
troops to step into a railroad car on the Neva and
step out of it on the Kur, is not likely to be carried
out for many years to come, for its cost would be
prodigious, and other military communications, that,
for instance, from Orenburg to Tashkend, are more
pressing. But as Southern Russia fills up by the
movement of population which is continually going
on from north to south, the Transcaucasians will
seem less and less remote, and will be connected by
more active relations of trade and social intercourse

with the European side of the Caucasus. Already
the opening of the railway to Poti on the Black Sea,
whence steamers run regularly to the Crimea and
Odessa, has made intercourse with the mother country
easier and more frequent, and strengthens the unity
of sentiment between Holy Russia and her children in
these outlying provinces.

Improbable, however, as the separation of Transcaucasia seems, its Russianization, in anything more
than administration, seems almost as distant. It is
not well governed, being like so much else in the
Empire both over-administered and ill-administered.
In material prosperity, in the diffusion of light,
morality, refinement, it is advancing very slowly.
Germans, or Frenchmen, or Americans, would probably have effected far more in seventy years of occupation than the Russians have done. But compare it
with the condition of Georgia or Mingrelia under their
own princes, or, still better, compare it with that of
the neighbouring territories of the Sultan or the Shah,
which are daily going back, where there is absolutely
no security for life, honour, or property, and its
fortunes appear happy indeed.

CHAPTER IV.

TIFLIS.

THE capital of **Transcaucasia** is a type **of the country.**
It is a city of contrasts and **mixtures, a** melting-pot
into which elements have been poured from half
Europe and Asia, and in which **they as yet show no**
signs of combining.

It stands on the Kur, which **is here a swift, turbid**
stream, just above the **point where it emerges from**
the upland country into the great steppe **that stretches**
away to the Caspian. **High hills of a** shaly limestone and schist enclose **it on all sides, those on the**
south rising some 800 to **1200 feet above the river.**
They are **not very picturesque hills, especially after**
May, when the herbage on **them is utterly burnt away**
by the **heats, and they stand out bare,** brown, and
stern, with **no colour except** when the setting sun
bathes them **for a** moment in a purple glow. Even
so, however, they give the city a character one would
not like to. **miss.** Besides, they shelter it **from the**
cold blasts **that** rush down **in** winter **from** the Caucasus, **so that** the winter climate is one of the
pleasantest **in** these latitudes, warm and equable,
yet **not nearly so** damp **as that** of the Black Sea

coast.[1] While the steppe of the Lower Kur is covered
with snow and swept by bitter north-easters, consump-
tive patients can here go out all the winter through.
The mean temperature of the year is a little lower
than that of Rome, which is in the same latitude, while
the mean of the adjoining steppe is that of Northern
France. On the other hand, Tiflis is intolerably hot
and close in summer. Down in this hollow, where not
a breath of air can reach you from the mountains
you descry, where the sun's rays are reflected from
bare slopes and white houses, where often not a
shower will fall for months together, one gasps and
pants, one is not merely scorched, but stifled. I have
repeatedly seen thunderstorms play all round the
town, sheets of rain descending a few miles off, and
the streets lit up at night by the flashes, when scarcely
a drop would fall in Tiflis itself. Add to this that
the water is scarce and indifferent, and the dust truly
Oriental, and it is easy to understand that summer is
not the time to enjoy the Transcaucasian capital.
So in summer, pretty nearly every one who can afford
it, and can get free from his official duties, makes off
to the hills. The court, that is to say, the Grand
Duke, who is the sun of this system, and his attendant
planets, the adjutants, go to Borjom, a charming spot
among wooded mountains eighty miles to the west-
north-west, in the upper valley of the Kur. Others
cross the Caucasus to Pjätigorsk or Kislovodsk,
favourite watering-places at the northern base of
Elbruz; a few go by way of Odessa to Europe.
Towards the middle of September they begin to

[1] Tiflis is 1335 feet above the sea : its annual rainfall 19 inches.

return, and by November society is again in full
swing.

The hills which I have mentioned break down
pretty steeply towards the river, and it is chiefly on
the lower slope of those lying on its right or south-
western bank, which are much the higher, that the
town is built, descending in terraces towards the
river, whose course is here (speaking generally)
south-east. At the east end of the city two rocky
spurs almost meet, the Kur forcing its way in
rapids and eddies between them. On the north-
east side stands the citadel, which is now also the
prison, and the ancient Georgian cathedral; behind
it, on a sort of terrace, are the enormous barracks.
The opposite rocks are crowned by the picturesque
ruins of a Persian fortress, whence we discover the
long wooded line of the outermost mountains of
Daghestan, and, in clear weather, the glittering snows
of Kazbek, rising over the watershed which divides
Europe from Asia. These irregularities of surface,
with the swift stream rushing through between precipitous banks, give a great charm to Tiflis, and
make it look much larger than it really is. The
views over it are very striking, not that the individual buildings are fine, for they are nearly all
modern, and, like so much modern Russian work,
handsomely uninteresting ; but the mass of houses
with groves and gardens interspersed, the stern
brown setting of hills, the motley throng just visible
upon the bridges, the glimpses of far-away mountains, make up a *coup d'œil* not easily forgotten. I

cannot recall any European city that resembles it. People have compared it to Prague, but Prague is as much inferior in situation as it is superior in architectural beauty.   Toledo, too, has been suggested, but the likeness seemed to me to begin and end with grim brown hills and a turbid stream.

Seen from above, Tiflis is one continuous city, interrupted only by public or private gardens here and there.   But in reality it consists of three perfectly distinct towns, unlike in their origin, their buildings, their population.   First, there is the Russian town, all new, bright, showy, and, externally at least, clean.   It is on the south-west bank of the river, rising steeply towards the hills, and is, of course, the fashionable residential quarter, as well as the region of the best shops, the opera-house, public offices, and so forth. The streets are wide and straight; the houses high, all new-looking, and all as like one another as in Paris or Chicago.   Rows of trees are planted in front of European shops with plate-glass windows.   This part, indeed, has only grown up within the last sixty years.   Here live the court—the Grand Duke has a handsome palace fronting to the principal street, called, in St. Petersburg fashion, Golovinski Prospekt—and, indeed, pretty nearly all the officials, besides a certain number of rich Armenians. You might fancy yourself in Odessa, or one of the newer and better suburbs of Moscow.

To the east of this Russian town, and lying deep down in the hollow along the river, is old Tiflis, a genuine Eastern city, with its narrow crooked streets, ill-paved or not paved at all, and houses of one or two stories only, the whole horribly dirty, yet incomparably more picturesque than the smart propriety of the modern town. Each of the principal trades has a street or streets, or a covered arcade in the bazaar, entirely to itself: thus in one street you find the dealers in arms, in a second the leather-sellers, in a third the jewellers, in a fourth the carpet merchants, in a fifth the furriers, on whose walls hang the skins of Caucasian bears and Hyrcanian tigers. The ground-floor room of the house is open to the street, from which it is generally raised a step or two; here the dealer squats on a piece of matting, surrounded by his assistants, with his wares hung or stowed round the walls behind and in the room which is visible at the back. If he practises a handicraft, he works at it here in the sight of all men, just as in some old-fashioned English villages the shoemaker may still be seen sitting in his front room open to the air, and hammering away at a solid boot sole, much more solid than anything that comes from an Eastern last. Thus, as you pick your way down the lanes, jostled into the middle by the crowd, and in the middle nearly run over by the impetuous droshkies, you can see the whole industry of the place in full swing; bread is being baked in one street, swords forged in another, cloth woven in a third. There is no department in which the artizans are particularly strong, except perhaps in the making of ornamental arms, such as pistols and daggers, and of silver cups and flagons, the designs on which are often very beautiful. One sees a great many exposed for sale, but

I fancy the best are of some considerable age; nor
is there much inventiveness in the modern work-
man; he goes on repeating these old models as if
he were a British architect, which is perhaps, in
the present dearth of invention, the best thing he
can do. The value of the old silver goods is well
known; it is little use hoping for a bargain where so
many Russian buyers are about, and where the sellers
are mostly Armenian. Pretty things, especially belts,
are still made in what is called niello work. The
jewellery rather disappointed us. So near Persia one
expects to see splendid turquoises at least, not to
speak of gold work emeralds and rubies, quite
abundant. Though we spent hours in the jewellers' street, it is possible we may have missed
the best shops, for out of the great number of turquoises shown us, though some were big, very few
were of a specially fine colour. It is true that
the small ones were considerably cheaper than in
St. Petersburg; perhaps the finest are bought up in
Persia to be sent direct thither or to Constantinople.
The settings are mostly very simple and uniform.
What pleased us best were the great dark rooms,
running away back from the streets, in which the
carpet dealers, most of whom are Persians or Tatars,
keep their goods stocked, the darkness being not only
pleasant in summer, but a sensible advantage to the
seller. Here a wonderful variety of all kinds of rugs,
mats, and carpets may be seen, the best, perhaps,
Persian from Tavriz and Khorassan, but plenty of
other kinds, little, if indeed at all, inferior, from

Shemakha and Nukha, on the road to Baku, and from Kurdistan and the valley of the Tigris. As everybody carries his rug with him when he travels, and as the rougher kinds are also used for packing bundles of more delicate goods, there is a considerable consumption of such articles beyond the needs of house furnishing, and a pretty large import trade in them from the east and south. We bought several and priced a great many more. Comparing these prices with those demanded in London for similar articles, we concluded that carpets are at Tiflis about forty per cent. cheaper, a difference which of course represents a good deal more than the cost of carriage thence to England.

The crowd, noise, and bustle of this Eastern town are at their highest on the bridge which in the middle of it spans the Kur, whose waves, breaking against the cliffs that enclose it, are hardly heard over the din of voices, loud and harsh as the voices of Orientals usually are. Hard by is the road leading to the neighbouring eastern gate, through which all the traffic flows in from Armenia, Persia, and the steppe; now a string of camels, now troops of donkeys laden with fruit or charcoal, now the rough, slow, solid-wheeled bullock carts of the country, now a party of mounted Cossacks clattering over the pavement. Piles of fruit from the German gardens strew the ground, mixed with huge bullock-skins full of Kakhitian wine. From the rocks above the grim walls of the citadel frown down, and beside them appears the grey cupola of the most ancient among the

Georgian churches ; nearer, and half hidden by the
confused mass of houses, you see the domes and
minarets of the rival mosques of the Sunni Tatars
and the schismatic Persian Shiahs. One can hardly
believe that a Russian Paris is only half a mile away.

Quitting this district, ascending the southern bank
of the river, and crossing it by the principal bridge,
which is adorned by a statue of Prince Woronzof, the
famous governor of Transcaucasia, one enters a third
quarter, equally unlike either of the two I have just
been trying to describe. You forget Russia, you
forget Asia : you fancy yourself on the banks of the
Swabian Neckar. This is the German settlement,
still called by everybody "The Colony," which was
originally quite a distinct town, and has only in the
recent growth of Tiflis become united to it by a continuous line of houses. It is inhabited by Germans,
the descendants of emigrants who came hither from
Würtemberg sixty years ago, driven from their homes
by a new hymn-book which their prince insisted on
forcing upon his subjects, and which they considered
too lax in its statements of doctrine. The Russian
government, always delighted to secure industrious
and peaceable colonists, received them warmly, placed
them first near Odessa, and ultimately, at their own
wish, transferred them hither. Here they have dwelt
ever since, not increasing much in numbers, though
some few have joined them from Germany, preserving
all their old ways and habits, cherishing their Protestant faith, and singing out of their dear old hymn-book.
Rows of trees run along the principal street ; breweries

and beer-gardens border it, where the honest burgher
sits at night and listens over his supper to a band, as
his cousins are doing at the same hour in the suburbs
of Stuttgart. Tidy little *Fraus* come out in the
evening cool to the doorsteps, and knit and chat
among their fair-haired Karls and Gretchens. They
have their own schools, far better than any which
Russian organization produces; they are nearly all
Protestants, with a wholesome Protestant contempt
for their superstitious Georgian and Armenian neighbours. They speak nothing but German among
themselves, and show little or no sign of taking to
Russian ways or letting themselves be absorbed by
the populations that surround them. It was very
curious to contrast this complete persistency of Teu-
tonism here with the extraordinarily rapid absorption
of the Germans among other citizens which one sees
going on in those towns in the Western States of
North America, where—as in Milwaukee, for instance
—the inhabitants are mostly German, and still speak
English with a markedly foreign accent. But of course,
when one thinks about it, the phenomenon is simple
enough. Here they are exiles from a higher civilization planted in the midst of a lower one; there they
lose themselves among a kindred people, with whose
ideas and political institutions they quickly come to
sympathise.

Unluckily these good Swabians have done less to
diffuse their superior civilization than might have
been expected. This is said to be the case with nearly
all the German colonies on Russian soil : they have

most of them retained their own industry and thrift,
while some of them, particularly the Mennonites
(who may be compared with our Quakers or Moravian
Brethren), have thriven wonderfully. But they have
not leavened and improved the general population of
the country. The difference of religion is probably at
the bottom of this separation. It prevents intermarriages, for there is a most objectionable law in Russia,
comparable to those which the English formerly enforced in Ireland, which requires the children of a
mixed marriage to be brought up in the Orthodox
Eastern faith even if neither of the parents has
belonged to that communion. And where there can
be no intermarriage, there is, after all, but little
familiar intercourse. However, I do not attempt to
explain the fact, but mention it as a curious instance
of the disappointment of what seemed a statesman-
like plan. For it was chiefly with the view of teaching
her Russian subjects habits of thrift and better modes
of agriculture that Catherine II. tempted so many
German colonies into Southern Russia ; as it was the
example of those colonies which induced these later
ones to follow.

The German population of Tiflis may, at present,
amount to some five or six thousand souls. Most of
them are artizans, or gardeners—gardening is almost
entirely abandoned to them by the lazy Georgians—
only a few are shopkeepers or merchants. Of course,
most of the men of science, and a pretty good proportion of government *employés*, belong to the *Culturvolk* ;
but these are mostly stray wanderers from the Baltic

Provinces, or from old Germany itself, not home-bred colonists. They are friendly, pleasant people, among whom an Englishman soon feels himself at home, and who are ready to show him every kindness. I should be ungrateful indeed not to acknowledge the help and advice we received from several among them, and which in some cases were given by persons to whom we had not brought introductions.

Although there are but three distinct towns in Tiflis, there are at least six distinct nations. Besides the Russians and Germans, of whom I have spoken already, the Georgians, Armenians, Tatars, and Persians, all contribute sensibly large elements to the population. The Georgians are at home, and may probably be the most numerous; amongst the motley faces in the streets their type seemed the most common. Most of them are nobles, as has been said already, and most of them are poor; they form probably one-third of the day labourers and servants. As the men generally wear European coats and trousers in the town, though in the country a dress much like the Circassian is common among the better class, they are not so easily recognised for Georgians as the women, whose singular head-gear—a square cloth cap ornamented with a kind of crown, from which there hangs down over the shoulders a long white gauze veil—makes them wonderful ornaments of the streets. Formerly they cultivated an Oriental reserve. I remember to have read some traveller who, writing forty years ago, says that in the town he could see none but old and withered faces.

They have changed all that now: no belles of Scarborough or Saratoga promenade a public garden with more nonchalance than the daughters of the first Georgian families in Tiflis. They are certainly a splendid race to look at, these Georgians, both men and women, but I doubt if they are anything more. They have never produced anything in literature or art; they have never had but one remarkable man, and that was a woman—I mean Queen Tamara; they fell into the hands of the Russians because they could not resist the effete despotism of Persia; and now though they do not really like the Russians, and will give you to understand as much on the sly, I do not suppose they would ever raise a finger against them. Perhaps their spirit has been broken by the long and unequal struggle which they, always a small nation, had to maintain against such bitter foes as Turks and Persians. One ought to compare them, not with European peoples, but with semi-civilized races who have been enslaved by foreigners. And it may well be that they have mended since the Persian yoke was broken, and will mend still further. Certainly they have, if the account which Chardin gives of them, in the seventeenth century, when Tiflis was held by a Persian garrison, was a fair one, or anything more than one of those proverbial bits of exaggeration by which travellers, long before the days of sensation writing, liked to heighten the effect of their narratives. This is what he says of our poor Georgians:—

"The Georgians are naturally very witty, and would be as learned men and great artists as any are in the world if they had the improvements of arts and sciences: but having a mean education and bad examples, they are drowned in vice, are cheats and knaves, perfidious, ungrateful, and proud. They are irreconcileable in their enmities, for though they are not easily provoked, they preserve their hatred inviolable. Drunkenness and luxury are such common vices among them that they are not. scandalous in Georgia. The churchmen will be as drunk as others: yea and they say that he that is not drunk at their great festivals of Easter and Christmas cannot be a good Christian, and deserves to be excommunicated. The women are as generally vicious as the men, and contribute more than they to that general debauchery which overflows the country."

The most conspicuous figures in the streets, next to the Georgian ladies, are the clerics, whose jolly faces are surmounted by huge cylindrical hats, from which depend long veils of a sort of black crape, while a robe of black serge, with immense sleeves, covers the body to the ankles. It is curious to any one who remembers France, Italy, or Spain, to see so many ecclesiastical countenances in which there is neither asceticism nor priestcraft, nor indeed any professional expression except a sort of vacuous and self-complacent good-humour, the good-humour of a lazy man who has plenty to eat and drink. When there meets you a keener or more restless glance, you may be sure that it comes from an Armenian eye.

The Armenians are a large and apparently an increasing element of the population, easily known by

their swarthy complexion and peculiar physiognomy.
They are the most vigorous and pushing people in
the country, and have got most of its trade into their
hands, not only the shop-keeping, but the larger mercantile concerns. A good many, too, are in the Russian
service, and have thriven in it; in fact, more than half
the *employés* in Transcaucasia are said to be Armenians. Like most successful people, they are envied
and ill-spoken of, possibly calumniated, by their less
energetic neighbours. Sharp men of business they
certainly are, thrifty, able to drive a hard bargain,
and sticking wonderfully together. Among them
there are several persons of learning and ability, and
as their education improves and their wealth increases, the number of such persons is likely to
grow; so that altogether one seems to see a considerable future before them. Although they get on
well enough with the Russians, they do not much mix
or intermarry either with them or the Germans, but
have a society of their own, which is quite self-
sufficing.

The Persians in Tiflis are said to number 10,000,
all of whom live in the older part of the city,
to whose picturesqueness those of the better sort
add a good deal by their long dark or yellowish
brown robes and pointed hats of black lambswool. Tiflis was once under direct Persian rule,
and for a much longer time under Persian supremacy, so that one may believe this Iranian population has remained here ever since, and need not
suppose any recent immigration. A few are mer-

chants, driving a trade in carpets, silks, and the
other goods of their country; the rest are handicraftsmen. Some trades they have almost appropriated, particularly that of masons, in which they
are said to excel all the other workmen of these
countries. They live upon next to nothing, are
steady workers, and have not yet learnt to organize
strikes.

The Tatars are probably about as numerous as the
Persians, but as many of them are carriers coming
to and fro from the Caspian coast and Persia, they
are more a floating than a settled population. They
are all poor people, have a good name for industry
and sobriety, do a great deal of the unskilled labour,
and keep all the baths, an important profession in
an Eastern city. All are of course Mohammedans,
some of the Sunni persuasion; but a probably large
number, especially of those from the Persian border,
are Shiahs.

Besides these six leading races, Tiflis is full of all
sorts of nondescript people from different parts of the
Caucasus. The nurses are all, we hear, Ossetes—
Georgian women object to domestic service—and
thus many children grow up able to speak that
interesting language, which used to be thought near
of kin to the Teutonic tongues, though their identification with the Germans, which rested only on two
or three words, and a taste for a liquor something
like beer, has now been abandoned.

Imeritians, Mingrelians, and even Abhasians from
the Black Sea coast, not unfrequently come here

looking for work; occasionally one recognises the delicate aquiline features and keen eyes of a Lesghian, armed to the teeth, from the mountains of Daghestan. Even Europe is not wholly unrepresented, for although there are very few Italians or English—of the latter I met three only: one a Russianized photographer, the second an agent of the Bible Society, and the third a new arrival, who had started a general store, and was doing a rattling business in cutlery and bitter beer— there are, besides Poles, plenty of Frenchmen, hotel-keepers, upholsterers, dyers and cleaners of cloth, confectioners, and, above all, hairdressers. So strangely mixed a population it would be hard to find anywhere, even in the East. You never can guess what language the men who pass you in the street are talking; it may be any one of some eight or nine that are spoken almost equally. We of course could only distinguish French and German, and sometimes Russian, but the friends who walked beside us would say from time to time: "These fellows are talking Armenian, or Tatar, or Georgian, or Osset, or Persian," as the case might be. The commonest is Russian, not that they are the most numerous class, but because, being the official language, it is the second language most frequently learned by persons of every nation in addition to their own. Thus pretty nearly all the Germans, at least the men, speak Russian, and I fancy most of the Armenians also, as they are excellent linguists, and more ambitious to rise than the Georgians. On the shop fronts are seen names written in Russian, French, German, Armenian, and Georgian, more rarely in Persian. There are very few Jews; perhaps the Armenians leave no room for them.

Tiflis, whose native name, Tbilisi, is said to be derived from a Georgian word meaning hot, and to refer to the warm springs, is a place of some historical note. Tradition says that the first fort was erected here by a lieutenant of the Sassanid kings of Persia in A.D. 380, and that at it, seventy-five years later, the reigning monarch of Georgia, Vaktang Gurgaslan, founded a city, to which, in the beginning of the following century, his son Datchi transferred the seat of government, attracted by the hot sulphureous baths. Compared, however, to the antiquity of the former capital, Mtzkhet (twelve miles to the north-west), which was founded by a great-great-great-grandson of Noah, Tiflis appears a settlement of yesterday. Like most cities in these countries, it has been so often destroyed in war that hardly anything remains from primitive times; nothing, indeed, except the old cathedral on the citadel hill, already mentioned, called the Melekhi, which is attributed to King Vaktang. Of these devastations, the most ruinous were those which it suffered from Timur in the fourteenth century, and from the savage Persian Aga Mohammed Khan in 1795, in the invasion which led the last Georgian king to cede to the Czar the country he could not defend. When the Russians came, it was a very small place, confined to the region round the lowest bridge, of which I have spoken already; even in 1834 it had but 25,000 inhabitants. Latterly, what with the general growth of the country, and with the concentration

M

of trade at this particular point, where several lines of
road meet the railway to the Black Sea, it has grown
very fast, and may now have a population of 80,000
or more. Building still goes on, and house rents are
inordinately high.

Its newness gives the city one merit, which most travellers, whatever they may say, will secretly appreciate. It has no sights. You have no picture galleries,
churches, monuments, museums, manufactories, arse-
nals, green vaults, and so forth, duly noted in your
guide-book, which a sense of duty, an odious feeling
that when you have returned home, you will be
ashamed not to have done them, drives you to see. It
is a place where you may settle down in your hotel and
do just as you please, saunter forth in the morning to
buy grapes, and mingle with the many-tongued throngs
in the meat and fruit market, doze away the sultry
afternoon upon a sofa, and in the evening cool drive
out to call on some friend, or sit in the public garden,
under the mellow southern moon, and hear the band
discourse military music till near midnight. As there
are no buildings older than the seventeenth century,
always excepting the little old Melekhi church, and
nothing at all remarkable since then, no collections,
except a museum, which is interesting, so far as it
goes, and very nicely arranged and kept, but small
when one considers the resources of the country in
the way of minerals, animals, and antiquities ; and a
botanic garden, also well managed by a German
botanist, but languishing for want of funds, there is
really nothing for the visitor to do except lounge and

amuse himself by watching the dresses and manners of the motley crowd. In fact, the town itself is a museum; the inhabitants are the sight of Tiflis, quite sufficient to keep curiosity alive for days and weeks together.

Besides a multitude of caravanserais and *duchans* (= small inns or taverns) frequented by the natives, there are three hotels, two of them at least, and I fancy the third also (which had only lately been set up), kept by Frenchmen, and situated in the fashionable new town near the market and the so-called Sololaki or new residential quarter. One of the two older hotels has an established reputation for good cooking and extortion; so we chose the other, and found it clean and reasonably comfortable. The charges are high, as usually in the East, but lower than those of St. Petersburg or Constantinople. Of the inner social life of the city, I cannot say much, for the good reason that I did not see it. All that any stranger could see would be that of the Russians and Germans, which is much like their life anywhere else; and at balls, dinner parties, and operas, one sees, after all, the merest outside of life. Moreover, September is not the season for society. The magnates were mostly away in the country, and to our vexation we found but few even of those men of letters and science to whom we had brought introductions. Time, however, did not hang heavily on hand. We had various preparations to attend to for our journey into Armenia, preparations which involved constant driving hither and thither through the town, to see people and make purchases. Everybody drives in Tiflis, down to the very beggars : a Georgian would think himself demeaned by walking more than a few yards while there were vehicles to be had. We had to hunt up an interpreter or courier, an enterprise which proved unexpectedly difficult in this city, which is polyglott, but unorganized, so that, though there may be twenty competent interpreters to be had, it is a mere chance if you hear of any of them. Above all, we had to obtain the requisite official permissions for our journey, letters of commendation and road pass-ports, entitling us to call for horses at the post stations. Without these documents you cannot go a step off the great roads in the Russian dominions, and very awkwardly even along them ; nor is the ordinary road passport (what is called a *podorojna*) enough—you must, in order to get on fast, have a crown *podorojna*, which gives special advantages. Fortunately, Russian officials are usually civil and friendly, very official, no doubt, yet less of martinets than Frenchmen or Prussians. Moreover, we had taken the precaution of bringing introductions from high authorities at St. Petersburg, so that every facility was at once offered to us, and, what is more, actually rendered.

When all this had been despatched, there remained he purchases to be made of articles to take back to England. Now purchasing is in the East a very dif-ferent and much more serious matter than any one ho has not been there can imagine. It is not merely that one must never give anything like the price demanded for an article : that goes without saying. But the process of bargaining must be conducted in a

leisurely and dignified way, must be interrupted by
coffee—or rather (in these countries) tea—and conversation, and, indeed, ought never to be concluded at the
first sitting or two, but adjourned from time to time
for further consideration. Our stay was not long
enough to permit all this to be done in due and solemn
form ; so probably we paid more for the carpets, belts,
daggers, and silks which we bought than we ought to
have done. But, on the other hand, we had, at least
with most of the dealers, the great advantage of being
unable to speak their tongue. All the eloquent pro-
testations of the seller came to us only through the
reducing medium of a German friend who had kindly
undertaken to interpret ; whereas our curt and dogged
refusals to give more than a certain sum produced
their full effect upon him. Thus business went on
apace, and down in the cool, dark bazaar we spent
only three hours in buying as many carpets ; carpets
which were fortunate enough to be approved of by
connoisseurs among our friends in England.

It was too hot for walks or drives in the outskirts
of the city, even had there been anything to see ;
which there is not, for, once beyond the houses, you
are in an utterly bare and dreary land, especially
dreary at this season, when the crops have been lifted
from the brown soil. There is but one walk which is
really worth taking ; a short walk which, as a guide-
book would say, no traveller ought to omit. The lofty
ridge of hills which rises behind Tiflis on the south-
west sends down a steep spur to the river, in the form
of a long, narrow, rocky ridge, called the Sololaki hill,

whose north side is turned to the town, while its back slopes down to the valley of a small stream called the Tsavkissi. Its bed is dry in summer, what little water there is being drawn off for the botanic garden and the supply of the town. One of the highest and best isolated tops of this ridge is crowned by the ruins of the Persian fortress which dominated the city; broken round and square towers connected by a line of walls, that stand picturesquely up against the sky. On another point are the remains of what local antiquaries pronounce to be a Persian shrine, a temple to the Sun or to Fire, dating from the times of the Sassanid kings, before the crescent of Islam was heard of. One climbs to the top of this ridge through the shady walks of the botanic garden, which lies on the declivity of it away from the town, looking across the dry and desolate glen of the Tsavkissi, on the farther side of which a multitude of tombstones stuck in the ground, unfenced and uncared for, shews where the Persians of Tiflis bury their dead. An ascent which grows steeper when one has left the trees of the garden ends suddenly at a sort of portal in the rocky ridge, and through this one sees all Tiflis lying at one's feet, the Oriental crowd on the bridge, the Russian sentries at the Grand Duke's palace in the Golovinski boulevard, the orchard-embowered houses of the Swabian colony beyond the river, the rush of whose waters one seems to hear amid the mixed hum and stir that rises from the busy streets. Behind are the wooded hills through which the Dariel road descends from the valley of the Aragva, and, still farther, ridge beyond ridge rising towards the central line of the Caucasus, where the snows of Kazbek glitter over all.

The mass of hills from which this Sololaki height is an offset rises farther to the west into a sort of upland plateau, where lies the pleasant little summer retreat of Kajori, the nearest to Tiflis of all those hill-stations to which its people retire during the heats. We went there—it was the only excursion we had time to make —to present ourselves to the general who was then acting as military adjutant to the Grand Duke Michael (the Lieutenant of the Caucasus), and who was therefore practically commander-in-chief and war minister for the Caucasian provinces.[1] It was a drive of some eight or nine miles ; so, in order that we might travel with proper dignity, our hostess procured for us a phaeton, which is the name in Tiflis for a two-horse vehicle, those with one horse being merely droshkies. I may say, in passing, that the Tiflis droshkies are much better than those of St. Petersburg or Moscow, and that there exists a regular tariff of charges, a blessing which the stranger who has spent many precious minutes in bargaining by finger-signs with a St. Petersburg driver over the fare is heartily thankful for. The road winds in a succession of curves up the hills south of the city, and then turns to the west along a gently rising table-land, broken here and there by valleys in which dwarf oaks shelter themselves, but mainly covered by large corn-fields, where teams of

---

[1] This distinguished officer, one of the ablest and most respected men in the Russian service, is, I believe, now commanding one of the divisions of the Russian army in Bulgaria.

twelve or sixteen oxen were ploughing up the
stubble.   The air grew fresher and fresher as we
mounted out of the oven where Tiflis lies, till in a
couple of hours we reached Kajori, where, at 5000 feet
above the sea and 3700 feet above Tiflis, we were revel-
ling in a climate like that of the middle slopes of the
Alps, keen cool breezes making even the powerful sun
enjoyable. There is a good deal of wood about, which
adds to the sense of coolness, and away to the south
large masses and ranges of mountains, unknown to us,
rose up one behind another, parts of the chain which
has been called the Anti-Caucasus, and which divides
Armenia on the south from Georgia and Imeritia.
Eastwards we discovered, among the far-off hills of
Daghestan, the snowy peak of Basarjusi (14,722 feet) ;
northward lay the Central Caucasus, with Kazbek
conspicuous in the midst, overhanging the depression
where the Dariel road crosses into Europe.   A more
delightful spot to be idle in can hardly be imagined
than this grassy upland, with its invigorating breezes
and prospects stretching over two hundred miles of
forest, dale, and mountain.

The prince Adjutant-General, however, to whom we
presented ourselves in his pretty little wooden villa,
was not idle.   Mounted Cossacks were galloping up
with despatches, waiting outside, and galloping off
again down the steep road to Tiflis with that air of
important haste which the bearer of despatches loves
to assume.   However, this did not prevent us from
receiving a cordial welcome, and enjoying a long and
leisurely conversation, resumed after dinner in the

open air, in which our host showed a mastery not only of European politics generally, but even of English party politics and the views and sympathies of our leading statesmen, which few of our own soldiers or diplomatists could have equalled. Remembering that conversation, I understand the temptation which an "interviewer" has to report what an eminent person says to him. But I will resist it.

Kajori is but a small place as yet, though with the growth of Tiflis it is likely to increase, and we visited only one other person there, General Chodzko, the distinguished engineer officer who in 1850 led a surveying party up Ararat. From him and his secretary, Mr. Scharoyan, I received a valuable suggestion for the climb, which we were thinking of trying, viz. to keep to the rocks rather than trust the snow, and many injunctions on no account to ascend alone. In the evening we returned to Tiflis, fortified with all the recommendations that could be desired to convey us along the road into Armenia, for which, on the next day but one, we started accordingly.

I seem to have given in these few pages but a meagre account of the sights of the Transcaucasian capital, wanting both in the practical precision of Baedeker and the wealth of illustrative learning and disquisition and quotation which is the glory of our great English series of guide-books. Even the picturesque side of the place suffers in the hands of a traveller who must own that he has no eye for costume. My excuse is that in Tiflis it is not the particular things to be seen in the city that impress

themselves on one's memory : it is the city itself,
the strange mixture of so many races, tongues,
religions, customs.   Its character lies in the fact
that it has no one character, but ever so many
different ones.   Here all these peoples live side by
side, buying and selling, and working for hire, yet
never coming into any closer union, remaining indifferent to one another, with neither love, nor hate,
nor ambition, peaceably obeying a government of
strangers who conquered them without resistance and
retain them without effort, and held together by no
bond but its existence.   Of national life, or municipal life, there is not the first faint glimmering :
indeed, the aboriginal people of the country seem
scarcely less strangers in its streets than do all the
other races that tread them.   It is hard to say what
the future has in store for such a town ; meantime it
prospers, delivered for ever from the fear of Persian
devastation, and, in spite of bran-new boulevards and
stuccoed shop-fronts, it is wonderfully picturesque.

CHAPTER V.

THROUGH ARMENIA TO ARARAT.

IN this chapter I propose to give some account of the route which leads from Tiflis through Armenia to the foot of Ararat and the borders of Persia, and of the ancient city of Erivan, the capital of a Russian government (= province) of the same name. Let me premise that the term " Russian Armenia," which it is often convenient to use, does not denote any political division. Armenia is merely a popular historical name for the countries which at one time or another formed part of the old Armenian kingdom.

On the 6th of September my companion and I rattled out of Tiflis in a comfortable tarantass, threading our way with difficulty for the first mile or two through the crowd of carts, pack-horses, and sometimes strings of camels which were entering the city laden with merchandise. Perhaps, however, I ought to say what a tarantass is. Two kinds of vehicle are used here, as in the Russian empire generally, for the conveyance of passengers—the *telega* and the *tarantass*. A telega is simply a small four-wheeled square or oblong cart, usually with sides, which give it the air of a box upon wheels, but sometimes without sides, a mere flat piece of board, on the edge of which you sit, letting your legs dangle over. Of its capacities, or incapacities, for comfort, I shall speak later on. The tarantass is in shape more like a large Norwegian carriole, but with four wheels : it is a seat, placed in the centre of a longish pole, which again is set on the axles of the wheels. This gives it a sort of elasticity ; in fact, the pole acts as a spring, just as in the American vehicle called a buckboard. It holds three persons, one beside the driver, and two on the seat proper, and is sometimes made with a hood to come up behind, which gives shelter in winter-time. There is just enough space in front of the sitter's knees to hold some light luggage, with a little box under the seat where you can stow away bread, tea, and grapes, the supplies with which we had started. Our tarantass, lent by a kind friend at Tiflis, had no hood, but in summer, and for a comparatively short journey, where there was no occasion to sleep much, this was no loss ; and otherwise it was satisfactory, and went as smoothly as tarantasses ever do. From the terrible sun one could get some protection by a white umbrella and dark spectacles, but the dust was less resistable ; it penetrated everywhere, even to the middle of our loaf of bread. Under any other cir-cumstances, life in such dust would have been a burden. However, we had just escaped from the furnace of Tiflis into the clear, dry, exhilarating air of the steppe ; we were going ahead into a really curious and seldom visited country—a country of which we had all our lives known the name, and little beyond the name; and we were in excellent health. So that even greater annoyances than this would have been willingly faced.

There is something startling, at least to a traveller fresh from Europe, in the suddenness with which, on emerging from a great Eastern city, one finds oneself in a wilderness. Here the country was already desolate steppe, just like that which lies north of the Caucasus between the Euxine and Caspian seas. However, I had better explain what the Russians mean by the term *steppe*, which is one of those a traveller comes to use so familiarly as to forget that it is not ordinary English. The steppe is not necessarily flat land, for the country north of the Sea of Azof, for instance, is rolling; nor low country, for some of the so-called steppes beyond the Caspian are on lofty table-lands. Nor is it barren; on the contrary, some parts are extremely fertile. It is simply open, treeless land, whether covered with grass, or with weeds, or with dwarf, thorny bushes, or only with stones and sand. Sometimes the soil is a rich loam, ready to produce magnificent harvests, and such is most of the Black Sea and Azof steppe; sometimes it is so thoroughly impregnated with salt, as in the part which lies round the west-north-western bay of the Caspian, as to be useless for agricultural purposes; sometimes, again, it is blank, downright desert, as useless as the sands of Sahara, or the stony deserts of Iceland. Which character it bears depends chiefly on the nature of the subsoil. If this is porous, sand or rock, for instance, the little rain that falls drains off at once, and the surface is condemned in these intensely dry countries to perpetual sterility. Here, in the valleys of the Kur and Aras, there is but little of the pure desert steppe, though the rainfall sinks sometimes to four or five inches a year; but on the other side of the Caspian, in the plateau of Ust Urt and the parts of Turkestan that lie south of the Aral Sea, desert is the rule, and a bit of cultivable land, with a spring or pond, the rare exception. Along the road we were traversing the steppe land is comparatively narrow. On the north one sees a long line of low wooded hills, outliers of and hiding the great range of the Eastern Caucasus in Daghestan; to the south-west other hills, bare, brown, and lumpy, rise up towards the edge of the Armenian plateaux, in whose recesses the patient industry of German colonists has here and there created, under sheltering woods, a little paradise of orchards. In the middle, between the two lines of hill, which lie some twenty or thirty miles apart, flows the Kur, in a wide, shallow valley, its banks fringed by willows and by gardens, irrigated from the stream by water-wheels. With a little more irrigation, the whole plain might shake with harvests, for now and then one finds a stream descending from the hills, the waters of which could be led in rills over this thirsty soil. At present there are no inhabitants to attempt this. Once in six or seven miles we pass a Tatar burying-ground, a dismal group of stones stuck erect, though most have now fallen over, in the bare steppe, with no enclosure round them nor any sign of care. Not far from the cemetery you discover, with some difficulty, groups of low, round-topped, earthen hovels, some like an English pigsty, some mere burrows in the clay, with no windows, and only a hole for a door. There is no wood close at hand, and the people are too idle or too poor to fetch it from a distance; besides which I suppose they prefer the troglodyte style of house for the sake of warmth. These huts are all deserted; the Tatars who inhabit them during winter have now driven their flocks up into the hills on the Armenian border to seek fresh pasture, and will not return till the approach of winter. One is puzzled to know how people so poor manage to live at all; probably the explanation is that they can live upon infinitely little, far less than a Western labourer needs. For the matter of that, they do not labour, but simply idle, though their countrymen in towns like Tiflis do and can work hard. Besides, they spend their time pretty much in the open air; and the race may perhaps have grown accustomed to abstinence by long ages of it. Silent and dreary as the steppe is, there is plenty of traffic along the road: strings of carts laden with merchandise, vehicles with merchants or officials, solitary riders, all armed to the teeth, with two or three daggers, and perhaps pistols also, stuck in their belt, and an extraordinary old gun of the matchlock type slung over their shoulder. At first we bowed or touched our hats to these wayfarers, whereat they seemed surprised, and did not return the compliment. Our companion solemnly warned us to salute no more, saying we should be taken for strangers ignorant of the ways of the country, and likely to be rich men;

and that even if none of those we met were thievishly
inclined, they might say something about us—probably
a disagreeable something—to other people along the
road who would be ready for mischief. In fact, the presumption here seems to be *omnis ignotus pro periculoso;*
and instead of civility you do well to scowl at those
you meet, and let them see that you too are armed.

This piece of country between Tiflis and Erivan is
said to be the chief seat of Transcaucasian brigandage,
and many are the tales one hears about it. Some,
which have a slightly romantic, Robin Hood sort of
flavour, I have given in an earlier chapter: I will add
two others which may be more historical. Not long
ago a band of less than a dozen mounted robbers seized
some merchants travelling along this road, disarmed
them, bound them, and led them into a hollow among
the hills. There they left them under the guard of
two of the band, and returned to a spot near the road,
where they seized one party after another of wayfarers,
and carried them, similarly bound and disarmed, into
the same hollow, till at last more than fifty were
collected. Then they proceeded to search and rob all
this crowd of victims, and dismissed them, unarmed
but unhurt. Only two or three years ago, the governor
of Erivan, who had been making efforts to clear his
government of these plagues, was encountered on a
journey by a troop of fully fifty brigands. Their
leader rode forward, and pointed out to his Excellency
that the escort of twenty Cossacks who accompanied
him need not attempt to resist the superior numbers
of the band. The governor admitted the justice of

this view, and surrendered, upon which they took from him his favourite horse, and sent him on his way lamenting. A few weeks later, the horse was returned, with a message from the chief that he had no wish to injure the governor, and desired that nothing should interrupt their friendly relations. "I took your horse only as a lesson to you not to interfere with my people as you have lately been doing: see that you do not repeat that mistake."[1]

The discourses on brigandage wherewith, like Bunyan's pilgrims, we beguiled the way received some point from our arriving, just as the shades of evening were beginning to fall, at the Red Bridge, the most favourite haunt of robbers on the whole road. Here, some twenty-five miles from Tiflis, a considerable stream comes down from the Armenian mountains on the right to join the Kur, and winds along the precipitous face of some low, bare hills that bound its valley on the south. In among these hills there are admirable lurking-places, whence the robbers can pounce out on you at a moment's notice when their scout has seen you crossing the bridge, and in whose recesses they could easily evade the pursuit of the Cossacks or the *tchapars* (= gallopers) who are now stationed at the north end of the bridge, where some of its dry, slightly pointed arches have been turned into dwellings. These tchapars are a sort of local police or militia, composed

---

[1] I give this story for what it is worth, having been unable to ascertain what foundation there is for it. A high Russian official to whom I mentioned it pooh-poohed it altogether (as, indeed, he could hardly have helped doing); another well-informed semi-official friend afterwards assured me that it was perfectly true.

not generally of Cossacks, but of the natives of the district, Georgians, Tatars, or Armenians, as the case may be, and about here probably Tatars. They are supposed to scour the country, and act as escorts to travellers whom the administration specially desires to protect. Unless rumour does them great injustice, they are often in league with the thieves; and if not, they are so sure to ride off at the first shot that one loses nothing (except a sense of dignity) by their absence. Along the road, at intervals of a few miles in the more hilly parts, there are placed little wooden scaffoldings, some fifteen feet high, with a ladder giving access to a small platform, where a tchapar or Cossack is set to keep a look-out over the adjoining slopes, and summon his comrades from the nearest station if he sees any suspicious characters about. We saw nobody aloft in any of these look-outs as we passed, and supposed from this, and from what people told us at the Red Bridge, that the road was safe at present. However, at the next station, which we reached about 9 o'clock P.M., the air was full of stories of "bad people," Tatars, of course, who had been seen hanging about; and we were besought not to go on by a pompous postmaster, who warned us that, as we were recommended to his care by the government, we owed it to him to be prudent, and that he would not be answerable for the results if we proceeded further that night. Whether there was really any risk, it was impossible for us to tell, but, anyhow, it was clear that there would be considerable difficulty in getting horses;

so on our companion's advice we halted till about.
4 A.M., "making ourselves comfortable" in the one
room which the post-house provided. This process
consisted in spreading out on the dirty floor a small
Shemakha rug which we had bought in Tiflis, and
lying down upon it with a pair of boots for a pillow.
As the floor was hard as well as dirty, and the room
full of other travellers, who went to and fro, and would
not suffer the window to remain open, it may be
imagined that we rose little refreshed to continue our
journey, and appreciated less than we ought to have
done the splendour of the sunrise that broke over the
far-off mountains of Daghestan, and lit up with a mo-
mentary glow the brown wastes of the steppe and the
desolate hills that enclose it. At the next station but
one (Akstafinsk), milk and eggs proved to be obtainable; so here we halted for breakfast, and bade farewell
to the Kur, whose course towards the Caspian could
be traced far down through the widening plain by
a winding line of green willows, poplars, and brushwood of various kinds fringing its marshy banks, and
harbouring fevers and wild boars. Our road turned
sharp to the west, up the valley of the Akstafa river,
which, as we neared the hills, grew verdant and cheerful, fields of maize alternating with thickets, while the
wild vine climbed among the oaks and planes, and
cottages raised above the ground replaced the Tatar
burrows. Still further up, the valley becomes a deep
and narrow glen between bold mountains, sometimes
of limestone, sometimes of schist, with masses of
columnar basalt and porphyry interjected. At one

point they come down to the river, and form a striking
gorge. Nothing could be prettier, or less like the
country we had just left. Bare reddish mountain
tops rose nearly 4000 feet above us, and 6000 or
7000 feet above the sea ; their densely wooded
sides descending steeply into the valley, along whose
narrow but level floor the clear stream rippled along
in little runs and pools, where surely trout must
play, the sunlight breaking through the bushes on
its sparkling shallows. We might have fancied ourselves in the Jura but for the intense dryness of the
hillsides and the paucity of life and cultivation ; for
there was but one small village in the twenty miles
between Akstafinsk and Delijan, a little town high
up among the hills, 4200 feet above the sea, where
we were forced to halt some hours to repair the
damaged wheels of our tarantass.

Delijan, to which some of the wealthier residents in
Tiflis retire during the summer heats, is not only an
exquisitely pretty spot, but of some consequence in
a military point of view, for here the main road to
Erivan, which we were following, is joined by a road
which runs west through the mountains, north of the
great mass of Ala Göz, to the fortress of Alexandropol, or Gumri, on the Turkish frontier, the principal
stronghold of Russia in these regions, where a large
force is always kept on foot, and the autumn manœuvres usually take place. This second road is now
of great military importance to the Russians, who
have sent along it most of their troops operating
against the Turks in Armenia ; so it is the more sur-

prising that it should be unfinished in parts. Either
they did not intend to fight Turkey so soon or they
have been strangely remiss.   Delijan itself, which lies
scattered up and down the steep hillside, at a point
where two glens meet, is inhabited partly by Armenians, partly by Molokans, a sect of Russian Dissenters
who have been deported hither by the Czars. Though
a Transcaucasian German whose acquaintance we had
made gave a bad account of them, declaring they
were "nearly as bad as the Armenians, full of deceit,
making a great pretence of religion, but using it as a
cloak for treachery and greed," I believe that they are
really a good sort of people, steady and industrious,
something like the Shakers of America, or what our
own Quakers may have been in their first days,
though, no doubt, far less intelligent and more superstitious. They are said to have neither baptism nor
the Lord's Supper, nor any regular clergy; and at
their religious meetings follow up the singing and the
extempore prayers which constitute the service with
an odd sort of dance and kissings all round. They
cling to all their old Russian habits, marry only
among themselves, and build their cottages of wood,
so that one easily distinguishes their settlements from
those of Armenians or Tatars, even before seeing their
beards and characteristically Russian physiognomy.
It is a pity there are not more of them in the
country.

From Delijan, which we left at seven o'clock in
the evening, the well engineered road mounts steeply
through a superbly wooded glen, whose beauties,

however, we lost in the darkness. It was midnight before we reached the post-house at the top of the pass, where we halted in the hope of a little sleep, having had none to speak of the night before. Sleep, however, was out of the question. It was bitterly cold, for we were at a height of 7000 feet above the sea, the room was small, and foul beyond description, and the stony floor one had to lie down upon swarmed—here, however, let a veil be dropped. Memory called up many disagreeable nights—nights in rock-holes on the Alps, nights under canvas amid Icelandic snow-storms, nights in Transylvanian forests, nights in coasting steamers off the shores of Spain, nights in railway waiting-rooms in England, but no night so horrible as this. Descending under the opening eyelids of the dawn from the pass, which lies among green and rounded hills, we were refreshed by the sight of a magnificent inland sea stretching away fifty miles to the southward, surrounded by high volcanic hills, all absolutely bare of trees, and in most places even of grass, but with a few small patches of snow lying here and there in their upper hollows.[1] It was the lake which the Russians call Goktcha (a corruption of the Tatar name, which means blue lake), and the natives Sevan, the Lychnitis of the ancients ; and we were now fairly in Armenia. Unlike the two other great lakes of that country, that of Van in the Turkish dominions and that of Urumia in the Persian, its waters are fresh,

---

[1] The top of the pass is 7124 feet above the sea. A little bit of the summit of Ararat is said to be visible ; we, however, did not see it.

and it discharges by a small river, the Zenga, into
the Aras. Of the various legends relating to it, one
is as old as the time of Marco Polo,[1] viz. that no fish
are found in it during the whole winter till the first
day in Lent, when, for the benefit of the faithful, who
in the Eastern world observe the fasts of the Church
more rigorously than any other of her ordinances,
they appear in immense numbers, and continue till
Easter Sunday. The mountains round it are all of
volcanic origin, and rise some 4000 to 5000 feet above
its surface, which is over 5870 feet above the sea.
Great part of it freezes in winter. The beach, at the
place where I bathed, was composed of large volcanic
pebbles, glued together by and incrusted with a thick
calcareous deposit, which forms all around the shores
a white line, marking the difference between the
summer and winter level of the water. Grand and
solemn as the view over it was, there was something
so dreary in these stern, dark brown mountains, and
long lines of shore, unrelieved by a tree or a spot of
cultivation, that one could understand why the people
of Tiflis prefer the woody hollows of Delijan or Borjom to a place otherwise so well fitted to become a
health-giving mountain retreat. The only village we
could descry lies just opposite the only island, whereon
is the ancient and famous Armenian monastery of
Sevan or Sevanga. Here a great fishery is carried on,
and, I grieve to say, at other times as well as during
Lent; in fact, Tiflis gets most of its fish from the lake,
which is a hundred miles nearer to it than is the

[1] See the fifth chapter of the second part.

Caspian. Even the Armenian fathers of the little
monastery in the lake, which at one time claimed to
be the seat of the Patriarch of the Armenian Church,
own with a sigh that the age of miracles is past.

Passing by the Molokan settlement of Elenovka,
situate at the point where the river issues from a
shallow arm of the lake, we came to another station,
where it was necessary to quit the post-road in order
to present ourselves to the vice-governor of Erivan,
who was then residing at a mountain nook called
Daratchitchak, the Simla of Erivan, whither its
upper classes escape from the frightful heats of the
Araxes plain, and whose name is interpreted to mean
Valley of Flowers." It is a drive of about eight miles
up a steep and rocky road into this pleasant little
recess among the hills, on whose higher slopes the
yellow corn had not yet been reaped, for they are full
7000 feet above the sea-level. Hamlets lie scattered
in the glens, and here and there woods of dwarf oak
hang on the steep sides of the glens, giving the landscape a softer and more cheerful look than this part
of Armenia generally has. At the top of the long,
steep slope down which the village of Daratchitchak
meanders stand three curious old churches, built of
huge blocks of a reddish volcanic stone, the masonry
exquisitely finished, as it usually is in the ancient
ecclesiastical edifices. The two larger of them have
been partly destroyed in some of the numerous Tatar
irruptions ; but the smallest is entire, covered, like all
Armenian churches, by a high polygonal cupola, and
has a pretty little portico, whose doorway is divided

into two by a miniature, elegantly carved, Romanesque column, supporting two slightly pointed arches, a charming piece of work, which reminded us of Western forms more than anything we had yet seen in these countries. It is said to have been built by a Mohammedan who had been converted to Christianity by listening, as he stood outside, to the sweet music of the mass, a legend which becomes credible only if it be supposed that Armenian church music has greatly degenerated during the last few centuries. He who listens to-day to its plain song will experience very different impressions from those attributed to the musical Muslim.

We were courteously welcomed by the vice-governor and his wife, a lady from St. Petersburg, and received from him a batch of letters commending us to various authorities further on. He smiled when we asked, through the lady, who acted as interpreter, about Ararat, told us that it had never been really ascended, though several travellers professed to have got up, and evidently thought the enterprise hopeless. After dinner we regained the post-road, and, when fresh horses had been obtained, drove on between two tremendous thunderstorms, the one shrouding the mountains round the Goktcha lake towards the east, the other hanging over the huge mass of Ala Göz, which now came into view on our west. This mountain consists of three sharp, rocky peaks, apparently parts of the rim of an ancient crater, rising out of an immense swelling upland some forty miles in circumference. The peaks, one of which is said to be inac-

cessible, and certainly looks as though it might afford
nice bits of climbing, are too abrupt to bear snow, but
we afterwards saw patches of white in the bottom of
the extinct crater between them.   It is even said that
there is a small glacier there ; I cannot think, however,
the snow is sufficient in quantity to feed one.   Ala
Göz is a curious instance of the untrustworthiness of
one's impressions about the height of mountains.
After Ararat, it is the loftiest summit between the
Caucasus and the Persian Gulf, 13,436 feet above
the sea, as high as the Schreckhorn or Piz Bernina.
If we had judged by our eyes, we should have put
it down at 9000 feet.   I have never seen so high a
hill look so inconsiderable, so perfectly mean and
trivial.   It is true that the point whence we first
caught sight of it was 5000 feet above the sea ; but
afterwards, looking at it from the plain of the Aras,
and from the top of Ararat, it seemed no higher,
owing, no doubt, to the gentleness of its lower slopes
and to the way one miscalculates distance in this
clear, dry atmosphere.

The rolling plateau which we were traversing is
mostly cultivated, partly by Armenians, partly by
Russian Molokans, and in a few places by emigrants
belonging to the Finnish tribe of Mordvins, who were
transplanted hither from the Middle Volga at their
own wish, and are said to be well satisfied with the
change.   At one village where we stopped to change
horses, it was easy to recognise the peculiar Finnish
physiognomy, broad and smooth faces, long eyes, a
rather flattish nose.   The harvest had just been got in,

and at every village the corn was being trodden out by
bullocks (unmuzzled, we were glad to see), who are
driven round and round on the hard earthen threshing-
floor, dragging a piece of wood the bottom of which is
studded with bits of iron or hard stone, and on the top
of which the driver, usually a woman, stands. It is a bare
and dreary country, like all the interior of Armenia,
perfectly brown, and apparently almost waterless ; but
the volcanic soil is very rich, and would support a
population far larger than that which now occupies it.
Everything is primitive to the last degree : there was
not even a morsel of food, nor a drop of *vodka* (the
common Russian spirit), to be had at the post-station,
where hunger forced us to stop for a sort of meal at
10 P.M. ; and we supported life entirely upon a huge
lump of bread which we had brought with us from
Tiflis, and hard-boiled eggs, which we had managed
to pick up at one of the more sumptuous stations
some way back. Fortunately tea was obtainable, even
in this abode of famine, and tea had become a solace
and support which the traveller in more favoured
regions can hardly understand. You can always have
it, and that promptly, if you carry, as everybody does,
the raw material about with you. Every post-house,
however simple, possesses a *samovar*, a huge brazen
urn with a cylinder in the middle, into which hot
charcoal is put to boil the water. As soon as you
enter the station, you call for the samovar ; in fifteen
or twenty minutes the hot water is ready. Then you
put in the tea, slice down the lemons, and tumble in
the sugar, which articles you have, of course, brought

with you, and in five minutes all your wretchedness is forgotten. One soon acquires, and on returning to England is loth to relinquish, the two characteristic Russian habits, of pouring out the tea the moment it has been made, without letting it stand to grow stronger by brewing, or "masking," as they say in Scotland, and of drinking tumbler after tumbler of it. (It is always taken by the Russians in glasses, not cups, and with incredibly large quantities of sugar.) Of course it is weak, but then it does your nerves no harm, and the flavour is usually so much finer than that of English tea that one cares little about the strength. Tea is the universal beverage of these countries, just as coffee is of the Levant and the Mediterranean generally; it is drunk by Armenians, Persians, Tatars, Turkmans, Kalmucks, Mongols, Tibetans, in fact, by the whole of Northern and Central Asia, all the way to China, just as much as by the Russians themselves. Of course, the kinds which the poor, and the nomad races, consume are very coarse. These commoner kinds come across Siberia or the desert in flat cakes or bricks—cakes so hard as to need a strong knife or hatchet to cut them; and in some parts they pound it up and drink it with butter and salt.

The last part of this third day's journey to Erivan was performed in the dark. The thunder-clouds had rolled away, and the moon appeared, a waning moon that feebly lit up the bleak landscape. At last, as we topped a hill, something like a faint white cloud appeared in the southern sky. "Look there," said one

of us, rousing his **nodding companion**; "**do you see**
that, the white thing yonder? high up? Do you know
what that is?"—"No," said the other, **sleepily**; "what
is it?" To which the first whispered **in** answer,
"That is Ararat." Then we both dropped asleep
again, at imminent peril to me on the box-seat of falling off, and were only awakened by the unutterable
jolting of the vehicle over the masses of loose volcanic
rock which form the principal street of Erivan. **It**
was no easy matter to find quarters, for the only **inn**
was not only shut up at 2 A.M. (the hour when we
arrived), but **had** closed itself altogether and ceased
to receive guests. Nothing but the argument which
overcame the unjust judge induced its people, when
all the dogs in the city had been roused by our
knockings, to open their courtyard door, and let us
sleep the sleep of utter weariness upon an ancient sofa
and a dismantled bedstead.

Erivan,[1] the capital of Russian Armenia, which next
morning stood basking in a sun that made it dangerous to go out except under an umbrella, is a
thoroughly Eastern town, with just a little Russian
varnish in one or two of its streets. It is Eastern of
the Persian type, which is very different from the Arab
Orientalism of Cairo or Tangier, or the half French,
half Osmanli Orientalism of Stamboul. Lying in a
hollow at the foot of the plateau which extends north-
wards towards the Goktcha lake, yet a little above

---

[1] Pronounced almost 'Yeryevan.' The stress of the voice is on the
last syllable, as **in** Tiflis (Teeflees), Etchmiadzin, Tavriz, and most of
these names.

the level of the Aras plain to the south, it covers with
its 30,000 people an area nearly as large as that of
Brussels or Sheffield. The streets are wide, the houses,
except a few modern Russian ones, of one story only,
built of clay or plastered brick, round an open courtyard, with no windows towards the street. Many
of them, especially in the outskirts, open off narrow
lanes between high mud walls, and are surrounded by
groves and vineyards. There are no shops, for all the
buying and selling goes on in the bazaar, a complex
of long straight brick arcades, in which the dealers
and handicraftsmen sit upon divans behind their
wares, sipping tea, or smoking out of their *kalians*,
or long flexible water pipes, and scarcely conde-
scend to answer you when you ask the price of an
article. Each trade has an arcade or two to itself;
the bakers are in one, the fruit-sellers in a second, the
shoemakers in a third ; in a fourth, carpets ; in a fifth,
leather goods, and so forth. Persians, Tatars, and
Armenians are all represented, the last being de-
cidedly more anxious to do business than the other
two. The bazaar begins to be crowded about 5 A.M.,
and thins off in the forenoon, reviving a little in the
quarters where food is sold towards the time of the
evening meal. In front of it lies the great *Meidan*, a
sort of square or open space, where the road to Persia
meets the road to Tiflis and Europe. Standing here
at 6 A.M., when the bazaar is at its height, one sees
the life of an Eastern town in its picturesque simplicity. The busy parti-coloured crowd is vibrating in
and out of the mouths of these arcades; men in

sheepskin hats, shuffling along in their loose, low-heeled
slippers, and women covered from head to foot with a
blue checked robe, are flocking hither to buy food from
every part of the city, and clustering like bees round
the stalls which bakers and fruit-sellers have set up
here and there through the *Meidan,* and where heaps
of huge green and golden melons, plums, apples, and,
above all, grapes of the richest hue and flavour, lie
piled up. Hard by stand the rude country carts or
pack-horses that have brought the fruit, with the
Armenian peasant in his loose grey cotton frock ;
while strings of camels from Persia or the Caspian
coast file in, led by sturdy Tatars, daggers stuck in
their belts, an old matchlock slung behind, and a
huge sheepskin cap overshadowing the whole body.
Sometimes a swarthy, fierce-eyed Kurd from the
mountains appears ; sometimes a slim and stealthy
son of Iran, with his tall black hat and yellow robe.
It is a perfectly Eastern scene, just such as any city
beyond the frontiers would present, save that in Persia
one would see men crucified along the wall, and both
there and in Turkey might hear the shrieks of wretches
writhing under the bastinado. One forgets Russia
till a mounted Cossack is seen galloping past with
despatches for Alexandropol, where the Grand Duke,
attended by the governor of Erivan, is now holding a
great review. It is just such a scene as Ararat, whose
snowy cone rises behind in incomparable majesty, may
have looked down upon any day for these three thousand years. As noon approaches, the babbling rills of
life that flow hither and thither in the bazaar are stilled ;

the heat has sent every one home to slumber, or at
least to rest and shade ; the fruit-sellers have moved
their stalls, the peasants have returned to the country ;
Ararat, too, has hid his silvery head in a mantle of
clouds.   Only the impatient Western traveller braves
the arrows of the sun, and tries to worry his Armenian
driver into a start across the scorching plain.

The population of Erivan is greatly mixed, and, of
course, no one knows the proportions of the various
elements.   Till 1827, when Paskievitch captured it,
and won for himself the title of Erivanski, it belonged
to Persia, and a good many Persians still remain in
it, fully a quarter of the whole number of inhabitants.
Nearly as many more may be Tatars, less than a
half Armenians ; the balance consists of Russian
officials and troops, with a few Greeks and other
nondescript foreigners, including, of course, several
Germans.   Go where you will in the world, as a
friend said to me who has traversed nearly every
part of it, you will always find a German ; they are
more ubiquitous than the English themselves.   Although it is the capital of a government which includes
nearly all Russian Armenia, it is a stagnant sort of
place, with little trade and hardly any manufactures.
Life flows on in the old channels, little affected either
by Russian conquests or by the reviving hopes of
the Armenian nation.   Like most towns in a country
which has been so often the theatre of destructive
wars, it has few antiquities, though it claims to have
been founded by Noah, and appeals to its name, which
in Armenian is said to mean " the Apparent," as evi-

dence that it was the first dry land the patriarch saw. Another tradition goes still further back, holding that it was Noah's dwelling before the Flood took place. Be this as it may, it has now no sights to show except the mosques and the ancient palace of the Shah, or rather of his lieutenant, the Sardar of Erivan. This palace is included within the citadel, a Persian fortress, strong by its situation on the top of a basaltic cliff, which rises over the river Zenga; strong also, according to Asiatic ideas, in its high brick walls running along the top of the cliff, though I do not suppose they could resist modern artillery for a day. Part of the fortress is now occupied by barracks, part is in ruins, but two or three chambers have been carefully kept up, and even to some extent restored in genuine Persian style, and give one a lively idea of the architectural style and taste of the only Eastern nation among which art can still be said to live, if indeed it lives even there. The roof, as well as the floors inside, are covered with bright blue, green, or yellow tiles, the older ones of which—you may pick them anywhere out of the ruins—are wonderfully vivid in colour. The walls and ceiling of the principal chamber, which is supposed to have been the audience chamber of the Sardar, are decorated with a profusion of small mirrors, or rather pieces of looking-glass, stuck together in a kind of mosaic, arranged alternately with paintings in excessively bright colours, representing the Shah chasing the lion and the stag, together with various emblematic devices, and patterns of roses and other flowers and shrubs, repeated all round. A

sort of stalactite ornament in coloured plaster is in a
style similar to that of the ceilings in the Alhambra ;
indeed, it has been supposed that some of the work
there bears traces of a Persian hand. The drawing is
stiff and conventional ; and though the tints are well
harmonized, they are almost too bright ; the effect is
rather gaudy than gorgeous. One is glad to refresh
the sated eye by looking through the one window
which opens to the south upon the stream foaming
down its rocky bed below, the women washing clothes
along its banks, Tatar carriers driving their teams over
the bridge, and beyond it the well-watered banks of
the Aras, an oasis of delicious green in this parched
and dusty land, with the two cloud-girt peaks of
Ararat rising five-and-thirty miles beyond.

The principal mosque lies behind the bazaar in a
maze of lanes separated by gardens and courtyards.
It forms one side of a square enclosure planted with
orange and other trees, with a tank in the middle, over
which four tall elm trees bend, the whole not unlike
in arrangement to, although smaller than, the famous
garden of that masterpiece of Mohammedan art, the
mosque at Cordova. Here, however, the mosque
itself, so far from being a vast and complicated
structure is more like what would be called in Italy
a *loggia*, open on one side to the garden, with a deep
and lofty horseshoe-shaped recess (the mosque proper),
much like a large round apse, or the half of a dome,
in the middle of this gallery, part of the interior of
which is covered with handsome tiles, and adorned
with texts from the Koran. The floor is bare and

open; there is, however, a small wooden pulpit, whence the officiating mollahs read or preach. A little way from the dome that surmounts the mosque, an elegant minaret rises, round and decorated with coloured tiles, like those of Turkey and Morocco, whereas at Cordova and Seville the minaret is a square brick tower. The rest of the gallery which surrounds the enclosure is appropriated to the mollahs attached to the mosque, or made to furnish resting-places for pilgrims, or school-rooms where boys are taught to read the Koran. This mosque belongs to the Muslims of the Shiah persuasion, that which prevails in Persia; and here they come to worship all day long, bowing and prostrating themselves towards the centre of the apse, which is of course in the direction of Mecca. Its ample proportions, the rich yet soft colours of its walls, the silence, the shade, the rustling of the boughs and murmuring of water in the adjoining garden, make it one of the most beautiful and impressive houses of prayer that I have ever seen.

In the same part of the town, not far from the bazaar, are placed most of the caravan-serais, as well as the baths. An Eastern bath has been so often described that he would be a bold traveller who should attempt to describe it again, though here in Persia it is not quite the same thing as in Constantinople or London. The *caravan-serai* (bower or resting-place of the caravan) is very unlike an inn according to our notions. It is a round or elliptical enclosure between high walls with a strong gate or gates to it. Round the inner wall runs a sort

of gallery, roofed, but open to the air, where the
traveller encamps with his cart or camels, providing
himself from the market with bread and wine, fodder-
ing his beasts himself, and getting nothing from the
innkeeper except space, a sort of shelter, and protection against nocturnal thieves.   Till lately there was a
European inn of some pretensions in the city, but
its landlord, according to the story told us, had some
months before been thrown into prison on a charge of
murdering one of his guests, a Greek banker, whose
imprudent display of money had roused his cupidity,
and the hotel was therefore closed.   The cries and
groans of the victim, whose throat was being cut, had
been heard by various people in the house, none of
whom stirred to help him.   Nobody doubted the innkeeper's guilt, but justice moves slowly in these
countries, and he may not have been tried, much less
executed, even now.   The inn in which we stayed
had, as I have mentioned, also been closed, and when
we returned to Erivan from a journey to Etchmiadzin,
it refused to admit us, till compelled to do so by the
police authorities.   Having been recommended by the
vice-governor to their attentions, we thought it would
be a pity to make no use of them, and accordingly
by their means forced an entrance and got a night's
shelter.

The most trivial details of Eastern life are fascinat-
ing to those whose childish imagination has been fed
by the Bible and the Arabian Nights.   To see people
sitting or sleeping on the flat roofs, or talking to one
another in the gate through which a string of camels

is passing, to visit mosques and minarets and bazaars, watch the beggar crawl into the ruined tomb of a Muslim saint, and ramble through a grove of cypresses strewn with nameless, half fallen gravestones, to stand by the baker or the shoemaker as he plies his craft in his open stall, and listen to the stories told by the barber, even when one does not understand a word, with the sacred mountain of the Ark looking down upon all, this seems like a delightful dream from far-off years, and one wakes with a start to perceive that it is all real, and that in the midst of it stands an un-sympathetic Frank, unable to rid himself of a sense of mingled contempt and pity for the "natives," anxious to examine what he has come so far to see, and then press on to something further. One considers how long it would take to tame down a restless Western spirit to the apathy, the acquiesciveness, the sense of boundless time before and around which these people have been steeped in for so many generations. Nevertheless, the light of common day does not wholly disenchant the East. True it is that every-day life here must be un-speakably dull, duller than in the quietest provincial town of France or England. For romance, in the novelist's sense of the word, there is infinitely less opportunity than among ourselves. The great move-ments of the European world seem much farther away than they had seemed to me six years before in America ; for the inhabitants, even those of the better class, had not the smallest interest in them. Even of the approaching rupture with Turkey, which was to bring war into this very plain, and of the forces

that were urging it on, no one (so far as we could
ascertain) knew anything, or had any means of knowing, except what might be given in some stray Russian
newspaper, brought here weeks after it had appeared.
Nevertheless, in spite of, perhaps indeed because of,
all this stillness and sameness, this want of literature
and discussion and news, the East retains its power of
fascination.   Setting aside the view of Ararat, and
one or two picturesque bits like the bazaar and the
mosque garden I have described, Erivan is not beautiful.   Its streets, not only the three new Russian
ones, but those that date from Persian times, are dull
or ugly with their long blank walls of brick or baked
clay, unbroken by a window, or a gable, or a shop.
They are as colourless as Bolton or Wolverhampton,
and not one-tenth so animated, for a vehicle is rarely
seen, and a foot passenger not often ; the women
steal along silent and shrouded.   But not only are
there here under one's eyes all those externals of
Oriental life to which literature, legend, and history,
from the book of Genesis downwards, have attached
so much romance ; there is also a deep impression
received from the sight of a society so unlike our
own, a society which has preserved that very old-
world character which seemed old-world even to the
Greeks more than two thousand years ago, a society
immovable in its beliefs, ideas, usages, with its fundamental conceptions so different from our own that
one hardly sees how it is ever to be carried along
in the general stream of the world's development, and
hardly wishes that it should.

With the end of our pilgrimage full in sight, and the moon, on whose light we must depend for night marches, waning fast, we had no wish to linger in Erivan, especially as the letters we bore enabled us to get horses without trouble or delay. Both in Tiflis and all the way along from Tiflis to Erivan, we had enquired about Mount Ararat, the side from which to approach it, the modes or chances of ascending it. Little, however, could be learnt except that the point we must make for was the frontier military station of Aralykh, lying on the right (western) bank of the Araxes,[1] about twenty-five miles from Erivan. It was to the colonel commanding a detachment of Cossacks at this point that our letters of recommendation from the Russian authorities were addressed. So far, then, our course was clear. Whatever might happen afterwards, whatever difficulties man or nature might oppose to the ascent of the mountain, we must make for Aralykh. Accordingly, on the morning of September the 9th, we drove off from Erivan under the blazing noon, having purchased and stowed away in the tarantass a good stock of bread, tea, and delicious grapes, grapes well worthy to have grown on Noah's vine. The road combined in a singular manner two apparently incompatible evils, roughness and softness. It was strewn with rocks, over which we jolted with a violence that obliged one to hold on for fear of being thrown out ; it was deep in dust, which rose

---

[1] Aras is, I believe, the Persian form of the name, Arax the Russian ; but it is quite as well known under the ancient name Araxes, which is at least as old as Herodotus. He, however, confounds our river with the Volga and the Oxus.

round us in blinding clouds. The hilly ground was
mostly steppe, unoccupied waste, which is doubtless
browsed on by Tatar flocks in spring, but in September was grey stony soil, covered with withered weeds.
Cultivation did not appear till we began to approach
the Araxes, where not only is the soil deeper, but
tiny canals from the river or the few tributary streams
which it receives from the left diffuse fertility.

This Araxes plain is much the richest part of Armenia, being both hot and well watered, while the
rest of the country is high, cold, and dry. It is, in
fact, a country of lofty open plateaux separated by
ranges of bare mountains; the plateaux 5000 to
7000 feet, the mountains 8000 to 12,000 feet above
the sea. The climate is therefore mostly a rigorous
one, running into violent extremes of winter cold, and
unrelieved in summer by the sheltering or moistening
influence of forests. The plateaux I have mentioned,
like that on which Erzerum stands, are covered with
snow till April, the passes of the mountains much
later; and of course little but corn and other distinc-
tively northern crops can be raised on them. But this
great valley of the Araxes which intersects the mountain land is here only 2700 feet above the sea, and as
the latitude is that of Seville or Baltimore, one is not
surprised to find the heat overpowering even in September, and to see fields of cotton and tobacco border-
ing the road. A prettier crop than cotton makes it
would be hard to name, with its yellow flowers, abundant low leafage and pods snowy white as they burst.
Here, too, one comes again upon the maize which we

had parted from in the valley of the Akstafa, on the other side of the mountains. The people make of it a kind of pudding or porridge something like *polenta*. Lines of lofty poplars sometimes enclose the road, and give a temporary defence against the sun for which we are duly grateful, though they hide Ararat, on which we had been keeping our eyes fixed since morning, hoping that the clouds which were shifting themselves uneasily round his top would part sufficiently to let us have a glimpse of it. The vineyards, loaded with purple fruit, would have been too great a temptation to men so hot and thirsty but that they were enclosed by high walls of mud, with a sort of crow's nest on a scaffolding in the centre, where a peasant was perched to watch for and scare away depredators.

In the villages we passed, the houses were all of clay, which looked as if it could scarcely resist a moderately energetic thunderstorm; their walls spotted with lumps of mud which have been stuck on wet where the original structure had begun to show holes or chinks. An Armenian house gets renewed in this fashion like an Irishman's coat, till there is none of the first fabric left. These houses are usually built at the side of or round a small courtyard, enclosed by a high mud wall with one door in it; round two or three sides of the yard the rooms are placed, which have no apertures for light—one can hardly say windows—except into the yard, and little or no furniture. In some the cattle are housed with the family; those of a better sort have a byre on the other side of the yard,

distinct from the living-rooms, and sometimes many
such small subsidiary erections. The interior is dark,
and with scarcely any furniture, perhaps a low stool
or two, and a rough carpet or piece of matting to sit
or sleep upon. In summer life goes on chiefly upon
the flat roofs, also of clay, where the men sit smoking
or eating melons, and where, or else in the gardens,
they sleep at night. These villages in the middle of
fields, surrounded by vineyards and by groves of the
elæagnus, with its handsome brown fruit, and apricot
or willow, are mostly inhabited by Armenians, who
labour on the soil, getting water from the Araxes
by a multitude of channels that run hither and thither
through the tilled land. Of the Tatars many are
shepherds, accustomed in summer to wander up to
the hills with their flocks ; some, however, have permanent dwellings in the plain, and do a little hus-
bandry. Their hamlets are generally even ruder and
meaner than the Armenian, and their way of life
more repulsive. All are, of course, Mohammedans,
and most of the Shiah persuasion, having been brought
over to it by the Persians, who so lately held these
regions. They are reputed to be more fanatical than
the Sunnis, often unwilling even to give the passing
traveller a bowl of water, and, if they give it, likely to
break the vessel he has drunk from lest his unclean-
ness should pollute them. Of course, they never intermarry with their Armenian neighbours, and never
speak their tongue. When communications have to
be made, Tatar is the medium, not only because
it is the *lingua franca* of all these countries, but

because the Armenians, who are quick at languages, learn it far more readily than the Tatars do Armenian. A good deal of traffic goes on along this road, which is the only highway from Tavriz,[1] the chief commercial city of Northern Persia, to Erivan and Russia generally. As far as the Persian border at Djulfa, it is fit for wheeled carriages; beyond that, one must take horses for ninety miles on to Tavriz. The people whom we met were mostly either Tatar carriers with camels or high piled carts of merchandise, or else Armenian peasants. They wear a simple dress, which consists of a brown cotton shirt, loose, rather short cotton trousers, and a prodigious hat of brown sheepskin, something like a Guard's bearskin, only bigger, which overshadows the whole man. It is, of course, an excellent non-conductor against the sun, but what a weight to carry! Except for the trouble of winding it on and off, a turban would be far more agreeable: turbans, however, are rare in these parts, even among Muslims, and, I fancy, still less common in Persia.

After five hours' driving from Erivan, and changing horses twice, we suddenly turned to the right off the post-road, with its double line of telegraph wires,[2] and, passing through some thickets, emerged on to a long stretch of open ground, marked here and there

---

[1] Pronounced Tavreez, and commonly spelt Tabriz. The Russian *b* is pronounced nearly as our *v*.

[2] One of these lines belongs to the Russian Government: the other is our own Indo-European, along which the Viceroy of India and the Secretary of State conduct their discussions. It is kept in order by Messrs. Siemens Brothers, and, I need hardly say, is kept in much better order than the Russian line.

with wheel tracks, across which we came in two or three miles to the banks of the Aras. Things have not changed much here in the last nineteen hundred years. The Araxes—*pontem indignatus Araxes*—is spanned by no bridge all down its course, and he who would cross its historic flood must swim, or wade, or ferry. Wondering how we were to get over, we looked with some concern as well as admiration at the wide stream, as wide as the Thames at London Bridge, that swept along between banks of clay which rose ten or twelve feet above the present level of the water, but which in winter are no doubt often covered. The driver, however, promptly ran his horses down the bank and plunged in; when to our astonishment the stream turned out to be only two feet deep. The water, the muddiness of which had prevented us from seeing how shallow it was, scarcely rose to the horses' knees, and did not come into the bottom of our low tarantass ; though its flow was so rapid that fording may be pretty dangerous after heavy rains above. On our way back, some days afterwards, we crossed in a ferry-boat stationed a little lower down, which is worked by a rope, and I had then the pleasure of a plunge into this famous river, whose water is not cold enough to do the most exhausted bather any harm. It seemed to have a fuller current than the Kur at Tiflis, yet a wonderfully scanty one, considering the length of its course ; this, of course, is easily explained by the great dryness of the country it drains.

Passing through a crowd of picturesque Kurds who had been driving their cattle through by the same ford,

and envying the big greyish-white buffaloes which were
cooling themselves in the water, we crossed a tract intersected by numerous channels drawn from the river for
irrigation, bordered with tall reeds, and enclosing fields
of rice, already reaped, and cotton whose pods were just
bursting with white fluff. In the reedy marshes which
these channels feed, there is abundance of wild hogs.
They come out at night, and ravage the rice-fields of
the Tatars ; and as the Mohammedan scruples of the
latter prevent them from touching, and practically
therefore from hunting down, this unclean animal, the
hogs have a fine time of it. If ever that Araxes valley
railway to India, whereof the Russians talk, comes to
be made, perhaps some of our military pig-stickers
will halt here on their way and give the Armenians
a lesson in that exciting sport. At last, after three or
four miles' driving, a cluster of bushes told us that a
village was near, and through them we discovered
the trim cantonments of our destination, the Russian
station of Aralykh.   Here there is always kept a
detachment of Cossacks, and the colonel in command
is the chief military authority over the skirts of the
two Ararats, charged to guard the frontier and look
after the predatory bands that are said to hang about
it.   The summit of Little Ararat is the meeting-
point of the Russian, Persian, and Turkish empires,
and every one knows that border lands have been
from time immemorial the haunts of dangerous or
turbulent characters, since they can find an easy
escape from the jurisdiction against which they have
offended into another that knows nothing about them.

Where, as here, there are three such jurisdictions, these risks are of course intensified, especially as there is no attempt made to keep order in the Turkish or Persian dominions, nothing that deserves to be called a police. So I dare say there would be a good deal of brigandage if there were anybody to rob, but the villages of the Aras valley are almost too poor to be worth plundering, and travellers, except on the main road to Tavriz, are very rare. The mountains are inhabited only by a few wandering Kurds. It will appear in the sequel that we saw, with our own eyes, no trace whatever of banditti. But as the colonel, who was a very sensible man, particularly begged us not to ramble more than a mile from the station, offering an escort if we wished to go farther, one could not but suppose there must really be some hidden dangers in these apparently deserted slopes. Robbers have for many generations been made an excuse for not exploring the mountain to find the Ark. In hearing about them, we were often reminded of the lines in *Bishop Blougram's Apology*—

> "Such a traveller told you his last news,
> He saw the Ark a-top of Ararat;
> But did not climb there since 'twas getting late,
> And robber bands infest the mountain's foot."

Aralykh is not fortified, for there is no attack to be expected from these wretched banditti, whoever they are, nor does Russia appear to fancy an invasion from Turkey or Persia likely enough to be worth guarding against. It is merely a row of wooden barracks, neatly painted, with a smith's and carpenter's shop, cottages for the army followers, and so forth, scattered round it, and a few trees, giving a little shade in summer and shelter from the violent winter winds. The situation is striking. It is exactly on the line where the last slope of Ararat, an extremely gentle slope of not more than two or three degrees in inclination, melts into the perfectly flat bottom of the Aras valley.[1] Looking up this slope, the mountain seems quite close, though in reality its true base, that is, the point where the ground begins to rise sharply, is fully four hours (twelve miles) distant. On this its north-eastern side, one looks right into the great black chasm, and sees, topping the cliffs that surround that chasm, a cornice of ice 300 or 400 feet in thickness, lying at a height of about 14,000 feet, and above, a steep slope of snow, pierced here and there by rocks running up to the summit. A little to the west of south, and about seventeen miles distant, rises the singularly elegant peak of Little Ararat, appearing from this point as a regular slightly truncated cone, which in the autumn is free from snow.[2] In the plain, and only a few miles off to the south-west, a low rocky eminence is seen, close to the famous monastery of Khorvirab, where St. Gregory the Illuminator, the apostle of Armenia, was for fourteen years confined in a dry well by his cousin, King Tiridates. So

---

[1] Aralykh is 2602 feet above the sea-level.

[2] The view of the two Ararats in the frontispiece is taken from Syrbaghan, a Tatar village about two miles south-west of Aralykh, and therefore shows the mountains in what is practically the same aspect as that described in the text. This view is drawn after one of Parrot's, with some alterations for which I am responsible.

at least says the Armenian Church. The very ancient
ruins on it are sometimes taken to be the site of the
famous city of Artaxata, which, according to Strabo,
was built for King Artaxias (who, revolting from
Antiochus the Great, founded an Armenian kingdom)
by Hannibal, after he had left Antiochus, and before
he sought his last refuge with Prusias of Bithynia.[1]
Others place Artaxata nearer to Erivan on the river
Medzamor, and at some distance from the present
bed of the Araxes, which, according to Tacitus
(Ann. xiii. 41) flowed under the walls of Artaxata.
It was one of the two capitals of Digran or Tigranes, the great Armenian conqueror, and captured
by Lucullus, when, after defeating Mithridates of
Pontus, he carried the Roman arms against Tigranes,
the son-in-law and ally of the latter, into these remote
regions, which even Alexander had not entered. A
century and a half later it was again taken and razed
to the ground by Corbulo, one of the generals of
Nero, and was subsequently rebuilt by Tiridates, a
protégé of Nero's, under the name of Neronia. When,
about A.D. 370, it was again taken and burnt by the
Persians, it is said to have contained a population of
200,000, 40,000 of them Jews.

---

[1] Strabo, xi. p. 528 : cf. Plutarch Lucull. c. 31. The story is doubted
by some historians, and among others by Mommsen (Röm. Gesch.
b. iii. c. ix.). If it be a fable, the evidence it gives of the fame of
Hannibal through the East is all the more striking. I may, however,
remark—(1) that the alleged building of Artaxata by Hannibal took
place only a century and a half before Strabo's time ; (2) that it does
not appear that any alibi can be proved for Hannibal at the time assigned for his visit to Armenia ; and (3) that there is apparently no
other instance of Hannibal's name appearing in Oriental legend, like
Alexander or Semiramis, as the reputed author of great works.

At Aralykh we were received with the utmost courtesy by the officer in command, Colonel Temirhan Aktolovitch Shipshef, a Mohammedan noble from the Kabarda, on the north side of the Caucasus, and a man of many and varied accomplishments. To our great regret, as he spoke no West European language, and we no Russian, our communications were comparatively limited ; but even the conversation carried on through an interpreting friend enabled us to perceive that he was well read, not only in military matters, but in general history and literature. He had a particular admiration for Cromwell, about the recent lives of whom he questioned us, and discoursed with great acuteness as well as knowledge on European politics and literature, including the works of two writers who seem to be favourites in Russia, the late Mr. Buckle and Mr. Herbert Spencer. Although a strict teetotaller himself, as a good Muslim ought to be, his table was well supplied with the choicest wines of Transcaucasia, as well as with a liquor to which the prohibition of the Prophet is supposed not to apply, and which, in spite of its high price, is largely consumed in these countries, English bottled porter. His house was spacious, with large, low rooms, all on the ground floor, and by closing the shutters we were able to get some cool during the day, especially as a slight breeze rose in the afternoon. At night, however, it was terribly hot, for we were enjoined to keep the windows shut to avoid the fever-producing miasma from the adjoining marshes. Even our concentrated solution of carbolic

P

acid, though it was strong enough to burn a hole in my forehead, did not wholly repel the mosquitoes whom these marshes rear. The pleasantest time was the evening, when we sat on the verandah beside our genial host, sipping tumbler after tumbler of delicious lemon-flavoured tea, and watching the exquisite colours of sunset die away in this lucent air into the balmy vivid night. Concerning Ararat we had much discourse, the upshot of which was that nobody at Aralykh knew anything of former ascents, nor of how it ought to be attacked, but that we should have horses and Cossacks to take us to Sardarbulakh, a small military outpost high up on the way which leads over the pass between Great and Little Ararat to Bayazid, and as much farther as horses or Cossacks could go. We could desire no more, so this was settled, and we were grateful. Though the colonel doubtless marvelled in his heart what could be our motive for a difficult and fatiguing expedition, the success of which was so uncertain, he was too polite to say so, talking as gravely about the matter as if he had been president of an Alpine club sending out his explorers with instructions. A day, however, was needed to make preparations, and while these went forward, we got the heads and spikes of our ice-axes fitted with shafts by a German carpenter attached to the station, and rambled out under umbrellas over the slope that rose almost imperceptibly to the south-east, an hour's walking on which seemed to bring us no nearer to the mountain. It was an arid waste of white volcanic ash or sand, covered with prickly shrubs (the commonest of them being that *Calligonum polygonoides* which supplies fuel to the Kurds in winter), among which lizards and black scorpions wriggle about. We ought, of course, to have gone— any energetic traveller would have gone—to examine the ruins of Artaxata, but the overpowering heat and the weariness of the last few days and sleepless nights, which began to tell as soon as we began to rest, made us too languid even for so obvious a duty. So we dawdled, and panted, and dozed, and watched the clouds shift and break and form again round the solemn snowy cone till another evening descended and it glittered clear and cold beneath the stars.

CHAPTER VI.

ARARAT.

NONE of the native peoples that behold from the surrounding plains and valleys the silvery crest of Ararat
know it by that name. The Armenians call it Massis,
or Massis Ljarn (*ljarn* meaning "mountain"), a name
which we may connect with the Masius of Strabo
(though his description of that mountain does not
suit ours) ; the Tatars and Turks, Aghri Dagh, which
is interpreted as meaning "curved mountain," or
"painful mountain"; the Persians, Koh i Nuh, "the
mountain of Noah," or, according to Sir John Chardin,
Sahat Toppin, which he interprets to mean "the
Happy Hillock." It has received among geographers
the name of Ararat, which the Russian use is now
beginning to spread in the neighbourhood, and which
the ecclesiastics at Etchmiadzin have taken as the
title of a monthly magazine they publish, only from
its identification with the Biblical mountain of the
Ark, an identification whose history is curious.

The only topographical reference in the Scripture
narrative of the Flood is to be found in the words,
Genesis viii. 4,—" In the seventh month, on the seventeenth day of the month," " the ark rested upon the

mountains of Ararat," which may be taken as equivalent to "on a mountain of (or in) Ararat." The word Ararat is used in three, or rather two, other places in Scripture. One is in 2 Kings xix. 37, and the parallel passage in Isaiah xxxvii. 38, where it is said of the sons of Sennacherib, who had just murdered their father, that "they escaped into the land of Ararat," rendered in our version, and in the Septuagint, "Armenia." The other is in Jeremiah li. 27, "Call together against her" (i.e. Babylon) "the kingdoms of Ararat, Minni, and Ashchenaz." The question then is, what does this Ararat denote? Clearly the Alexandrian translators took it for Armenia; so does the Vulgate when it renders in Genesis viii. 4 the words which we translate, "on the mountains of Ararat," by "super montes Armeniae." This narrows it a little, and St. Jerome himself helps us to narrow it still further when, in his commentary on Isaiah xxxvii. 38, he says that "Ararat means the plain of the middle Araxes, which lies at the foot of the great mountain Taurus." Besides, Moses of Chorene, the well-known Armenian historian of the fifth century, speaks of a province or district he calls Ajrarat, lying on the Araxes, and which some have tried to identify with the name of the Alarodians in Herodotus. Now as our modern Mount Ararat, Aghri Dagh, is by far the highest and most conspicuous mountain of that region, no one who looked at it, already knowing the story of the Flood, could doubt that it was the first part of the dry land to appear as the waters dried up, so much does it rise above all its neighbours.

The identification, therefore, is natural enough : what it is of more consequence to determine is how early it took place ; for as there is little or no trace of an independent local tradition of the Flood, we may assume the identification to rest entirely on the use of the name Ararat in the Hebrew narra- tive. Josephus (*Ant. Jud.* bk. i. ch. iii.) says that the Armenians called the place where Noah descended the disembarking place (ἀποβατήριον), "for the Ark being saved in that place, its remains are shown there by the inhabitants to this day," and also quotes Nicolas of Damascus, who writes that "in Armenia, above Minyas, there is a great mountain called Baris (is this word the Armenian Masis ?), upon which it is said that many who escaped at the time of the Flood were saved, and that one who was carried in an ark came ashore on the top of it, and that the remains of the wood were preserved for a long while. This might be the man about whom Moses, the law-giver of the Jews, wrote." This ἀποβατήριον has usually been identified with the town of Nakhitchevan (called by Ptolemy Naxuana), which stands on the Araxes, about thirty-five miles south-east from our mountain, and whose name the modern Armenians explain as meaning "he descended first,"[1] which would seem to show that in the first century of our era—and how much sooner we cannot say—the Armenians living round the mountain believed it to be the Ark moun-

---

[1] Nöldeke, however, to whose 'Untersuchungen zur Kritik des alten Testaments' the curious reader may be referred for a learned discussion of the subject, is informed by a competent Armenian scholar that this etymology is, as might have been supposed, impossible.

tain. They might have **heard of the Bible** narrative
from Jews, who were already beginning to **be scattered**
through these countries (there **is a story** that some of
those carried away by Shalmanezer were settled in Armenia and Georgia) ; they might know the **Chaldaean**
legend of the Flood, which **was** preserved by Berosus,
to whom Josephus so **often refers, and a version of**
which has been found on **clay tablets** in the ruins **of**
Nineveh and **deciphered by the late Mr. George Smith.**
The curious **thing is that this** Chaldee legend fixed
the spot of **Noah's landing in a quite different region,**
although one **which was sometimes included in the**
wide and loose **name Armenia, viz. in the** mountain
land (called by **the Jews Qardu) which rises to the**
east of the Upper Tigris, that **is, north-east** of
Nineveh and Mosul, in the direction **of Urumia.**
This country was called in **ancient times Gordyene,**
a name which appears **in the Hebrew Qardu, and**
in our modern name Kurds, as well **as in the**
Karduchi of Xenophon. As its mountains, although
far less lofty than **our** modern Ararat, are of great
height, and visible far away **into the** Assyrian plain
(Mr. Layard saw Aghri Dagh from the summit of one
of them), it **was natural for the** inhabitants of **that**
plain to assume that they **were the highest on earth,**
which the **Deluge would be the last to cover, and**
where the vessel **of safety would come to land.** The
Jews also, probably at the time of **the Captivity, took**
up this notion, and it **became the dominant one among**
them, is frequently given in the **Talmud,** and by
Josephus himself, **in** a passage (*Ant. Jud.* **xx.** ii. 2)

where he mentions that in the country of Adiabene, and in the district of Carrae (others read " of the Cardi " = Kurds), there were preserved the remains of the Ark. Probably he thought that the disembarking place mentioned in the beginning of his treatise was here, for he quotes Berosus as stating that it was among the Kurds, who in those days are not mentioned so far north as they wander now. Berosus' words are, "It is said that there is still some part of this ship in Armenia at the mountain of the Cordyaeans (πρὸς τῷ ὄρει τῶν Κορδυαίων), and that some people carry off pieces of the bitumen, which they take away and use chiefly as amulets for the averting of mischief." But probably Josephus' ideas of the geography of these regions were vague enough, and he may not have known that from the land of Ajrarat, on the middle Araxes, to Gordyene it is more than 200 miles. From the Jews, this idea that Gordyene was the Biblical spot passed to the Syrian Church, and became the · prevailing view throughout the Christian East, as it still is among the Nestorians, who dwell hard by. It passed also to the Muslims ; and Gudi, the mountain where the Ark rested according to the Koran, is usually placed by them in the same Kurdish land, near the spot where there seems to have stood for several centuries (it was burnt in A.D. 655, but may have been rebuilt later) a convent to which tradition pointed as the guardian of the sacred fragments. Those who assume, as many Oriental scholars do, that the original tradition of the Flood is to be found in Assyria, naturally prefer this

latter identification, since the mountains of Southern
Kurdistan, the Qardu land, are quite high enough to
satisfy the narrative, and must have been always
familiar to the Chaldees, whereas the Araxes valley
lies far away to the north, and the fact that its
summits are really loftier would in those times be
little known or regarded. Without the aid of our
modern scientific appliances, men's ideas of relative
height are even vaguer and less capable of verification
than their ideas of distance. On the other hand, the
view which holds the Ararat of the Bible to lie in
Northern Armenia, near the Araxes, can appeal not
only to the undoubted fact that there was in that
region the province called Ajrarat, but also to the reference to a " kingdom of Ararat " in Jeremiah li. 27,
which could hardly apply to Gordyene.[1] And one
does not see why the Old Testament writers, whose
geographical knowledge was in some points a good
deal wider than is commonly assumed, should not
have heard of the very lofty summits that lie in this
part of Armenia. Full liberty is therefore left to the
traveller to believe our Ararat, the snowy sovereign of
the Araxes plain, to be the true Ararat, and certainly
no one who had ever seen it rising in solitary majesty
far above all its attendant peaks could doubt that its
summit must have first pierced the receding waves.

The modern Armenian tradition of course goes for
nothing in settling the question, for that tradition
cannot be shown to be older than our own era, and is
easily accounted for by the use of the word Ararat in

[1] See Nöldeke, *ut supra.*

the book of Genesis, which the Armenians, when Jews
or Christians came among them, would of course
identify with their Ajrarat. Once established, the
tradition held its ground, and budded out into many
fantastic legends, some of them still lingering in
Armenia, some only known to us by the notices of
passing mediæval travellers. Marco Polo, whose
route does not seem to have led him near it, says
only, in speaking of Armenia :—" Here is an exceeding
great mountain : on which it is said the Ark of Noah
rested, and for this cause it is called the mountain of
the Ark of Noah. The circuit of its base cannot be
traversed in less than two days ; and the ascent is
rendered impossible by the snow on its summit,
which never dissolves, but is increased by each successive fall. On the lower declivities the melted snows
cause an abundant vegetation, and afford rich pastures
for the cattle which in summer resort thither from
all the surrounding countries." But the Franciscan
friar, William of Rubruk, who, in 1254, a little before
Marco Polo's time, had on his return from Kara-
korum passed under Ararat, says that here upon the
higher of two great mountains above the river Araxes
the Ark rested, which mountain cannot be ascended,
though the earnest prayers of a pious monk prevailed
so far that a piece of the wood of the Ark was brought
to him by an angel, which piece is still preserved in a
church near by as a holy relic. He gives Massis as
the name of this mountain, and adds that it is the
mother of the world : "super Massis nullus debet
ascendere quia est mater mundi."

Sir John Maundeville, of pious and veracious memory, has also a good deal to tell us. After speaking of Trapazond (Trebizond), and stating that from there "men go to Ermonye (Armenia) the Great unto a cytee that is clept Artyroun (Erzerum), that was wont to ben a gode cytee and a plentyous, but the Turkes han gretly wasted it," he proceeds:—"Fro Artyroun go men to an Hille that is clept Sabisocolle. And there besyde is another Hille that men clepen Ararathe: but the Jews clepen it Taneez, where Noes Schipp rested: and zit is upon that Montayne: and men may see it a ferr in cleer wedre: and that Montayne is well a 7 Myle high. And sum men seyn that they have seen and touched the Schipp; and put here Fyngres in the parties where the Feend went out whan that Noe seyd ' *Benedicite.*' But thei that seyn such Wordes seyn here Wille, for a man may not gon up the Montayne for gret plentee of Snow that is alle weyes on that Montayne nouther Somer ne Winter; so that no man may gon up there: ne nevere man did, sithe the tyme of Noe: saf a Monk that be the grace of God broughte on of the Plankes down, that zit is in the Mynstre at the foot of the Montayne. And besyde is the Cytee of Dayne that Noe founded. And faste by is the Cytee of Any, in the whiche were 1000 churches. But upon that Montayne to gon up this Monk had gret desir; and so upon a day he wente up and whan he was upward the 3 part of the Montayne he was so wery that he myghte no ferthere, and so he rested him and felle to slepe; and whan he awoke he fonde himself liggynge at the foot of the Montayne. And then he preyede devoutly to God that he wolde vouche saf to suffre him gon up. And an Angelle cam to him and seyde that he scholde gon up; and so he did. And sithe that tyme never non. Wherfore men scholde not beleeve such Woordes."

This laudable scepticism of Sir John's prevailed, for it has long been almost an article of faith with the Armenian Church that the top of Ararat is inaccessible. Even the legend of the monk, which, as we find from Friar William, is as old as the thirteenth century, is usually given in a form which confirms still further the sacredness of the mountain. St. Jacob (Hagop), as the monk is named, was consumed by a pious desire to reach and venerate the holy Ark, which could in seasons of fair weather be descried from beneath, and three several times he essayed to climb the steep and rocky slopes. Each time, after reaching a great height, he fell into a deep sleep, and, when he woke, found himself at the foot of the mountain. After the third time, an angel appeared to him while he still lay in slumber, and told him that God had forbidden mortal foot ever to tread the sacred summit or touch the vessel in which mankind had been preserved, but that on him, in reward for his devout perseverance, there should be bestowed a fragment of its wood. This fragment he placed on the sleeper's breast, and vanished; it is that which is still preserved in the treasury at Etchmiadzin, or, as others say, in the monastery of Kjeghart; and the saint is commemorated by the little monastery of

St. Jacob, which stands, or rather stood till 1840, on the slopes of Ararat, above the valley of Arghuri, the spot of the angel's appearing. Every succeeding traveller has repeated this tale, with variations due to his informant or his own imagination : so, though the reader has probably heard it, I dare not break through a custom so long established. Among these repeaters is Sir John Chardin, who travelled through Armenia and Persia towards the end of the seventeenth century, and whose remarks upon it are as follows. They show the progress which criticism had been making since the days of the earlier Sir John.

"This is the Tale that they tell, upon which I shall observe 2 Things. First, that it has no coherence with the relations of ancient authors as Josephus, Berosus, or Nicolaus of Damascus, who assure us that the Remainders of the Ark were to be seen, and that the people took the Pitch with which it was besmeared as an Antidote against Several Distempers. The second, that whereas it is taken for a Miracle that no Body can get up to the Top : I should rather take it for a greater Miracle that any Man should climb up so high. For the Mountain is altogether uninhabited, and from the Halfway to the Top of all, perpetually covered with Snow that never melts, so that all the Seasons of the Year it appears to be a prodigious heap of nothing but Snow."

Whether Chardin himself believed the Ark to be still on the top of the mountain, does not appear. In two views of it which he gives, showing also Erivan and Etchmiadzin, the Ark appears, in shape exactly

the Ark of the nursery on Sunday afternoons, poised
on the summit of Great Ararat. But this may be
merely emblematic; indeed I have not found any
author who says he has himself seen it, though plenty
who (like the retailers of ghost stories) mention other
people who have.

Religious fancy has connected many places in the
neighbourhood with the Biblical narrative. Not to
speak of the sites which have been suggested in the
Araxes valley for the Garden of Eden, the name of
Arghuri itself is derived from two Armenian words
which mean, " he planted the vine"; it is taken to
be the spot where Noah planted that first vineyard
which is mentioned in Genesis ix. 20: and till 1840,
when the village was overwhelmed by a tremendous
fall of rocks, shaken down by the great earthquake of
that year, an ancient vine stock, still bearing grapes,
was pointed out as that which had been planted by the
patriarch's hands. The town of Marand, the Marunda
of Ptolemy (in Armenian = "the mother is there "), is
said to be called after the wife of Noah, who there died
and was buried; and (as has been mentioned already)
the name of another still considerable town, Nakhitchevan, in the Araxes valley, is explained to mean,
" he descended first," and has therefore been identified
with the ἀποβατήριον of Josephus aforesaid. There too
was shown, perhaps is still shown, the tomb of Noah.
Modern historians and geographers have been hardly
less fanciful than Armenian monks: some derive the
Tatar name Aghri or Arghi Dagh from the word
Arca. Some imagine a relation between this and

the *Argo;* others connect the word *baris* (mentioned above as an ancient name for the mountain) with a supposed Oriental word meaning "boat" (see Herodotus, ii. 96), or with the Armenian *bariz* (= exit); in fine, there is no end to the whimsical speculations that attach themselves to the mountain. What is certain is that the word Ararat, though it is a genuine old Armenian name for a district, and is derived by Moses of Chorene from *Arai jarat,* "the fall of Arai," a mythical Armenian king slain in battle with Semiramis, has never been the name by which those who lived round the mountain have known it, albeit it is found in the Armenian version of the Bible just as in our own.

Of the other legends that cluster round the mountain, I shall mention only two. One of them connects it with the so-called Chaldaean worship of the stars, and affirm that upon it stood a pillar with a figure of a star; and that before the birth of Christ twelve wise men were stationed by this pillar to watch for the appearing of the star in the east, which three of them followed, when it appeared, to Bethlehem. The other, of a very different kind, relates to a spring which bursts forth on the side of the Great Chasm, above the spot where the convent of St. Jacob stood. There is a bird called by the Armenians *tetagush,* which pursues and feeds on the locusts whose swarms are such a plague to this country. Now, the water of this sacred spring possesses the property of attracting the tetagush, and when the locusts appear, the first thing to be done is to fetch a bottle of it, and set it on the

ground near them, taking care not to let it touch the
ground upon its way. The bird immediately appears ;
the locusts are devoured, and the crops are saved. It
is a pity the Canadians have no *tetagush* to set at their
destroying beetle.

Before finally quitting the realm of fancy for that of
fact, I will repeat an observation by which more than
one orographer of distinction, struck by the remarkable geographical position which Ararat occupies,[1]
has suggested a sort of justification for the Armenian
view that it is the centre of the earth. It stands in
the centre of the longest line of the old continent,
stretching from the Cape of Good Hope to Behring
Straits. It is also in the line of the great deserts and
of the great inland seas from Gibraltar to Lake
Baikal, that is, in a line of almost continuous depressions. It is almost exactly equidistant from the
Black Sea, the Caspian, and the northern end of the
great Mesopotamian plain, which at no distant period
was probably also part of the ocean bed.

Taking the two Ararats together, they form an
elliptical mass of about twenty-five miles in length
from north-west to south-east, and about half that
width. This mass rises on the north and east out of
the alluvial plain of the Aras, whose height is here
from 2800 to 2500 feet above the sea, and on the
south-west sinks into the valley or rather plateau of
Bayazid, which lies between 4000 and 5000 feet above
sea-level, and also discharges its waters towards the

---

[1] See Ritter, ‘Erdkunde,’ vol. x., who quotes K. von Raumer
on the point.

Aras. It is therefore quite isolated on all sides but
the north-west, where a depression or col about 7000
feet high connects it with a long ridge of volcanic
mountains, which, under the names of Pambak, Synak
Dagh, and Parly Dagh, runs away to the westward
between the basins of the Aras and Murad Su
(Eastern Euphrates), and connects itself south of
Erzerum with the great range of the Bingöl Dagh, or
north-eastern Taurus, as well as with the southern
offsets of the Anti-Caucasus. Over against it to the
north, nearly forty miles away, rise the three volcanic
pinnacles, fragments of a broken crater rim, of Ala
Göz (13,436 feet); to the east, beyond the wide
valley of the Aras, is the great plateau of the Kara
Bagh, some of whose highest volcanic tops exceed
11,000 feet, while on the south, beyond Bayazid and
the Upper Euphrates, ranges nearly equally lofty run
away down towards the Lake of Van in the south and
the Lake of Urumia in the south-east. Orographically
and geologically, Ararat is connected with all these,
but the plain immediately around it is wide enough to
give it that air of standing quite alone which so greatly
contributes to its grandeur, and speaks so clearly of
its volcanic origin.

Out of the great elliptical mass I have described
rise two peaks, their bases confluent at a height of
8800 feet, their summits about seven miles apart. The
higher, Great Ararat, is 17,000 feet above the sea-
level,[1] the lower, Little Ararat, 12,840 feet. They are

---

[1] The different measurements of the height of Ararat vary a little.
Parrot, by the barometer, made it 17,325 English feet; Fedorof, by

very similar in geological structure, but sufficiently
dissimilar in appearance, like the sisters in Virgil—

> "Facies non omnibus una
> Nec diversa tamen, qualem decet esse sororum "—

to enhance the effect of one another. For while Little
Ararat is an elegant cone or pyramid, rising with
steep, smooth, regular sides into a comparatively
sharp peak, Great Ararat is a huge, broad-shouldered
mass, more of a dome than a cone, supported by
strong buttresses, and throwing out rough ribs or
ridges of rock that stand out like knotty muscles from
its solid trunk.   The greatest length of this dome is
from north-west to south-east. Towards the north-
east, that is, on one of its long sides, it descends very
abruptly towards the Aras plain, forming in places
ranges of magnificent black precipice, capped with ice-
beds many hundreds of feet in thickness, and pierced
by a profound glen or chasm. On the opposite or
south-west side the fall is somewhat less rapid ; towards the south-east, where the peak faces Little
Ararat, it is steep indeed, but in most parts not precipitous (this is the side up which I ascended) ; while
towards the north-west the declivity is longer and
more gentle, a succession of terraces, separated by
moderately difficult slopes, falling away into an immense fan-shaped base, which spreads far into the
Araxes plain. This is, therefore, the side on which
occur the only considerable fields of snow or rather
névé (the others being too abrupt for much snow to

trigonometry, 17,130 feet ; some other observer gives 17,260 feet,
which has been commonly adopted in England ; General Chodzko,
who ascended in 1850, makes it 16,916 feet..

lie), and it was by advancing over them that Parrot effected the first ascent of the mountain. The upper slopes, where not snow-covered, are extremely rough and broken, seamed by gullies, the larger of which are no doubt volcanic fissures, the smaller probably produced by winter storms, rising here and there into lofty towers and ridges of rock, and strewn with prodigious masses of loose stone, broken by the weather into wildly fantastic shapes. All this part, above 10,000 or 11,000 feet, is almost wholly bare of vegetation. The middle part of the declivity is somewhat less rugged, and the lowest slopes of all, by which the mass subsides into the plain, are singularly smooth and uniform. On the north-east side these basal slopes, as I may call them, are two. First comes one which rises from the Aras marshes at an angle of about $2\frac{1}{2}$ degrees for some six miles, and then another, which rises for, say, four miles, at an angle of $4\frac{1}{2}$ degrees. After this second, the steep part of the mountain begins. Its average angle on the north-west declivity is about 17 degrees, on the south-east 25 to 30 degrees.

Both peaks are entirely composed of igneous rock, and there is no question that they belong to what may be called the grand volcanic system of North-western Asia, the main lines of whose action are indicated in a general way by the direction of the chief mountain chains, such direction being supposed to correspond to axes of elevation, or, as it is sometimes expressed, to lines of fissure. Along these lines of fissure, continuously or at intervals, the igneous masses forming the highest part of such chains were from time to time ejected. One such line, or perhaps more than one, is represented by the Caucasus, where, besides the granitic mountains on the axis, there are several comparatively modern volcanic summits, such as Elbruz, Kazbek, and Basarjusi. Another line of elevation, marked by volcanic outbursts, appears in the north-eastern ranges of Taurus ; another in the range dividing the upper valleys of the Kur and Aras. Still nearer to Ararat, the great mass of Ala Göz, on the north, and the continuation of that mass to the east and south-east in the mountains that surround the Goktcha lake, are all volcanic, composed chiefly of trachyte rock. The valley of the Aras itself is filled by recent alluvial deposits, out of which rise isolated palæozoic hills composed of carboniferous limestone or Devonian strata, which appear again farther to the south, in the hills through which the Aras takes its way to Nakhitchevan and the Persian border ; while farther to the south and west, newer sedimentary rocks range southwards, pierced here and there by the volcanic outbursts which reach as far as Lake Van.

The only geologist of eminence who has carefully examined Ararat is Hermann Abich, now one of the patriarchs of the science ; and probably the best thing I can do is to abridge his view of its structure and history, so far as I can gather it from the various papers which he has contributed to different scientific journals.[1] He holds the inner and original part of

___

[1] See in particular his paper, "Ararat in seiner genetischen Bildung," in the *Transactions* of the German Geological Society for 1870, in which

the mass to be composed of trachyte and trachytic
tuffs, poured out at a comparatively early period in
dome-shaped hills, three of which, placed along a line
of fissure running nearly north-west and south-east,
were Little Ararat, Great Ararat, and the rounded
plateau called, from a small pond or pool upon it
(*ghöll* = lake, in Tatar), Kip Ghöll, which lies about
four miles north-west by west of the top of Great
Ararat. The eruptive forces which raised these hills
having, after an interval of quiescence, resumed their
activity in comparatively recent times, probably in
what we call the pleiocene age, violent splittings and
burstings of the trachytic rocks went on, mainly along
the old lines of fissure, and vast quantities of lava of
a doleritic or basaltic character were poured out from
various points along these fissures. The pressing-up
from beneath of the edges of the fissures gave to the
summits of both Great and Little Ararat their present
form ; no eruptions taking place from the actual tops,
although some of the fissure-vents which discharged
streams of doleritic lava were not far below these
summits, while a number of minor cones were raised
and craters formed along the sides of the mountain,
especially to the south-east of Great Ararat, and on
Kip Ghöll, where several large and well-marked cra-
teriform hollows may be still made out. Along with
this splitting, there went on a process of elevation,
by which the southern edge of one huge cleft was
raised to be the present summit of Great Ararat,

the views expressed in his paper contributed to the *Transactions* of the
Geological Society of Paris in 1850 are slightly modified.

while its other side remained at, or sank to, a much lower level; other rifts were also formed at right angles to the principal axis, one of which was the origin of the remarkable chasm on the north-east side of the mountain, which bears much similarity to the famous Val del Bove on Etna. Its present shape and dimensions—it is nearly 9000 feet deep, and surrounded by monstrous precipices—are probably, like those of the Sicilian valley, due to subsequent erosion; but there may well have been eruptions from it in some earlier stage. A somewhat similar, but smaller, chasm penetrates deep into the mountain on the opposite or south-western side.

According to this theory, there never was a great central crater at the summit of either Great or Little Ararat. The forms of those two peaks are due to the elevating and rending forces which, operating on pre-existing trachytic masses, squeezed up the edges of the clefts they opened into comparatively sharp points, while prodigious and long-continued eruptions sometimes from these clefts, sometimes from cones of eruption built up round the principal orifices along their line, increased the external volume of the mountain, and in the case of Great Ararat turned it from a comparatively sharp cone, similar to Little Ararat, into the broad-shouldered, grandly buttressed mass which it now presents. Unlike these two loftier summits, Kip Ghöll would appear to approach more nearly the normal type of a modern volcano, having been built up, not so much by a general upheaval, as by external accretion from the lava, scoriæ, and ashes,

ejected from its craters; and the gentler inclination
of the northern slope of the peak of Great Ararat
would be accounted for by the fact that behind Kip
Ghöll to the south-east, in the direction of that peak,
there were other similar craters which filled up the
depression between it and Kip Ghöll, and gave to the
north-west face of the mountain its present appearance of a series of descending terraces. Subsequent
denudation continued through many thousands, or
millions, of years, and that process of decay and
levelling which all mountains undergo has worn down
the inequalities of the sides, has given to Little
Ararat its figure of a wonderfully regular pyramidal
cone, has filled up some and scooped out others of
the fissures on Great Ararat until the former seem to
be merely shallow troughs running down the mountain face, while the latter are profound gorges such as
the great chasm, has obliterated many of the lateral
craters by breaking down their rims and raising the
level of their bottoms.

    To criticise this theory, which perhaps retains too
much of the old upheaval doctrines of von Buch
and Élie de Beaumont to be altogether acceptable to
British geologists, would require far wider geological
knowledge than I possess, as well as a more careful
study of Ararat itself than I had time for. The
existence, however, of the great fissures to which Herr
Abich attributes so much is unquestionable; one in
particular, on the south-east side of the mountain,
runs down for many thousand feet, bordered by lofty
cliffs of black or reddish porphyritic trachyte, and has

every appearance of having discharged currents of lava.
I can also confirm what he says as to the absence of
any trace of a crater on the summit of Great Ararat.
The top (which I shall describe in the following
chapter) forms a small undulating plateau of snow,
with two rounded heights or bosses rising out of it;
there is no appearance of a circular hollow, and
although the cap of *névé* is thick enough to obscure
in some degree the structure of the rocky ground
beneath, it could hardly have its present form if there
really lay underneath it sharp cliffs surrounding a
basin, such as are seen in most volcanoes. Nothing,
for instance, could be less like the snowy summit of
Hekla, where there is a beautiful crater almost surrounded by an *arête*, than is the top of Ararat.
Similarly, the top of Little Ararat is nearly flat, with
many vast blocks and masses of rock on it, but no
central depression, no rim of cliffs. It would, however, be rash to infer from the absence of a crater now
that none ever existed on these summits, for many
volcanoes might be cited whose central crater has
been almost or even quite obliterated, though the
general structure of the mountain enables us to conclude its former existence.[1] It may therefore be that
on Great Ararat the crater had been, at the time
when volcanic action through its chimney ceased,
almost filled up within by the ejection of solid matter
from that chimney, so that the crateral form had

[1] Instances may be found referred to in Mr. Scrope's treatise on
Volcanoes, and Professor Judd's book on Volcanoes, where this
question is particularly discussed.

almost disappeared.   Or, again, it is possible that,
in the immense period that has elapsed since the
last eruption from the summit, the sides of the
crateral basin which then existed have been completely broken down by decay, the destructive action
of the atmosphere being doubly powerful at this
prodigious height, where frosts and storms are constantly raging.   Or, lastly, the summit, as we now
see it, may be the remains of one side of a large
crater, the other sides having been destroyed by
some paroxysmal eruption, as the one side of Somma,
the ancient Vesuvius, was destroyed in the tremendous outburst of A.D. 72.

Supposing that there once existed a central vent of
eruption, opening at the top of Ararat, it would be in
the usual order of volcanic phenomena for this main
vent, whose presence had determined the height and
original shape of the mountain, to pass into a state of
quiescence while the minor eruptive points on the
flanks still remained active, and perhaps became more
numerous.   A great volcano has been compared to a
great tree, which dies down from the top.   When the
explosive forces become weaker, they are no longer
able to raise the molten masses from within to the
height of the central orifice, but produce a crack
somewhere in the sides ; this becomes a crater, is
perhaps raised into a cone, and through it minor
eruptions go on.   The repetition of the process mul-
tiplies these secondary vents all round the great
central chimney, which probably continues to emit
steam and light ashes, but no longer discharges molten

rock, while the parasitic cones and craters cover the skirts of the mountain with large deposits of scoriæ and ash, and send into the plain below far-reaching streams of lava. This is the process now going on in many famous volcanoes, of which I may again take Hekla as an instance. Although the soil of its central crater is still hot in some places, and emits a little sulphurous vapour, no eruption has issued thence for a long time; and the last one, that of 1845, was from a chasm about 1000 feet below the top. So, too, most of the lava flows of Etna have taken place from lateral vents; no less than 700 of which have been counted on its sides. Such parasitic craters are very conspicuous on Ararat. On the north-west there are several on the large dome-shaped heights of Kip Ghöll; on the south-east, a good many lie close together on the ridge which unites Great to Little Ararat, behind the spring and station of Sardarbulakh, some of them looking as fresh as if they had been burning last week. The most conspicuous secondary cone of eruption is one which rises boldly on the east-south-east slope, between Sardarbulakh and the top, and from the plain below looks like a huge tooth stuck on the mountain side.[1] Its top is about 13,000 feet above the sea-level. From these craters all sorts of volcanic materials have been ejected, trachytes, andesites, and basalts of various descriptions, with pitchstones, ashes whose consolidation has formed

[1] It appears in the frontispiece as a black projection from the snowy east-south-eastern side of the mountain, and goes by the name of Tach Kilissa.

tuff beds, scoriæ like the slag from a furnace, pumice, and in some places at the south-western foot of the mountain, obsidian, a sort of volcanic glass, black or dark green like the glass of a bottle. A remarkable bed or dyke of this obsidian is also to be found between .Erivan and Daratchichak, where it crosses the high-road ; it is made by the workmen of Tiflis into handsome ornaments, but is less clear and glossy than that of the famous obsidian mountain Hrafntin-nuhryggr, in Iceland.

When the fires of Ararat became extinct is mere matter of guess ; it may have been six thousand or sixty thousand years ago. All that can be said is that no record exists of any eruption in historical times. Stories indeed there are in the Armenian historians of mountains emitting fire and smoke—this is alleged to have happened in A.D. 441—and of darkness prevailing for thirty days, but they do not point to Ararat in particular, and are too vague to enable us to set any store by them. A German traveller named Reineggs alleges that in February 1785, from a great distance to the north-east, smoke and flames were seen to issue from Ararat, but nobody has believed his entirely unconfirmed assertion. No other volcano in these countries, or indeed in Western Asia at all, can be shown to have been active within time of human memory, although, as has been said already, there are hundreds of extinct volcanic chimneys between Constantinople and Afghanistan. It is only in hot springs, naphtha wells, sometimes in those bubbling pools of mud which are called

mud volcanoes, and which occur at both ends of the
Caucasus, and now and then in a *solfatara*,[1] a hollow
or crevice emitting vapours which deposit sulphur,
and, above all, in earthquakes, that the presence of the
terrible subterranean forces reveals itself.

One of the most remarkable features of Ararat is
the surprising height of the line of perpetual snow.
This, which in the Alps averages 8500 to 9000 feet,
which in the Caucasus varies from 10,000 feet on the
south-western to 12,000 feet on the northern slopes, rises
here to nearly 14,000 feet.[2] It is, of course, different on
different parts of the mountain ; lower on the north-
west, not only because the sun does not strike there
with such force, but also because the slopes are more
gentle.   They descend, as I have said, in broad
terraces, which are covered with glittering fields of
unbroken *névé*, while on the steeper south-east declivity the snow appears chiefly in vast longitudinal
beds, filling the depressions between the great rock
ridges that run down the mountain, giving it, as Parrot
has remarked, the appearance, from a distance, " of a
beautiful pointed collar of dazzling white material on
a dark ground."   One at least of these rock ridges
continues bare of snow to within a hundred feet of the
summit, a fact which cannot be completely explained
by their inclination, since it is not always too steep
to permit snow to lie, nor even by the fact that they
are mostly covered by loose volcanic blocks, off which

[1] Such a solfatara is said to exist among the mountains to the south-
west of Little Ararat.

[2] One observer puts it as high as 14,200 feet : this seems to me a
trifle too high.

snow melts more readily than from a smooth, solid surface ; it is probably, therefore, to be also referred, as Abich suggests, to the decomposition of the minerals contained in the rock. The lowest point at which I noticed a permanent snow-bed on the exposed south-east side is about 12,000 feet above the sea ; but in the deep dark valley on the north-east of the mountain, which is sometimes called the Great Chasm, sometimes the Valley of St. Jacob, from the little monastery aforesaid, the snow descends even lower. Here is to be found the only true glacier on the whole mountain, those glaciers of which the older travellers talk as seen on its upper sides being either mere beds of *névé* or, in one or two instances on the north-west slope, what are sometimes called glaciers of the second order. In the chasm, however, there is not merely an accumulation of masses of half melted ice that have fallen from the prodigious ice-wall that fringes the top of the cirque in which this chasm ends, but really a glacier, small and almost covered with blocks and stony rubbish, but with the genuine glacier structure, and united to the great snow mass of the mountain above by one or two snow-filled glens which run up from its head. It is nearly a mile long, and from 200 to 400 yards wide, with its lower end about 8000 feet, its upper nearly 10,000 feet above the sea-level, and bearing a *moraine*.

The great height of the snow-line on Ararat, which seems extraordinary when we compare it with the Alps or the Caucasus, which lie so little farther to the north—Ararat is in latitude 39° 42′, Elbruz in latitude

43° 21′, Mont Blanc in latitude 45° 50′—becomes easy of explanation when it is remembered how many causes besides distance from the equator govern the climate of any given spot. The most powerful influence in determining the point at which snow remains through the year is the rainfall. It is the greater moisture of the air that fixes the snow-line on the outer Himalaya, immediately north of the Bay of Bengal, at about 14,000 feet above the sea, while, as one advances north into Tibet, it rises steadily in the drier air, till it reaches 19,000 feet. So on the part of the Caucasus which looks towards the Black Sea, and receives the south-western rains coming thence, the snow-line is 2000 feet lower than on the colder, but far drier, north-eastern slopes. Now Ararat stands in an exceptionally dry region, whose rainfall is only 10 or 12 inches in the year:[1] there is, therefore, much less snow to fall than in the Alps. Besides, it is isolated, with only a small area of very great height, whereas Elbruz and Mont Blanc are surrounded by large snow masses little less elevated than themselves. The great Araxes plain, hemmed in on the north and east by bare and lofty mountains, which reflect, like the walls of a garden, every ray of light and heat, may be called a sort of huge bath or caldron filled with hot dry air, which is continually rising out of this caldron along the sides of Ararat and these other peaks, melting its snows and absorbing whatever moisture the storms of the higher regions have

[1] The annual rainfall at Aralykh is 6·08 inches ; at Alexandropol, 90 miles to the north-west, 14·68 inches.

deposited on it. Hence it is that, while in winter the whole country, except the Aras valley below Erivan, is covered with a thick mantle of snow, this has in September melted off every exposed summit except Ararat himself, though upon some of the others, and especially on Ala Göz, it may still be discovered sheltering itself in northward-lying hollows.

The upward rush of air from the plain produces another phenomenon on Ararat which is the first thing to strike every observer. The top is generally, at least during the months of summer and autumn, perfectly clear during the night and till some time after dawn. By degrees, however, as the plains begin to feel the sun, their heated air mounts along the sides of the mountain, and, when it reaches the snow region, is condensed into vapour, and forms clouds. Springing out of a perfectly clear sky, usually about three or four hours after sunrise, these clouds hang round the hill till sunset, covering only the topmost 3000 feet, constantly shifting their places, but never quite disappearing, till sunset, when they usually vanish, the supply of hot air from below having stopped, and leave the peak standing out clear and sharp in the spotless blue. So it stands all night, till next morning brings the envious clouds again. The phenomenon is just the same as that which those who climb the Southern Alps, to gain a view over the plains of Italy, have so often noted and reviled; one sees it to perfection in Val Anzasca, where the south-east face of Monte Rosa is nearly always cloud-wrapped after 11 A.M. Here, however, it seems even stranger, for the other mountains round the Araxes plain, being unsnowed, remain perfectly bare and clear; through the whole sky there is not a cloud except round this one snowy cone. It is a phenomenon which the explorer of Ararat has to lay his account with, and which makes it useless to hope for a perfect view, except in the early morning.

Although the snow-fields on the mountain are not very extensive, they are quite large enough to supply streams to water its sides; and the want of such streams is due to the porous character of the volcanic soil. At the height of about 13,000 feet, one finds plenty of lively little brooks dancing down over the rocks from the melting snows. But as they descend, they get lost in the wilderness of loose stones that strew the middle slopes of the mountain, and are only faintly heard murmuring in its deep recesses, mocking with sweet sounds the thirsty wayfarer. Towards the base these streams sometimes, though rarely, reappear in fountains, as they usually do in limestone countries; but they are then even more quickly swallowed up in the alluvial soil of mud and consolidated ash which, sloping gently eastwards, extends from the foot of the rocks to the bed of the Aras. Hence Ararat is painfully dry throughout; one finds it hard to imagine it dripping and steaming after a flood. Sometimes you see a gully whose torn sides and bottom strewed with rounded blocks show that in winter a torrent rushes down; but all autumn long you may wander round and round it, meeting scarcely a brook and rarely even a spring. This is strange and dreary to a traveller accustomed to the mountains of Western Europe, all alive with streams, or even to one coming straight from the Caucasus. Nevertheless, the middle zone of Ararat is covered with good pasture, greener than on most of the Armenian mountains, for here the proximity of the snows moderates the temperature, and there is a reasonable dewfall, besides the showers which the great mountain gathers. This middle zone extends from about 5000 feet above the sea to 11,000 or 12,000 feet. Below it, towards the valley of the Aras (I speak particularly of this north-eastern side, because it is the only one I know from personal observation), the lower declivities composed of whitish clay or sand, strewn here and there with lumps of grey or yellowish trachyte, are covered by a sort of steppe vegetation almost of the desert type—dwarf shrubs or bushes, often prickly, with few leaves and a much branching stem, some herbaceous flowering plants, and one or two grasses growing in stray tufts, especially *Dactylis littoralis*, on which a cochineal insect lives. Being utterly parched and quite without continuous herbage, this region is unprofitable, touched neither by plough nor spade, and without inhabitants. On the other hand, the upper slopes, from 11,000 or 12,000 feet upwards— the limit varies a little in different parts of the mountain—are bare of vegetation, except that a few of the hardiest species creep up to the snow-line: it is all loose gravel or bare rock, perfectly dry, and with nothing bigger than a lichen growing on it. Between these two regions of barrenness and solitude lies a

R

tract over which the nomad Kurds wander with their
flocks and herds, seeking the upper pastures during
the heat of summer, and in winter retreating before
the snow to the edge of the steppe land. Here and
there they have planted two or three little fields of
wheat or barley, and by them built sorry grass-covered
huts, but by far the greater number live entirely on the
milk and flesh of their cattle, and, when the winter cold
becomes too severe, migrate quite down into the
valleys that surround the mountain, where, at least
on Turkish soil, they often quarter themselves on the
Armenian villagers. Their favourite summer camping
grounds on the mountain are two, the high open plain
which lies between Great and Little Ararat, 7000 to
8000 feet above the sea, whereof more anon, and
the before-mentioned alpine plateau of Kip Ghöll, a
comparatively level tract, where waters descending
from the snow-beds above have formed a small lake
or rather pond, about half an acre in size, and made an
oasis of fine herbage at a height of nearly 12,000 feet.
Enormous blocks of stone, which have fallen from the
sides of the neighbouring extinct craters, lie around,
and give good shelter: it is the pleasantest high
station on Ararat, and the best from which to ascend
the summit with tolerable comfort. Except these
Kurds, a few Tatars at New Arghuri, where there
is a little bit of cultivation, and possibly some casual
Persian robbers straying upon the slopes, there is not
a human being all over the vast area of the two
mountains.

Not only this pastoral zone, but the whole moun-

tain, is, like Central Armenia generally, singularly
bare of wood. Here and **there a single tree,** of no
great height, may be **discerned in sheltered** situa-
tions, about 5000 or 6000 feet above the **sea** ; but the
only wood of **any extent is** on the **skirts of** Little
Ararat, at a height **of** 7500 feet, and is composed **of**
low birches. The Kurds cut it down for firewood, **so**
perhaps it may be merely the relic of a much **larger**
forest. No coniferous tree is to be seen anywhere ;
nor even an isolated birch **at a** greater height than
8000 feet. **In the** month of September, when **I**
visited the mountain, everything is parched ; the
flowers which love the middle slopes have nearly all
withered, and most even of the alpine plants **have**
lost their petals. It is, therefore, **an** unfavourable
time for botanizing ; and as **I** passed over the best
botanical region, between 8000 and 12,000 feet, in
the darkness **of** the night both going and returning,
there was little chance of observing or gathering rare
species. Those **which** I saw mostly belonged to the
same genera as **the** alpine plants of Europe ; such as
Gentiana, Campanula, Saxifraga, Draba, Cerastium.
One Cerastium in **particular ascends to an** enormous
height, fully **14,000 feet.** On the whole, **the flora,**
though interesting, seemed **to be scanty.** This is
usually the case on **volcanic** mountains, partly **be**-
cause so large **a part of** their surface is **covered by**
bare stones or rock, partly **because they are so** dry,
partly, perhaps, owing to the presence of iron or
sulphurous ingredients in the soil. The *Cryptogamia,*
except lichens, are particularly poor, as always in a

dry air; very few mosses were to be seen, and no ferns, except two scrubby bits of our common English *Lastrea Filix mas.* In full summer the show of plants is doubtless finer, especially in the middle part of the mountain, where I passed for a mile through thickets of rose-bushes hanging on the steep sides of a rocky buttress.

Of wild creatures, other than human, there is no great variety, which is natural enough when one considers the want of wood and shelter, but is perhaps not what might have been looked for by those who hold that on this spot all the species of animals were once seen together, descending to disperse themselves over the globe. On the upper crags, the ibex, or wild goat (it is not quite clear which), as well as the wild sheep (*Ovis Musimon*), are found; and a small species of fox has been seen on the snows 15,000 feet above the sea. Lower down there are wolves and lynxes, and in the marshes of the Araxes abundance of wild swine. The botanist Tournefort says he saw tigers, but nobody has believed him; perhaps they were wild cats or leopards. The tiger is found on the south-west shore of the Caspian, round Lenkoran, but there is no evidence of it so far west as this. So far as my own observation goes, the mountain is very ill supplied with life: I saw no quadrupeds, scarcely any birds, except a few vultures and hawks, not many insects even. Of lizards and scorpions, there is great plenty on the lowest slope, but these, of course, belong rather to the fauna of the plains.

From what has been said already, the reader will

probably have gathered how utterly unlike Ararat is,
not only in details, but even in general effect, to any
great mountain in those ranges, such as the Alps or
Pyrenees, with which we are most familiar. It is so
dry, so bare and woodless, so generally uniform in its
structure, having neither spurs running out nor glens
running in, even the colours of its volcanic rock have
so little variety, that a traveller, especially an artist,
might think it unpicturesque and disappointing. Even
of scenery of the sterner sort, precipices and rock
gorges, there is not much to be seen on the mountain
itself, save in the Great Chasm, whose head is surrounded by appalling cliffs, and on the upper south-
eastern slope, where ranges of magnificent red crags
run down from the summit. The noble thing about
Ararat is not the parts but the whole. I know
nothing so sublime as the general aspect of this huge
yet graceful mass seen from the surrounding plains ;
no view which fills the beholder with a profounder
sense of grandeur and space than that which is unfolded
when, on climbing its lofty side, he sees the far-
stretching slopes beneath, and the boundless waste of
mountains beyond spread out under his eye. The
very simplicity, or even monotony, of both form and
colour increases its majesty. One's eye is not
diverted by a variety of points of interest : all the
lines lead straight up to the towering, snowy summit ;
which is steep enough on the upper part to be beautiful, while its broad-spread base and rocky buttresses
give it a sort of stately solidity. The colour is as
simple as the form. From a gently inclined pedestal

of generally whitish hue, formed, as has been said, of
volcanic sand and ashes, the steep slopes rise in a
belt of green 5000 feet wide; above this is another
zone of black volcanic rock, streaked with snow beds;
highest of all the cap of dazzling silver. At one
glance the eye takes in all these zones of climate and
vegetation from the sweltering plain to the icy pinnacle, ranging through more than 14,000 feet of
vertical height. There can be but few other places in
the world where so lofty a peak (17,000 feet) soars so
suddenly from a plain so low, 2000 to 3000 feet above
the sea, and consequently few views equally grand.
The great summits of the Himalaya, like those of the
Alps and the Atlas, rise from behind high spurs and
outliers, at some distance from the level country;
while the giants of the South American Cordilleras
and of Mexico, all of them, like Ararat, volcanic, rise
out of high plateaux, and therefore lose to the eye a
good deal of their real height. Orizaba, for instance,
though 17,000 feet high, stands on a base of 7000 feet
in height; Chimborazo reaches 21,000 feet, but the
plateau of Riobamba beneath it is nearly 10,000 feet
above sea-level. The Peak of Teneriffe springs up
out of the sea, but its height, 12,000 feet odd, falls
considerably short of that of Ararat, and this seems
to be true, also, of the lofty volcanoes along the coast
of Northern Japan. Any one who is familiar with
the Alps, which I take as best known to us, must
have been surprised to notice how seldom he saw,
near at hand, any single unbroken mountain slope of
great vertical elevation. A few points one remem-

bers, such as **Courmayeur, where** nearly 12,000 feet of Mont Blanc are seen ; or **Val Anzasca**, where, from a valley about 4000 feet above **the** sea, Monte Rosa ascends, in what the eye thinks a precipice, to 15,000 ; or Randa, below Zermatt, where the peak **of** the Weisshorn, 11,000 feet above the spectator, seems to hang over his head. These instances, however, **are** instances of a view from a valley, where other hardly inferior heights **lie round**; here in Armenia the mountain raises himself, solitary and solemn, out **of a** wide, sea-like **plain**.

The only exception, so **far as I know**, to the admiration which it has excited in **the minds of the modern** travellers who have seen it is supplied by **the** famous French botanist Tournefort (in **the beginning** of the eighteenth century), who says, " This mountain, which lies between the south and south-south-east of the Three Churches (the Tatar name for Etchmiadzin) is one of the most dismal and disagreeable sights on the face of the earth." [1] One wonders whether a time will again come when men of taste will think so differently from ourselves.

Ararat has, at present, another claim to importance, in which, **so far** as I know, it is singular among famous mountains. It is the meeting-point, the cornerstone, of three great empires. On the top of its lower peak, Little Ararat, the dominions of the Czar, the **Sultan**, and the **Shah, the** territories of the three chief forms of faith that possess Western and Northern Asia, **converge to** a point. From this point

[1] I quote this from Parrot.

the frontier between Persia and Turkey trends off to
the south-south-west, while that of Turkey and Russia,
running along the ridge that joins Little to Great
Ararat, mounts the latter, keeps along its top in a
north-west direction, and then turns west, along the
watershed of volcanic mountains, Pambak and Synak,
which divides the Russian province of Erivan, including the middle valley of the Aras, from the Turkish
pashalik of Bayazid. This is no accident, nor has
Ararat been taken as a boundary merely because
it was a convenient natural division ; it is rather
a tribute to the political significance of the name
and associations of the Mountain of the Ark. When
in 1828 the Czar Nicholas, having defeated the Persians, annexed the territory round Erivan, his advisers insisted on bringing Ararat within the Russian
border, on account of the veneration wherewith it is
regarded by all the surrounding races, and which is
reflected on the sovereign who possesses it. To the
Armenians it is the ancient sanctuary of their faith,
the centre of their once famous kingdom, hallowed
by a thousand traditions. He who holds Ararat is
therefore, in a sense, the suzerain of the most vigorous
and progressive Christian people of the East. To the
Mohammedans, Persians, Turks, Tatars, and Kurds,
the mountain, though less sacred, is still an object of
awe and wonder from its size, its aspect, and the
general acceptance among them of the tale of the
Flood. In these countries one still sees traces of that
tendency, so conspicuous in the ancient world, but
almost obliterated in modern Europe, for men of one

race and faith to be impressed by the traditions and superstitions of another faith, which they may even profess to disbelieve and hate. No Irish Protestant venerates the sacred island in Lough Derg; but here the fanatical Tatars respect, and the Persian rulers formerly honoured and protected, Etchmiadzin and many another Christian shrine; while Christians not unfrequently, both in the Caucasus and farther south through the eastern regions of Turkey, practise pagan or Mohammedan rites which they have learnt from their neighbours, and even betray their awe for the sacred places of Islam.

A remarkable result of this superstitious reverence for Ararat is to be found in the scarcely shaken persuasion of its inaccessibility. A Persian Shah is said to have offered a large reward to any one who should get up; but nobody claimed it. There is also a story told of a Turkish pasha at Bayazid who was fired with an ambition to make the ascent, and actually started with a retinue for the purpose. He meant however to do it on horseback, and in fact went no farther than his horse would carry him, which was of course a long way below the snow-line. The first recorded ascent was made, in A.D. 1829, by Dr. Frederick Parrot, a Russo-German professor in the university of Dorpat, whose name is attached to one of the pinnacles of Monte Rosa. He was beaten back twice, but on the third attempt reached the top with a party of three Armenians and two Russian soldiers. The description he gives is perfectly clear and intelligible; and its accuracy has been in most respects confirmed by subsequent observers. There is not, and ought never to have been, any more doubt about his ascent than about De Saussure's residence on the Col du Géant ; and the enterprise, considering how little was then known about mountain climbing, the most modern of all our arts or sciences, and how much superstitious prejudice he had to overcome in order to persuade the natives to aid or accompany him, was not unworthy to be compared with that of the great Genevese. Nevertheless, in spite of the evidence he produced, that of two Russian soldiers who had gone with him, in spite of his own scientific attainments, and the upright and amiable character which shines through every line of his book, Parrot's account was disbelieved, not only by the people of the neighbourhood, but by several men of science and position in Russia and elsewhere, and he died before justice had been done to his success. Two of the Armenians whom he took with him to the summit, on being examined, declared that they had ascended a considerable distance but had seen much higher tops rising above them ; and this became the conviction of the whole country-side. When Herr Abich made his ascent in 1845—it was the third, the second having been that of Spassky Aftonomof, who went up in 1834 in order to ascertain whether it was really true that the stars are visible at noon from the tops of the highest mountains—he reached the eastern summit, which is only a few feet inferior in height to the western, and six minutes' walk from it, and finding the weather threatening, returned without going on to

the western. The consequence was that, when, anxious
to destroy the popular superstition, he produced his
companions as witnesses before the authorities at
Erivan, to make a regular deposition, they turned
round on him, and solemnly declared and swore that
from the point which they had reached a great part of
the horizon was covered by much more lofty mountains. This of course actually strengthened the
Armenian belief, nor did it yield to the fact that
General Chodzko, while conducting the triangulation
survey of Transcaucasia, reached the top with a large
party, moving slowly upwards from August 11 to
August 18, and stayed there three days in a tent
pitched on the snow. A party of Englishmen who
ascended in 1856, from the Turkish side, were assured
by Turks and Kurds that the mountain was inaccessible, and considered themselves the first to climb it,
evidently doubting both Parrot and Abich. And at
this moment, I am persuaded that there is not a person
living within sight of Ararat, unless possibly some
exceptionally educated Russian official in Erivan, who
believes that any human foot since Father Noah's has
trodden that sacred summit. So much stronger is
faith than sight ; or rather, perhaps, so much stronger
is prejudice than evidence.

As I have mentioned these ascents, a word or two
may be said regarding the routes taken. Parrot had
his head-quarters at the then existing monastery of
St. Jacob, on the edge of the great chasm of Arghuri ;
he mounted from this to the west ; encamped on the
second occasion at Kip Ghöll, on the third and suc-

cessful one at a point somewhat higher than Kip
Ghöll, just under the perpetual snows, and reached
the summit by a long march over the terraces and
generally gentle slopes of *névé*, which sink from it on
the north-west side.   This way is not to be recommended to a solitary climber, because the ice slopes
are occasionally steep enough to require some step
cutting—they repulsed Abich on his third attempt—
and here and there a crevasse may be met with ;
however, a solitary ascent is not to be recommended
in any case.   But I believe it to be, on the whole, the
easiest and least fatiguing route, and the best for
a party.   Notwithstanding which, it seems to have
been only once followed since Parrot's time.   Abich's
fourth and successful ascent in 1845—he deserves
scarcely less credit than Parrot for the tenacity with
which he clung to his purpose under so many difficulties—was made up the south-eastern face from
Sardarbulakh ; and it was on this side that both
Chodzko and the Englishmen of 1856 mounted.   As
I shall have to describe it in giving my own experiences, nothing more need be said of it here, further
than to remark that it is probably the best route for
a single man or a very small party, since it involves,
at least in the autumn, very little snow work.   No
one seems to have climbed the south-western slope
looking towards Bayazid and the alpine lake Balykh
Ghöll ; but Herr Abich, who has reconnoitred this
side, told me in Tiflis that he believed it to be quite
practicable.   The chief advantage of the south-eastern
route, besides the scantiness of snow, lies in the fact

that it is entirely in Russian territory, so that one
need have less apprehension of robbers, and can use
the Cossack station at Sardarbulakh (of which more
anon) as a base of operations.

The last event of importance in the history of
Ararat is the great earthquake of 1840. I have more
than once spoken of the profound chasm which, on
the north-east side of the mountain, over against
Aralykh, runs right into its heart. This chasm ends
in a sort of cirque hemmed in by tremendous walls of
black or grey lavas and tuff conglomerates, capped
by other precipices of ribbed blue ice, while at the
bottom of the cleft, almost covered by masses of
stone that have fallen from above, is to be found the
only true glacier on the hill. Near the mouth of this
chasm there formerly stood a pleasant little Armenian
village of some two hundred houses, named Arghuri,
or Aghurri, whose inhabitants, raised above the heats
of the plain, and out of the track of war, had led a
peaceful pastoral life for many generations, dwelling
in the midst of their orchards and vines, feeding
their flocks in the alpine pastures above them, and
cultivating a few fields where the generally stony soil
permitted the spade or plough to be used, and the
stream from the glacier spread vegetation over the
slopes. They boasted not only of the Patriarch's
vine, bearing grapes delicious to eat, but which
Heaven, in memory of the fault they betrayed him
into, had forbidden to be made into wine; but also of
an ancient willow trunk, which had sprung from one of
the planks of the Ark. Not far above the village, on

the spot where the angel of the legend had appeared
to the monk, stood the little monastery of St. Jacob,
eight centuries old, and still higher was a tiny shrine
beside a spring of bright clear water, the spring of
the *tetagush* legend; while on the opposite side of the
glen the Persian Sardar or viceroy had erected a
sumptuous summer villa to which he was accustomed
to retire from the scorching heats of Erivan. Setting
apart the wandering Kurds, this was the only inhabited
spot on the mountain, the place in which its traditions
centred, and where they were faithfully preserved.
Towards sunset in the evening of the 20th of June
1840 (old style), the sudden shock of an earthquake,
accompanied by a subterranean roar, and followed by
a terrific blast of wind, threw down the houses of
Arghuri, and at the same moment detached enormous
masses of rock with their superjacent ice from the cliffs
that surround the chasm. A shower of falling rocks
overwhelmed in an instant the village, the monastery,
and a Kurdish encampment on the pastures above.
Not a soul survived to tell the tale. Four days
afterwards, the masses of snow and ice that had
been precipitated into the glen suddenly melted, and,
forming an irresistible torrent of water and mud,
swept along the channel of the stream and down
the outer slopes of the mountain, far away into the
Aras plain, bearing with them huge blocks, and covering
the ground for miles with a deep bed of mud and
gravel. Even now, after thirty-seven years, the traces
of this convulsion are distinctly visible; in some
places the precipices from which the masses fell show

a fracture mark fresh as of yesterday. The direction of the shocks, which were felt as far as Tiflis, the Caspian, and the Lake of Urumia, was from the centre of Great Ararat, towards the north-east. It was reported in Europe at the time that Ararat had broken out in eruption; but for this story there is no foundation: the dust which accompanied the great rock fall was probably mistaken for smoke by those who saw it from a distance. Doubtless the blast was produced by the fall of the rock masses. Since then a few huts have again arisen somewhat lower down the slope than the site of Old Arghuri and without the mouth of the chasm; here dwell a few Tatars—for the Armenians (several, happening to be away from the village, escaped) do not seem to have returned to the desolated spot—and pasture their cattle on the sides of the valley which grass has again begun to clothe. But Noah's vine and the primeval willow, and the little monastery where Parrot lived so happily among the few old monks who had retired to this hallowed spot from the troubles of the world, are gone for ever; no Christian bell is heard, no Christian service said, upon the Mountain of the Ark.

CHAPTER VII.

THE ASCENT OF ARARAT.

AT 8 A.M., on the morning of the 11th of September, we set out from Aralykh to ascend the mountain. We had arranged to start at sunrise, knowing how terrible the heat would be for the first part of the road, but to get a large party under way is always troublesome, and certainly not least so in these countries, where there is no sense of the value of time, and no conception of the conditions of a successful mountain expedition. Indeed, what with the collecting of the soldiers, the packing of provisions, the hundred little things that occur to one's mind at the last moment, a compass, snow spectacles, warm gloves, and, above all, the indispensable lemons, more than three hours would have been consumed had we been in any hands but those of our genial and energetic host. The last thing was to write a few lines home, wondering what the next lines would have to report, and then we filed out of the cantonment amid adieux and good wishes given in strange tongues. We were nine in all, six soldiers of the Cossack detachment, the gentleman who had undertaken to interpret, and our two selves. The soldier in command was a

Kurd named Jaafar, a man of great mental as well as bodily force, in whom the colonel reposed full confidence, and whose singularly keen and expressive glance made us wish that we could have held some direct communication with him. Remembering that on the same day of the year, five years ago, I had started to climb the Schreckhorn, and three years before, the Maladetta, it amused me to think how unlike this cavalcade of ours was to the parties of loud-voiced Englishmen and stalwart guides that issue from an Alpine inn before daylight to "do" some stimulating peak or pass. We were all mounted, though certainly on no fiery chargers, and might rather have been taken for a reconnoitring or marauding party, sent to plunder some village across the Persian border, which lay six miles off. The Cossacks were of course fully armed and equipped, while my friend and I, in addition to pistols stuck in the belt, brandished heavy ice-axes, the management of which, together with that of the bridle and a big white umbrella, required some dexterity. An umbrella and a horse do seem rather incompatible, not only with one another, but with a mountain ascent; but we would willingly have looked even more ridiculous for the sake of some protection against the fiery shower of beams that descended from the cloudless sky, and was reflected from the whitish wastes over which we took our way.

We were traversing, in a southerly direction, the outermost and extremely gentle slope of Ararat, a region of fine sand or hard yellowish clay, covered with dwarf, prickly, almost leafless bushes, but no

S

grass, and with no creatures save butterflies and lizards
of every hue scuttling about.   Each mile was like the
last ; the want of landmarks on the almost level expanse prevented us from noticing our progress ; and
the air was so clear that, when we had marched for
three hours, the mass of the mountain seemed no
nearer than it had done from Aralykh.   Looking up
the smooth and featureless slope, we had, of course,
grossly underestimated the distance which separated
us from the base of the cone.   Such heat we had
never felt before.   Probably it was only the thrice
blessed umbrellas that saved us from a sunstroke,
since we had no better head protection than light felt
wide-awakes, whereas the Cossacks cover their solid
skulls with thick caps of sheepskin.   Yet it was not
an enervating heat : the air had that fresh stimulating
quality which is said to make travelling in the Arabian
desert so healthy ; and the sight of the glittering
peak above, which was now, like an Eastern beauty,
beginning to draw over its face the noonday veil of
cloud, seemed to shoot a thrill of coolness through
our burning veins.

After a time the ground became rougher as we
came to a region where winter torrents had cut deep
gullies in the volcanic soil; the slope, too, grew steeper,
and the air was fresher as we mounted, while a stray
cloud or two, detached from the mountain, deigned
us a passing shadow as it sailed across the blue.
About noon we were fairly on the side of Ararat himself, and felt that every step was a gain.   Here
there projects from the body of the mountain, as a

glance at the frontispiece will show, a huge rounded, dome-shaped spur or buttress, 7091 feet in height, and evidently formed by eruptions from one or more volcanic vents rising through it : it is, in fact, one of the largest of the parasitic cones, or groups of cones, mentioned in the preceding chapter. Its name is Takjaltu, not to be confounded with another Takjaltu much farther to the north-west, in the upper Araxes valley. We made for the point where this mass joins Great Ararat, following a path which mounts between them, and crosses a succession of rocky ridges that descend steeply from the east side of the latter.

Pursuing our way along the hillside, we had to dip into more than one rocky ravine, but nowhere was there a stream at the bottom : everything dry as a chalk down in Sussex. This path brought us out on a little grassy plain, hemmed in by two of these ridges, and on the third or eastern side by the heights of Takjaltu, where to our surprise several tiny fields appeared, and one or two men and women at work in them, with a cluster of huts, built of stones and earth, standing near. Jaafar rode across to the men to inquire if any Kurds could be got to take our baggage up the mountain, on the backs of oxen, while we halted in the hope of a drink from the well that was said to be somewhere near. At last a man came, carrying a rude bowl, but as it was filled with liquid mud instead of water, we preferred thirst. The men were Kurds, and this was one of their few autumn or spring settlements on the mountain. As it lies 6000 feet

or more above the sea, they do not stay in it through
the winter : at this season they were beginning to descend hither from the higher pastures. Remounting, we
continued to coast round the mountain towards the
south, scaling several more of the black rocky ridges
that descend its flank, the path being in some places
so steep and rugged that we were obliged to dismount and lead the horses. Among these rocks there
grew rose-bushes enough to have inspired all the
poets of Persia. They were pretty even in berry, but
imagine what the scene must be in July, when the
whole mountain-side is gay with these delicate pink
blossoms, whereof I saw only one left now in September, and the sweet scent fills the keen mountain
air. On rounding the last ridge, the conical peak of
Little Ararat came in view, its base about two miles
distant, across an open slope, and just beneath us,
nestling under the ridge, was a Kurdish encampment.
Four or five tents stood side by side on the greensward,
supported on low poles or stakes, and covered with
curtains of black goat's hair, the ends loosely fastened
to the tops of these stakes, and the centre raised on cross
poles. The walls, if one can call them so, are formed
of matting or plaited reeds, and a similar strip of
reeds, with sometimes a rug or a piece of cloth thrown
over it, runs along between, and purports to divide
the women's apartment in each tent from that of the
men. It is more for the sake of form than to secure
privacy, for every corner of the establishment is
clearly visible to a person standing outside. To
slake our thirst, they brought us bowls of sourish

milk mixed with water, a frequent drink in these countries, and we found it refreshing, if less palatable than the fresh milk of a Swiss *châlet*.

Five minutes' more riding up the grassy slope brought us to the spot for which we had so often, and latterly, time drawing on, so anxiously, enquired, the well of Sardarbulakh. As the only high permanent camping-ground on the mountain, and the place which will be chosen for an alpine hotel, if such a thing ever comes into existence on Ararat, Sardarbulakh is entitled to a few words of description.[1] It stands nearly in the middle of a wide semicircular valley, or rather a sloping plain, between the two Ararats. Towards Great Ararat, which bears about west, the ground rises, at first gently, then steeply, in a series of rocky ridges of nearly equal height, separated by long, narrow hollows, and mostly running nearly west-north-west and east-south-east. About five miles, as the crow flies, from this plain these ridges merge in the great cone, whose summit may be some six or seven miles from Sardarbulakh in a straight line through the air, though more than twice that distance to walk.

On the opposite or south-south-east side of this small plain, Little Ararat springs up 5000 feet, in an almost perfect truncated pyramid, with steep, smooth sides, grassy, except where they are seamed by deep cuts, running from top to bottom, into the sand and gravel with which those smooth sides are covered. Its

---

[1] Sardarbulakh does not appear in the view, as it lies back, just behind the top of the buttress which shows between the two Ararats.

base may be two, its top about four, miles distant in
a straight line drawn along the earth. If Great Ararat
is the most majestic, Little Ararat may claim to be the
most elegant of mountains ; the eye is never tired of
its beautiful lines. The two peaks are connected by
a rough-topped ridge which forms the back of the
sloping plain I have described, and also marks the
frontier between the Russian and Turkish empires.
Over it is the path to Bayazid,[1] distant some nineteen
miles to the south-west, while five miles to the east,
on the north-eastern side of Little Ararat, one enters
the territories of the Shah. The place is therefore
particularly well suited for predatory operations, since,
when the marauders are attacked on any one of the
three soils, they can promptly retire into one of the
other two, and snap their fingers at justice, just as
evil-doers in England used to be fond of establishing themselves on the boundary between two counties,
where they could slip away from the sheriff of either.
Hence Russia, who cares more about the security
of the subject than her neighbours do, has placed
here a sort of small frontier guard, consisting of seven
or eight armed Cossacks, who remind the mountain

---

[1] Bayazid, a decaying town with a half ruinous citadel, was the first
Turkish fortress which the Russians captured in the present war. They
approached it from the east, through Persian territory, as the snow was
then (early in May) too deep both on the pass between the Ararats, and
the other passes west of Great Ararat which lead to it, to permit the
passage of an army. As everybody knows, the garrison they placed
there was surrounded by a large Turkish force, consisting mainly of
Kurds, who butchered a great part of this garrison, while it actually was
surrendering under an agreement, and beleaguered the few who saved
themselves in the citadel till they were relieved by General Tergukasof.

Kurds of **the existence of** the Czar, and keep an eye on the border depredators, **who**, lurking about in Persia or Turkey, now and then swoop down on the Aras valley **for a** little booty. Before 1828, when Persia still held all of what is now the Russian side of Ararat, this plain of Sardarbulakh was a regular stronghold of the robber Kurds, who not only spoiled and murdered travellers attempting to pass this way to Bayazid, but constantly plundered the villages **of** the plain and the **two** highways of commerce which pass along the two sides of the mountain, one of them from Tiflis and Erivan to **Tavriz**, the other from Trebizond and Erzerum to the same place. **Now all** is changed. The Kurds recognize the Czar as a power that makes for righteousness : they probably regret the good old times, but so long as they are on this side the mountain, they spare the Armenian peasant and the traveller, well knowing that on the other side they may play what pranks they please.

The height above the sea of this sloping plain varies from 8818 feet, which is given as the height of the pass leading **to** Bayazid, and 7000 feet ; and Sardarbulakh in the middle is 7514 feet. Its lumpy volcanic hillocks—I have called it a plain, but it is far from being level—are covered with good grass ; and about a mile off, near the foot of Little Ararat, appears the only **bit of wood on the whole** mountain—a grove of low birches, **whose dimensions** the wasteful Kurds are rapidly reducing. Near the birch trees is a sort of subterranean village, **huts** formed by hollowing out the ground and laying a few boughs, covered with turf, across the top, through which comes such light as can penetrate. These huts are often uninhabited: I I fancy it is mostly when cold weather comes on that the Kurds take to them. There is a tale told that they were once an Armenian village, inhabited by people whom the Sardar had transported hither, but who forsook the place when his power ended. Sardar, or Sirdar, a name with which Anglo-Indians are familiar, means general or governor, and was the title of the Persian governor of Erivan. Sardar-bulakh is therefore translated as the Sardar's well. It is, of course, the presence of drinkable water that has made the Kurds and Cossacks fix themselves here, for (as has been said already) there is no other constant spring nearer than the valley of Arguri, four hours' journey. Probably some Persian viceroy may have stationed a garrison here in the old days when they carried on constant wars with the Turk. A pleasanter frontier post to be sent to out of the hot valley of the Aras could not be imagined; exquisitely keen fresh air, noble prospects over the plains and mountains to the east, and a superb peak on either hand. It is just the place which those who love the Riffel or the Aeggischhorn would enjoy. However, we thought little more of these charms than probably the Persian officers did long ago, when they grumbled at being banished from the luxuries of the city, for it was two o'clock, and we were still many hours from the base of the cone. Every one who had spoken to us about the ascent had wound up with the same advice: " Whatever chance of success you have "—only one

of our informants (Mr. Scharoyan, in Tiflis, who
ascended with General Chodzko) thought we had
any—"depends on your sleeping very high up, close
to the snows, and starting before dawn to try the
main peak." Knowing that we were out of training,
and that, as we should have to find our own way up,
plenty of time would be needed, we recognized the
force of this advice, and were most anxious to get to
the foot of the cone, a point 11,000 feet high, by
nightfall. To push straight on was impossible, for
horses could go no farther, and the Cossacks absolutely refused to carry even the few things we needed
for a bivouac: it was therefore necessary to procure
Kurds for the purpose, and that was a slow business.
Minutes and half-hours slipped away while they were
being found and brought to Jaafar, who had been
charged by the colonel with the arrangements for our
expedition. When they came, the bargaining began,
and that seemed interminable. We knew nothing of
what was going on, for even with Jaafar, who spoke
Russian, we could not communicate directly, and
were, of course, one remove further from the Kurds,
whose tongue the companion who was interpreting
did not understand.

It is always vexatious to be checked by difficulties
and delays of merely human origin in a mountain expedition; and here we were in full sight of our goal,
the glorious snows seeming to beckon us on, while the
minutes which might make all the difference to success were being wasted in wranglings we could not
abridge or even understand. Once or twice we struck

in to urge that, at all hazárds and whatever the cost, a start should be made ; but to little purpose, for the Kurds, like true children of nature, found difficulties in every course proposed, and were, so far as I could make out, not so much pleased by the prospect of earning what to them was a fortune as anxious to improve the occasion by squeezing out more. Perhaps the idea of working at all was distasteful to them : one generally finds in wild and simple people a greater disposition to prefer their inclination to their interests, and in particular more disinclination to earn money by doing anything they are not accustomed to, than in civilized man. Jaafar's plan had been to send our baggage on the backs of Kurdish oxen as far up as a place which they call the Hermitage, where, however, there is no anchorite's cell, but only a grassy hollow among the rocks with sometimes a little water, and let us either sleep there, 2000 feet higher than Sardarbulakh, or else, leaving the animals there, get on as much farther as we could before nightfall.

But these discussions had now brought us to half past four o'clock. At least half an hour more would be consumed in packing and preparations for departure. There would then remain little more than an hour's daylight to reach a higher camping ground, where, of course, we should have much less chance of sleep than here below in the tent which the Cossacks had vacated for us. Yielding, therefore, most unwillingly to circumstances, and believing that we were practically abandoning our chances for the morrow, I suggested that we should remain and sleep at Sardarbulakh,

and make a start upwards as soon as the moon
rose, shortly after midnight. This idea, like anything
which delayed a move, was accepted. Jaafar en-
gaged four Kurds to go with us and carry what
baggage we had, some wrappings to sleep in, and a
little food—it would have been a load for one Swiss
porter and a half—and told off no less than seven
Cossacks to act as a guard, not merely a guard of
honour, it seemed, but an actual guard to defend us
against these four ferocious Kurds, who looked to me
wild indeed, but by no means terrible. However,
so it was settled. Whether, having really no say in
the matter, we ventured to suggest that seven Cossacks
were not needed, I hardly remember, but believe we
were told that the Cossacks refused to go at all unless
they were allowed to go in that number. The terrors
of the mountain and the Kurds would have been too
great for a smaller detachment.

While all this was going on, there was another scene
in progress which served to appease our impatience.
The two Cossack tents stood on a grassy slope, about
forty yards above the well which gives its name to the
place ; and to this well there now came, driving their
flocks before them, another band of Kurds, who had
just crossed the flanks of Little Ararat from Persia in
search of fresher pasture. The well is an elliptical
hollow, about ten feet long by five broad, surrounded
by a sort of rude, loose wall of lumps of lava, with the
water in it, when we first saw it, about three feet deep.
One could see where the spring rose into it from under
the wall, sweet, clear, and cool. As the water lay too

deep sunk for cattle to reach it, troughs were set up
all over the pasture round ; Kurdish boys and girls
brought brazen bowls and carried the water in these
to fill the troughs, whence the patient creatures drank.
The sheep, whose bleatings filled the air, were mostly
either light brown, or black, or white, not much larger
than those of the Scotch Highlands ; the goats, however, were thoroughly Oriental, mostly white, with
long, soft hair, and large, pendant ears, just like the
scapegoat of Mr. Holman Hunt's picture.   For nearly
two hours the process of watering went on, boys and
girls and women coming and going round the well,
and ladleing out the water till hardly any was left in
the bottom, permitting us sometimes to help them, but
scarcely looking at the strangers from Frangistan, so
incurious were they, or so intent on the work of the
hour.   All were wonderfully hardy and sinewy, the
women mostly scorched and withered, but the girls' and
boys' faces pretty and full-coloured, the carriage of all
perfectly graceful.   The men, of whom there were but
few, wore a sort of coat coming nearly to the knee,
sometimes woollen and striped, sometimes, oddly
enough, of a coarsely printed chintz, with trousers that
reached well below the knee, leaving the lower part of
the leg to be covered by wrappings and the strings
of the shoe or sandal.   Every one was armed with a
knife or sword, at least, sometimes huge old pistols,
sometimes a musket or matchlock besides.   On the
head was a woollen cap, having strips of silk or cotton
cloth wound round it to form a rude kind of turban.
The women's dress was rather brighter in colours, and

their striped or embroidered short petticoats, below
which cotton drawers descended to the ankle, were extremely pretty; the cap was generally of scarlet cloth;
in their nostrils and ears jewels were hung, while round
their necks they bore a profusion of ornaments, strings
of gold and silver coins and beads, and coloured
stones; even the bareheaded girls, whose plaited locks
fell over the shoulders, had always such a necklace.
Unlike their Mohammedan sisters of the plains, their
faces were unshielded by a veil, and they showed no
shyness or timidity in the presence of the Cossacks
and ourselves. Each, like the Fates in Catullus, bore
a distaff in one hand, with a lump of wool upon her
wrist, and this they plied as they drove the flocks
before them.

So picturesque a scene, or one that brought so
vividly to mind the first simple life of the world, un-
changed in these earliest seats of mankind, we had
never seen before. In the foreground were the beautiful flocks, the exquisite colours of the women's
dresses and ornaments, their own graceful figures, the
stir and movement beside the clear pool, the expanse
of rolling pasture around with its patch of tender little
birchwood. On each side a towering cone rose into
heaven, while in front the mountain slope swept down
into the broad valley of the Aras, and beyond stern
red mountains ranged away, ridge over ridge, to the
eastern horizon, all bare and parched, with every
peak and gully standing sharp out through the clear
air, yet softened by distance into the most delicately
rich and tender hues. Here, where a picture of primi-

tive life close at hand was combined with a vision of broad countries, inhabited by many peoples, stretching out to the shores of the inland sea of Asia, one seemed at a glance to take in and realize their character and history, unchanging in the midst of change. Through the empires of Assyria and Persia, and Macedon, through Parthian Arsacidæ, and Iranian Sassanidæ, through the reigns of Arabian Khalifs, and Turkish Sultans, and Persian Shahs, these Kurds have roamed as they roam now, over the slopes of the everlasting mountains, watering their flocks at this spring, pitching their goat's hair tents in the recesses of these lonely rocks, chanting their wildly pathetic airs, with neither a past to remember nor a future to plan for.

When our plans for the ascent had been settled there was just time left for a stroll up the slope towards the pass leading to Bayazid. I scrutinised the south-east face of the great cone, which looked in the marvellously clear air much nearer than it turned out to be, and sketched out mentally a line of attack for the morrow. Clouds still clinging to the summit made it difficult to say whether there might not be impracticable precipices in the upper part. There was, of course, no light to be had from either Kurds or Cossacks : the former never go higher than the limits of pasture, and the latter have no motive to go nearly so high. One could therefore only rely on the general structure of the ridges, which seemed to promise a route either up the edges of the snow-beds or along the rocky crests that rose between them. Returning at sunset to the tent, we found some

Cossacks sent out to meet us by the watchful Jaafar, who feared we might be picked off by stray marauders, and looked rather reproachfully at us for having gone forth alone. It was very odd; I suppose now that there really may have been a risk, but the habit of security was so strong that, in gazing about on those silent slopes, we could no more expect robbers than we should have done on the Wengern Alp.

Supper was prepared, the Cossacks cooking theirs and ours in a big pot over a fire kindled on the hillside, which lit up their figures and the still more picturesque figures of the Kurds, who crouched round it just like the brigands in an opera scene. The Russian has a turn for cooking; the Cossack, though his taste may be less refined, rivals the Zouave in the power of getting on in a bivouac. After the meal, which consisted of boiled mutton and milk, both procured from the Kurds, we had some of the unfailing tea, and lay down for a little sleep. Four years before we had shared a tent under the snowstorms of Iceland, an experience which somewhat diminished the romantic pleasure young travellers find in life under canvas. Here, to be sure, we were twenty-five degrees nearer the equator; but then we were 7500 feet above the sea, with a breeze shaking the tent walls and forcing us to cover down their bottom, piling up stones and hay outside, and to turn every shred of clothing into account. One feels little inclined for sleep on these occasions; we stayed long outside watching the Cossacks and the stars, by whose light it was just possible to make out the lines of Little

Ararat in front. The silence of the mountain was astonishing. No calling of torrents to one another, such as one hears in the Alps, no rippling of rills or rustling of boughs, not even the noise of a falling stone, only the whistling of the west wind, the home wind, over the pass. About nine we crept into the tent and fell asleep. Waking at midnight, which was lucky, for the rest were deep in slumber, we roused them by degrees, and packed up what we needed, while they gathered the food and the rugs as well as they could in the darkness, making four bundles, one for each Kurd. The moon had risen over the Kara-bagh mountains beyond Aralykh, but she was so far gone in waning that there was only sufficient light to see a yard or two around you.

About 1 A.M. we got off, thirteen in all, and made straight across the grassy hollows for the ridges which trend up towards the great cone, running parallel in a west-north-westerly direction, and enclosing between them several long narrow depressions hardly deep enough to be called valleys. The Kurds led the way, and at first we made pretty good progress. The Cossacks seemed fair walkers, though less stalwart than the Kurds; the pace generally was better than that with which Swiss guides start. However, we were soon cruelly undeceived. In twenty-five minutes there came a steep bit, and at the top of it they flung themselves down on the grass to rest. So did we all. Less than half a mile farther, down they dropped again, and this time we were obliged to give the signal for resuming the march. In another quarter of an hour they were down once more, and so it continued for the rest of the way. Every ten minutes' walking—it was seldom steep enough to be called actual climbing—was followed by seven or eight minutes of sitting still, smoking and chattering. How they did chatter! It was to no purpose that we continued to move on when they sat down, or that we rose to go before they had sufficiently rested. They looked at one another, so far as I could make out by the faint light, and occasionally they laughed; but they would not and did not stir till such time as pleased themselves. We were helpless. Impossible to go on alone; impossible also to explain to them why every moment was precious, for the acquaintance who had acted as interpreter had been obliged to stay behind at Sardarbulakh, and we were absolutely without means of communication with our companions. One could not even be angry, had there been any use in that, for they were perfectly good-humoured. It was all very well to beckon them, or pull them by the elbow, or clap them on the back; they thought this was only our fun, and sat still and chattered all the same. When it grew light enough to see the hands of a watch, and mark how the hours advanced while the party did not, we began for a second time to despair of success.

I can say very little about the ground we traversed in the darkness, except that it was quite waterless, and that I fancy we passed, in a grassy hollow at about 9000 feet above the sea, the spot which they call the Hermitage, which seems to be the site of

T

General Chodzko's meteorological camp of July and August 1850. He told me there was a spring there, but either it is dry at this season or else we missed it. There was pasture in many places, but we saw no cattle; doubtless they had already been driven down to the lower slopes. What we were able to remark and enjoy was the changing aspect of the sky. About 3 A.M. there suddenly sprang up, from behind the Median mountains, the morning star, shedding a light such as no star ever gave in these northern climes of ours, a light that almost outshone the moon. An hour later it began to pale in the first faint flush of yellowish light that spread over the eastern heaven, and first the rocky masses above us, then Little Ararat, throwing behind him a gigantic shadow, then the long lines of mountains beyond the Araxes, became revealed, while the wide Araxes plain still lay dim and shadowy below. One by one the stars died out as the yellow turned to a deeper glow that shot forth in long streamers, the rosy fingers of the dawn, from the horizon to the zenith. Cold and ghostly lay the snows on the mighty cone; till at last there came upon their topmost slope, 6000 feet above us, a sudden blush of pink. Swiftly it floated down the eastern face, and touched and kindled the rocks just above us. Then the sun flamed out, and in a moment the Araxes valley and all the hollows of the savage ridges we were crossing were flooded with overpowering light.

It was nearly six o'clock, and progress became easier now that we could see our way distinctly. The

Cossacks seemed to grow lazier, halting as often as before and walking less briskly; in fact, they did not relish the exceeding roughness of the jagged lava ridges along whose tops or sides we toiled. I could willingly have lingered here myself, for in the hollows, wherever a little soil appeared, some interesting plants were growing, whose similarity to and difference from the alpine species of Western Europe alike excited one's curiosity. Time allowed me to secure only a few; I trusted to get more on the way back, but this turned out to be impossible. As we scrambled along a ridge above a long narrow winding glen filled with loose blocks, one of the Kurds suddenly swooped down, like a vulture, from the height on a spot at the bottom, and began peering and grubbing among the stones. In a minute or two he cried out, and the rest followed: he had found a spring, and by scraping in the gravel had made a tiny basin out of which we could manage to drink a little. Here was a fresh cause of delay; everybody was thirsty, and everybody must drink, not only the water which, as we afterwards saw, trickled down hither under the stones from a snow-bed 700 feet higher, but the water mixed with some whisky from a flask my friend carried, which even in this highly diluted state the Cossacks took to heartily. When at last we got them up and away again, they began to dawdle and straggle; after a while two or three sat down, and plainly gave us to see they would go no farther. By the time we had reached a little snow-bed whence the now strong sun was drawing a stream of water, and halted on the rocks beside it for breakfast,

there were only two Cossacks and the four Kurds left
with us, the rest having scattered themselves about
somewhere lower down. We had no idea what instructions they had received, nor whether indeed they had
been told anything except to bring us as far as they
could, to see that the Kurds brought the baggage,
and to fetch us back again, which last was essential
for Jaafar's peace of mind. We concluded therefore
that, if left to themselves, they would probably wait
our return, and the day was running on so fast that
it was clear there was no more time to be lost in
trying to drag them along with us.

Accordingly I resolved to take what I wanted in
the way of food, and start at my own pace. My
friend, who carried more weight, and had felt the
want of training on our way up, decided-to come no
farther, but wait about here, and look out for me
towards nightfall. We noted the landmarks carefully,
the little snow-bed, the head of the glen covered
with reddish masses of stone and gravel, and high
above it, standing out of the face of the great cone
of Ararat, a bold peak, or rather projecting tooth of
black rock, which our Cossacks called the Monastery,
and which, I supposed from the same fancied resemblance to a building, is said to be called in Tatar
Tach Kilissa, " the church rock." It is doubtless
an old cone of eruption, about 13,000 feet in height,
and is really the upper end of the long ridge we
had been following, which may, perhaps, represent a
lava flow from it, or the edge of a fissure which at
this point found a vent. In the frontispiece it will

be seen as a black projection from the south-east
ridge of the cone. We were now at a height of
about 12,000 feet. Everything lay below us, except Little Ararat opposite, and the stupendous cone
that rose from where we sat, its glittering snows
and stern black crags of lava standing up perfectly
clear in a sea of cloudless blue. Tempting it was,
but it was also awe-inspiring, and as the summit was
hidden behind the nearer slopes, I could not tell
what the difficulties of the ascent might be. Still
less could we have learnt them from our companions.
The Kurds never come higher on the mountain than
their flocks can find pasture, and on this side at least
the pasture does not reach so high as where we were.
Moreover, they have a superstitious reverence for the
mountain, scarcely less than that of the Armenians:
only, while the Armenian faithful believe it to be
guarded by angels, the Kurds hold it to be the
favourite haunt of devils and Jinn, who are ready to
take vengeance on the disturber of their revels. The
shepherds, therefore, avoid the heights as much as
possible. This, however, was neither here nor there ;
for had they known never so much, they could not
have given us the benefit of what they knew.

It was an odd position to be in : guides of two
different races, unable to communicate either with us
or with one another, guides who could not lead and
would not follow, guides one-half of whom were
supposed to be there to save us from being robbed
and murdered by the other half, but all of whom,
I am bound to say, looked for the moment equally

simple and friendly, the swarthy Iranian as well as
the blue-eyed Slav.

At eight o'clock I buckled on my canvas gaiters,
thrust some crusts of bread, a lemon, a small flask of
cold tea, four hard-boiled eggs, and a few meat
lozenges into my pocket, bade good-bye to my friend,
and set off. Rather to our surprise, the two Cossacks
and one of the Kurds came with me, whether persuaded
by a pantomime of encouraging signs, or simply curious
to see what would happen. The ice-axe had hugely
amused the Cossacks all through. Climbing the ridge
to the left, and keeping along its top for a little way,
I then struck across the semicircular head of a wide
glen, in the middle of which, a little lower, lay a snow-
bed, over a long steep slope of loose broken stones and
sand. This slope, a sort of talus or "screes," as they
say in the Lake country, was excessively fatiguing
from the want of firm foothold, and when I reached the
other side, I was already so tired and breathless, having
been on foot since midnight, that it seemed almost
useless to persevere farther. However, on the other
side, I got upon solid rock, where the walking was
better, and was soon environed by a multitude of rills
bubbling down over the stones from the snow-slopes
above. The summit of Little Ararat, which had for
the last two hours provokingly kept at the same
apparent height above me, began to sink, and before
ten o'clock I could look down upon its small flat top,
studded with lumps of rock, but bearing no trace of a
crater. Mounting steadily along the same ridge, I
saw at a height of over 13,000 feet, lying on the loose

blocks, a piece of wood about four feet long and five inches thick, evidently cut by some tool, and so far above the limit of trees that it could by no possibility be a natural fragment of one. Darting on it with a glee that astonished the Cossack and the Kurd, I held it up to them, made them look at it, and repeated several times the word " Noah." The Cossack grinned, but he was such a cheery, genial fellow that I think he would have grinned whatever I had said, and I cannot be sure that he took my meaning, and recognised the wood as a fragment of the true Ark. Whether it was really gopher wood, of which material the Ark was built, I will not undertake to say, but am willing to submit to the inspection of the curious the bit which I cut off with my ice-axe and brought away. Anyhow, it will be hard to prove that it is not gopher wood. And if there be any remains of the Ark on Ararat at all—a point as to which the natives are perfectly clear—here rather than the top is the place where one might expect to find them, since in the course of ages they would get carried down by the onward movement of the snow-beds along the declivities. This wood, therefore, suits all the requirements of the case. In fact, the argument is, for the case of a relic, exceptionally strong : the Crusaders who found the Holy Lance at Antioch, the archbishop who recognized the Holy Coat at Treves, not to speak of many others, proceeded upon slighter evidence. I am, however, bound to admit that another explanation of the presence of this piece of timber on the rocks at this vast height did occur to me. But as no man is bound to discredit his own relic, and such is certainly not the practice of the Armenian Church, I will not disturb my readers' minds, or yield to the rationalizing tendencies of the age by suggesting it.

Fearing that the ridge by which we were mounting would become too precipitous higher up, I turned off to the left, and crossed a long, narrow snow-slope, that descended between this ridge and another line of rocks more to the west. It was firm, and just steep enough to make steps cut in the snow comfortable, though not necessary; so the ice-axe was brought into use. The Cossack who accompanied me—there was but one now, for the other Cossack had gone away to the right some time before, and was quite lost to view—had brought my friend's alpenstock, and was developing a considerable capacity for wielding it. He followed nimbly across; but the Kurd stopped on the edge of the snow, and stood peering and hesitating, like one who shivers on the plank at a bathing-place, nor could the jeering cries of the Cossack induce him to venture on the treacherous surface. Meanwhile, we who had crossed were examining the broken cliff which rose above us. It looked not exactly dangerous, but a little troublesome, as if it might want some care to get over or through. So, after a short rest, I stood up, touched my Cossack's arm, and pointed upwards. He reconnoitred the cliff with his eye, and shook his head. Then, with various gestures of hopefulness, I clapped him on the back, and made as though to pull him along. He looked at the rocks again, and pointed to them, stroked his knees, turned up and pointed to the soles of his boots, which certainly were suffering from the lava, and once more solemnly shook his head. This was conclusive; so I conveyed to him by panto-mime that he had better go back to the bivouac where my friend was, rather than remain here alone, and that I hoped to meet him there in the evening, took an affectionate farewell, and turned towards the rocks. There was evidently nothing for it but to go on alone. It was half-past ten o'clock, and the height about 13,600 feet, Little Ararat now lying nearly 1000 feet below the eye.

I am no disciple of that doctrine of mountaineering without guides which some English climbers have of late preached zealously by example as well as precept, and which others, among them so high an authority as my friend Mr. Leslie Stephen, have wisely set them-selves to discourage. But if there is any justification for the practice, that justification exists when guides are not to be had. Here not only had the Cossack and the Kurd refused to come on, but they really could not have been of use if they had. They were not guides in any sense of the word; they were an escort. They had never been so high in their lives before, knew nothing either of climbing in general or of this particular mountain, were not properly equipped for the work. In fact, their presence could have been no gain in any way, except that, if one of us had hurt himself on the rocks, the other two might have carried him down or taken news to the party below. There was no ground for complaining of them, seeing that the mountain was terrible not only by its legends, but

by its solitude and silence ; and the idea of going to
the top for the sake of getting to the top would have
been quite incomprehensible to them. What had happened was so obviously what might have been, and
indeed had been, expected, that it would have been
folly for a man to come so far unless he was now prepared to proceed alone. The weather looked pretty
steady, although clouds were gathering round the
top, and there seemed to be so little snow on this
side that the usual risks of solitary mountaineering
were absent, and a single climber would be just as
well able to get along as a party. Convincing myself by these reasonings that there was nothing rash
in proceeding, I fell to work upon the trachytic
crags in front, but found them so nasty that it soon
became necessary to turn off to the left (west).
There I emerged on a very long, straight slope of
volcanic stones, fragments of trachyte, basalt, amyg-
daloid, and so forth, lying at so high an angle (probably
over 33 degrees) that they were often rolling down of
themselves, and always gave way under the foot and
hand, so that I slipped down nearly as much as I
went up. It was nearly two hours' incessant toil up this
bit of "screes," owing partly to its nature, but chiefly
to the state of fatigue and breathlessness in which I
found myself, and which was no doubt due to the
thinness of the air. Having never before experienced,
even on the top of Monte Rosa, any of the discomforts
ascribed to this cause, I had fancied that my present
sensations, which had begun in crossing the first slope
of stones at a height of only 12,300 feet, were caused

simply by want of training and of sleep.   Now, however, when between every two steps one had to stop and gasp for breath, it was plain that the rarity of the air must be the real cause, though there was no headache, nausea, gushing of blood from the nose and ears, nor any other of those symptoms of mountain sickness on which the older travellers dilate.   Oddly enough, it grew no worse as I mounted ; in fact, was felt rather less at 17,000 feet than at 13,000.   Why this was so, or why I should have felt it so low on Ararat at all, I cannot explain : the phenomena of the subject are odd altogether, and seem to deserve more study than they have received.   In the Alps, for instance, there are said to be mountains, such as Mont Blanc, where these sensations are experienced far more frequently than on other hills at the same height. Doubtless there is a good deal of difference between one man's susceptibility and another's, and even between the same man's states at different times ; but there seem to be also further differences in the mountains themselves which it would be interesting to examine.

The practical question at this moment was whether with knees of lead, and gasping like a fish in a boat, I should be able to get any farther.   Another element of difficulty was added by the clouds, which had now established themselves, as they usually do at this hour, a good way down from the top, and might prevent me from finding it, or at least beguile me into a wrong track, which there would not be time to retrace so as to reach the desired goal.   I had not seen the

summit that morning, and was obliged to guess at its
whereabouts from the direction of the ridges running
up the face of the cone (I say "cone" for convenience,
though it is really more a dome than a cone, and
is so huge that in climbing the sides you do not
think of it as a cone at all).   With these grounds for
reflection I sat down to eat an egg and take stock of
the position.   The conclusion was that, whenever a
"bad place" presented itself, or three o'clock arrived,
it would be prudent, indeed necessary, to turn back
were the top never so near.   "Bad places" are more
serious things when one is alone, especially in descending, not so much because you lose the help of a
companion as because they are more likely to affect
the nerves and oblige the climber to proceed with
more deliberation.   In this case, moreover, time was
everything, because the place of bivouac must be
reached by 6 P.M., after which there would be no light
fit for walking, and a night without food or wrappings
in the open air, even at 12,000 feet, might have had
permanently disagreeable results.   In coming to this
decision, there was a sense of relief; and both lungs
and legs were so exhausted that the bad place, or
three o'clock, would have been almost welcome.

This repulsive stone slope abuts at its upper
extremity upon a line of magnificent black cliff, from
which there were hanging several glittering icicles,
200 feet long, frozen waterfalls in fact, produced by
the melting of the snow on a snow slope behind.
Before reaching this, I had grown so weary of the
loose stones, up which it was difficult to advance except

by a succession of spurts with the aid of hands and ice-
axe, as to turn still farther to the left, and get on to
another rock-rib, composed of toppling crags of lava,
along whose farther or western side, the *arête* itself
being too much broken, it was possible to work one's
laborious way over the fallen masses. Here a grand
sight, perhaps the grandest on the whole mountain,
presented itself. At my foot was a deep, narrow, im-
passable gully, a sort of gigantic *couloir*, in whose
bottom snow lay where the inclination was not too
steep. Beyond it a line of rocky towers, red, grim,
and terrible, ran right up towards the summit, its
upper end lost in the clouds, through which, as at
intervals they broke or shifted, one could descry, far,
far above, a wilderness of snow. Had a Kurd ever
wandered so far, he might have taken this for the
palace of the Jinn.

This gully is, no doubt, one of those ancient volcanic
fissures with which the mountain is seamed, and from
which great part of its lava has been discharged.
The same phenomenon appears in most volcanic
regions : in Iceland, for instance, tremendous eruptions have taken place from similar rifts or *gjás*, as
they are called there, opening on the sides or even at
the base of a mountain. This particular fissure, which
runs north-west and south-east, is on the main the
axis of the mass, midway between the craters of Kip
Ghöll on the north-west and Little Ararat on the
south-east, and indicates the line along which the
volcanic forces acted most powerfully. Following its
course towards the base of the cone, I could see that

line prolonged in a series of small cones and craters along the top of the ridge which connects Great and Little Ararat. Some of those craters, into which I looked straight down from this point, were as perfect as if their fires had but just cooled, each basin-shaped hollow surrounded by a rim of miniature black cliffs, with heaps of ashes and scoriæ piled on their sides. In the bottom of one or two water had gathered in greenish tarns or pools.[1]

Not knowing how far the ridge I was following might continue passable, I was obliged to stop frequently to survey the rocks above, and erect little piles of stones to mark the way. This not only consumed time, but so completely absorbed the attention that for hours together I scarcely noticed the marvellous landscape spread out beneath, and felt the solemn grandeur of the scenery far less than many times before on less striking mountains. Solitude at great heights, or among majestic rocks or forests, commonly stirs in us all deep veins of feeling, joyous or saddening, or more often of joy and sadness mingled. Here the strain on the observing senses seemed too great for fancy or emotion to have any scope. When the mind is preoccupied by the task of the moment, imagination is checked. This was a race against time, in which I could only scan the cliffs for a route, refer constantly to the watch, husband my strength by morsels of food taken at frequent

---

[1] These little cones appear in the frontispiece between the base of Great and the base of Little Ararat, immediately to the right of the top of the projecting buttress which is seen in front between the two Ararats.

intervals, and endeavour to conceive how a particular block or bit of slope which it would be necessary to recognise would look when seen the other way in descending.

Keeping mostly on the south-western side of this same rock-rib, and mounting at last to the top of it, I found myself on the edge of a precipice, which stopped farther progress in that direction. From this precipice, the summit, or at least the place where it must lie, since there was a great deal of cloud about in these higher regions, could be made out, barely 1000 feet above me. Fortunately, the clouds were really clouds, and not a generally diffused mist, so that, when I was not actually in them, it was possible to see clearly all round. Two courses were open. One, which would probably have been the better, was to bear off to the right, and get up the low cliffs at the top of the long stone slope which I had deserted, on to the upper slopes of rock, or gently inclined snow, which lead to the top. The other was to turn back a little, and descend to the left into a vast snow basin lying immediately south-east of the summit, and whose north-west acclivity formed, in fact, the side of the summit. This acclivity looked a likely place for crevasses, though I do not remember to have seen any, and was steep enough to require step cutting. Its névé would have been quite practicable for a party, but not equally so for a single man, who might have had some trouble in stopping himself if once he slipped and went off. Luckily there was on the east side of the basin, close under the range of

precipice on a projecting point of which I was standing,
though separated from it by a narrow snow-bed, a steep
slope of friable rocks, quite free from snow, which ran
up to a point where the clouds hid them, but where
there seemed no sign of any cliff to bar the way.
Forced to decide between a course which was difficult,
but almost certainly practicable, and another probably
easier, but possibly impracticable, I could not hesitate
long in choosing the former.   Retracing my steps a
little from the precipice, and climbing along the border
of a treacherous little ice-slope, where there was fortunately some handhold on the rocks enclosing it, I
got into the great snow basin aforesaid, just where the
gully or fissure I have already mentioned descends
from it, and attacked the friable rocks. Their angle (38
to 43 degrees) would have made them simple enough
if they had only been firm, but they were so rotten [1]
that neither hands nor feet could get firm hold, and I
slipped down and scrambled up and floundered about
pitiably, having no longer steel enough in the muscles
for a rush.   Among these rocks I was saluted by a
violent sulphurous smell, much like that of a battery
of cannon just fired off, and perceived at the same
time patches of whitish and reddish-yellow stuff
efflorescing from the ground, reminding me of similar
deposits noticed on Hekla and the half extinct
volcano of Krabla in Iceland. This was delightfully
volcanic, and I began to look about for some trace of

---

[1] The rock was exactly what is called in the Venetian Alps *croda
morta*, a term so happily descriptive (especially when compared with
the *vivum saxum* of the ancients) that it ought to be made technical.

an eruptive vent, or at least for hot vapours betraying the presence of subterranean fires. Nothing of the kind, however, was to be seen. The shape of this basin makes it probable that it was really a former seat of volcanic action ; but the smell and the efflorescences are no doubt due—as Abich, who (as I afterwards learnt) had observed them, remarks—to the natural decomposition of the trachytic rock, which is full of minute crystals of iron pyrites (sulphide of iron). This, in disintegrating under the moisture of these heights, gives off sulphuric acid gas, whence the smell, and combines with the lime and alumina present in the felspar of the same rock to form sulphates of lime and alumina, mixed with more or less sulphate of iron or chloride of iron, which gives the reddish or yellow hue. Lumps of these and other minerals are seen lying about; I found one, a piece of gypsum, with handsome crystals, on the surface of the snow close to the top. Abich further suggests that the process of chemical change which goes on so briskly here may be one cause of the freedom of these rocks from snow, an extraordinary phenomenon when one considers that they run up to very near the summit (17,000 feet), and, though steep, are less steep than many ice walls in the Alps or the Caucasus lying, in equally exposed places, far nearer to the lower limit of perpetual snow, which on Ararat averages 14,000 feet. Not only is some heat evolved in the decomposing process, but the sulphates thereby formed themselves act as solvents, just as common salt does when you sprinkle it on an ice-covered door-step.

U

All the way up this rock-slope, which proved so fatiguing that for the fourth time I had almost given up hope, I kept my eye fixed on its upper end to see what signs there were of crags or snow-fields above. But the mist lay steadily at the point where the snow seemed to begin, and it was impossible to say what might be hidden behind that soft white curtain. As little could I conjecture the height I had reached by looking round, as one so often does on mountain ascents, upon other summits, for by this time I was thousands of feet above Little Ararat, the next highest peak visible, and could scarcely guess how many thousands. From this tremendous height it looked more like a broken obelisk than an independent summit 12,800 feet in height. Clouds covered the farther side of the great snow basin, and were seething like waves about the savage pinnacles, the towers of the Jinn palace, which guard its lower margin, and past which my upward path had lain. With mists to the left and above, and a range of black precipices cutting off all view to the right, there came a vehement sense of isolation and solitude, and I began to understand better the awe with which the mountain silence inspires the Kurdish shepherds. Overhead the sky had turned from dark blue to an intense bright green, a colour whose strangeness seemed to add to the weird terror of the scene. It wanted barely an hour to the time when I had resolved to turn back; and as I struggled up the crumbling rocks, trying now to right and now to left, where the foothold looked a little firmer, I began to doubt whether there was

strength enough left to carry me an hour higher. At
length the rock-slope came suddenly to an end, and
I stepped out upon the almost level snow at the top
of it, coming at the same time into the clouds, which
naturally clung to the colder surfaces. A violent west
wind was blowing, and the temperature must have
been pretty low, for a big icicle at once enveloped the
lower half of my face, and did not melt till I got to
the bottom of the cone, four hours afterwards. Unluckily, I was very thinly clad, the stout tweed coat
reserved for such occasions having been stolen on a
Russian railway. The only expedient to be tried
against the piercing cold was to tighten in my loose
light coat by winding round the waist a Spanish *faja*,
or scarf, which I had brought up to use, in case of
need, as a neck wrapper. Its bright purple looked odd
enough in such surroundings, but as there was nobody
there to notice, appearances did not much matter.
In the mist, which was now thick, the eye could
pierce only some thirty yards ahead ; so I walked on
over the snow five or six minutes, following the rise
of its surface, which was gentle, and fancying there
might still be a good long way to go. To mark the
backward track, I trailed the point of the ice-axe
along behind me in the soft snow, for there was no
longer any landmark : all was cloud on every side.
Suddenly, to my astonishment, the ground began to
fall away to the north ; I stopped, a puff of wind drove
off the mists on one side, the opposite side to that by
which I had come, and showed the Araxes plain at
an abysmal depth below. It was the top of Ararat.

Two or three minutes afterwards another blast cleared the air a little to the west, which had hitherto been perfectly thick, disclosing a small snow valley, and beyond it, a quarter of a mile off, another top, looking about the same height as the one I stood on. Remembering, what I had strangely forgotten on the way up, that there are two tops—one sees them distinctly from Erivan and Aralykh—I ran down the steep, soft sides of the snow valley, across it in the teeth of the blast, and up the easy acclivity to the other top, reaching it at 2.25 P.M. It is certainly the higher of the two, but the difference is not great, only some thirty feet or so, and I cannot understand how General Chodzko comes to speak of it as amounting to thirty-six metres.[1] The longitudinal depression between them is 100–150 feet deep. Both tops are gently sloping domes or broad convex hummocks of snow, on which there is not a trace of rock, nor a trace of the crosses which first Parrot and afterwards Chodzko set up, just as little as of Noah's ship itself. One thought of the pictures of childhood, the Ark resting on a smooth, round grassy eminence, from which the waters are receding, while the Patriarch looks out of the window, and compared them with this snow-filled hollow, just large enough to have held the vessel comfortably, raised 15,000 feet above the surrounding country. Neither is there any sign of a crater. You

[1] See his brief account of his ascent in a communication to the French Alpine Club, published in their 'Transactions' for 1876. Herr Abich, to whom I wrote on seeing this, tells me he cannot understand it either. From the north-eastern top (not having time to go on to the western) he thought the difference very slight.

might describe the whole top as a triangular undulating plain, rather more than half as big as the Green Park in London, descending gently on the north-west, with extensive terraces like fields of *névé*, less gently towards the north-north-east, but steeply on all other sides, and on the east breaking off, after a short snow-field, in the tremendous precipices that overhang the chasm of Arguri. There was nothing about it to suggest an extinct volcano, were it not known to be one. But in the ages that have elapsed since the time when eruptions took place from the great central chimney of the dome, a time probably far more remote than that when the minor cones that stud the flanks of the mountain were active, all sorts of changes may have taken place, and the summit we now see may be merely the bottom of an ancient crater, whose craggy rim has been altogether broken away. Looking around, it was hard to imagine that volcanic fires had ever raged on such a spot, robed as it now is in perpetual winter.

Immeasurably extensive and grand as the view was, it was also strangely indefinite. Every mountaineer knows that the highest views are seldom the finest ; and here was one so high that the distinctions of hill and valley in the landscape were almost lost. Ararat towers so over all his neighbours, much more than Mont Blanc or even Elbruz do over theirs, that they seem mere hillocks on a uniform flat. The only rivals are in the Caucasus, which one can just make out all along the northern sky. Kazbek and Elbruz, the latter 280 miles away, are visible, but I could not be

sure that I saw them, for the sky was not very clear in
that direction. More distinct were the mountains of
Daghestan, rising 150 miles off, over the nearer ones
that engirdle the Goktcha Lake, a little bit of whose
shining levels appeared. Beyond the dreary red-
brown mountains of the Karabagh one strained to
discover a line that might be the Caspian or the plain
of the lower Kur, but, of course, at such a distance
260 miles) it would be impossible to distinguish a sea-
surface. Besides, the Caspian is below the horizon;
so one must reject, unless the aid of refraction be
called in, the stories of mariners who, sailing on it,
have been able to make out the white cone of Ararat.
Nearer at hand, only forty miles to the north, rose
the huge extinct volcano of Ala Göz, with its three
sharp black rocky peaks enclosing an ancient crater,
in whose bottom were patches of snow; and, nearer
still, the dim plain of Erivan encircled the mountain
to the north and east, with the Araxes winding like
a faint streak of silver through it. A slight rise in
the ground showed where Erivan itself lay, but the
bright green of the orchards and vineyards round
it was lost at this distance, though, standing in the
market-place of the city, Ararat seems to tower
right over the spectator's head. Looking due west,
the extreme ranges of Taurus mingling with the
Bingöl Dagh in the neighbourhood of Erzerum were
hidden by the clouds which the wind kept driving up;
but north-west the upper valley of the Araxes could
be traced as far as Ani, once the capital of the Armenian kingdom, and the great Russian fortress of

Alexandropol, and the hills where Kars, its enemy,
looks forth defiance. To the south and south-west
the eye ranged over a wilderness of bare red-brown
mountains, their sides seamed by winter torrents that
showed in the distance like dark lines, not a tree nor
a patch of green on their scorched and arid slopes,
scarcely even a fleck of snow on their tops, though
many rose more than 10,000 or 11,000 feet above the
sea. Prominent among them was the long stern line
of hills that enclose the upper course of the Euphrates
(the Eastern Euphrates or Murad Su), whose source
could be distinguished about forty miles to the south,
beyond the hollow where Bayazid lies, the houses of
which were hidden by a low ridge. Still further to
the south, from the shores of the Lake of Van, rose
the great volcanic peak of Sipan Dagh, and to the
south-east the stupendous masses of Savalan Dagh,
that look over all Azerbijan to the waves of the
Caspian. Neither the Lake of Van nor the still
larger Lake of Urumia was visible ; for both, though
high above the sea, are enclosed by lofty hills. But
far beyond them, more than two hundred miles
away, I could just descry the faint blue tops of
the Assyrian mountains of Southern Kurdistan, the
Qardu land, where Chaldee tradition places the fragments of the Ark, mountains that look down on
Mosul and those huge mounds of Nineveh by which
the Tigris flows. Below and around, included in
this single view, seemed to lie the whole cradle of
the human race, from Mesopotamia in the south to
the great wall of the Caucasus that covered the

northern horizon, the boundary for so many ages
of the civilized world. If it was indeed here that
man first set foot again on the unpeopled earth, one
could imagine how the great dispersion went as the
races spread themselves from these sacred heights
along the courses of the great rivers down to the
Black and Caspian Seas, and over the Assyrian plain
to the shores of the Southern Ocean, whence they were
wafted away to other continents and isles. No more
imposing centre of the world could be imagined.
In the valley of the Araxes beneath, the valley which
Armenian legend has selected as the seat of Paradise,
the valley that has been for three thousand years the
high-road for armies, the scene of so much slaughter
and misery, there lay two spots which seemed to mark
the first and the latest points of authentic history.
One, right below me, was the ruined Artaxata, built, as
the tale goes, by Hannibal, and stormed by the legions
of Lucullus. The other, far to the north-west, was the
hollow under the hills in which lies the fortress of Kars,
where our countrymen fought in 1854, and where the
flames of war were so soon again to be lighted.

Yet how trivial history, and man the maker of
history, seemed. This is the spot which he reveres as
the supposed scene of his creation and his preserva-
tion from the destroying waters, a land where he has
lived and laboured and died ever since his records
begin, and during ages from which no record is left.
Dynasty after dynasty has reared its palaces, faith
after faith its temples, upon this plain ; cities have
risen and fallen and risen again in the long struggle

of civilization against the hordes of barbarism. But of all these works of human pomp and skill, not one can be discerned from this height. The landscape is now what it was before man crept forth on the earth; the mountains stand about the valleys as they stood when the volcanic fires that piled them up were long ago extinguished. **Nature** sits enthroned, serenely calm, upon this hoary pinnacle, and speaks to her children only in the storm and earthquake that level their dwellings in the dust. As says the Persian poet:

> " When you and I behind the veil are passed,
> O but the long long while the world shall last,
> Which of our coming and departure heeds
> As the Seven Seas should heed a pebble's cast."

Yet even the mountains change and decay. Every moment some block thunders from these crags into the glens below. Day by day and night by night frost, snow, and rain are loosening the solid rock, and the ceaseless action of chemical forces is dissolving it into its primal elements, setting free the gases, and delivering over the fragments to torrents that will sweep them down into the plain. A time must come, if the world lasts long enough, when even the stately peaks of Ararat will have crumbled away and be no more. "Of old hast thou laid the foundations of the earth: and the heavens are the work of thy hands. They shall perish, but thou shalt endure: they all shall wax old as doth a garment; and as a vesture shalt thou change them, and they shall be changed: but thou art the same, and thy years fail not."

Withal I am bound to say that the view, spite of

the associations it evoked, spite of the impression of
awe and mystery it gave, was not beautiful or splendid, but rather stern, grim, and monotonous. The
softer colours of the landscape seemed to be lost; the
mountains, seen from above, and seldom showing
well-marked peaks, were uncouth, rough-hewn masses.
One had a sense of vast sterility and dreariness as the
vision ranged over this boundless expanse of brown,
and sought, almost in vain, a point to recognize. For
most of these huge mountains are nameless on our
maps; and these bare valleys are peopled by races of
whom we know little except that they live now much
as they may have lived when that first dispersion of
mankind took place. Then suddenly, while the eye
was still unsatisfied with gazing, the curtain of mists
closed round again, and I was left alone in this
little plain of snow, white, silent, and desolate, with a
vividly bright green sky above it and a wild west
wind whistling across it, clouds girding it in, and ever
and anon through the clouds glimpses of far-stretching
valleys and mountains away to the world's end.

The awe that fell upon me with this sense of utter
loneliness made time pass unnoticed; and I might
have lingered long in a sort of dream had not the
piercing cold that thrilled through every limb recalled
me to a sense of the risks delay might involve. It was
half-past two o'clock, so that only four hours of daylight remained; there might be some difficulty in retracing the morning's path, even by the help of the
piles of stone set up: a night on the mountain without
food or wrappings would be a more serious matter

than any obstacle that had yet presented itself. Besides, as night approached, my friend below would grow anxious ; the rather as he could not communicate with the Cossacks, and their stock of provisions would scarcely enable them and him to wait till the next day. It was clear therefore that the hope of descending the summit towards the west and north for the sake of better examining its structure, which no one seems to have properly described, must be abandoned. So I ran down the easy slope into the little valley between the two tops, climbed the snow wall of the eastern one, and followed the marks made by my ice-axe in the snow back to the spot where I had left the rocks. The mist was now so thick that it would otherwise have been impossible to hit the right direction ; for though I had a compass, on a volcanic mountain like Ararat, with plenty of iron in the rocks, one could not have trusted it. I have seen the needle on the basaltic top of Ben Nèvis point every way in succession. Once on the slope of friable rock, the way was pretty clear, since a snow-bed lay on each hand, though the treacherous nature of the surface made caution necessary and progress slow. Towards the bottom I was tempted to try a glissade on the narrow left-hand snow-bed, but it turned out to be much too rough and too hard for the purpose ; so my glissade ended in a slip and some bruises, the only little mischance which befel me during the day.

A few minutes more brought me to the upper end of the great fissure of eruption already mentioned, along whose eastern side I had climbed in the morning, partly on the slope, partly on the top, of the rock-rib or *arête* which encloses it on the east. Surveying the declivity below me from the top of this rock-rib, it seemed possible to descend by a route considerably shorter than that which I had then followed, viz. by striking diagonally across the slopes of loose rock towards the east-south-east, instead of due south-east down the cone. Taking this line, which presented no great difficulty except where the loose, angular blocks became so large that much time was lost in climbing over and among them, I dropped down at last upon a large snow-bed,[1] and in crossing it had the ill-luck to break off the spike of my ice-axe, which had been unskilfully fixed by the military carpenter of Aralykh. It was well that the inclination was not steep enough to make the rest of the way dangerous ; by caution and the use of the head of the ice-axe to cut steps or take hold of the ice, I got safely across, and on to another mass of loose rocks, down which I pursued the same south-eastward course, and thought I began to recognize the long ridge up which we had toiled in the morning. To the left rose the sharp peak which is called, in Tatar, Tach Kilissa, and at the foot of it, on

[1] This snow-field stretches right up to the top of the mountain, and would afford a practicable route to it, although a tiresome one, for in most parts of it the inclination is steep enough to make step-cutting necessary. At the point where I crossed, it is a kind of tongue from a wider snow-field above, up which Messrs. Freshfield and Tucker and their Swiss guide seem to have made their spirited attack on the mountain in 1868. They went (as far as I can gather) from Sardarbulakh right up past Tach Kilissa, and were prevented from reaching the summit only by illness, the result of long travel in Russian telegas. See the very interesting account of their expedition in Mr. Freshfield's 'Central Caucasus.'

the top of the ridge I have just mentioned, was the
spot where my friend and the Cossacks had halted;
the spot I had now to make for. By this time the
sun had got behind the south-western ridge of the
mountain, and his gigantic shadow had already fallen
across the great Araxes plain below, while the red
mountains of Media, far to the south-east, still glowed
redder than ever, then turned swiftly to a splendid
purple in the dying light.

Quickening my pace as the risk of missing the
encampment became greater, feeling, in fact, that it
was now a race against the onward striding night in
which defeat would be serious, I caught sight at last
of two Cossacks loitering on the edge of the slope of
sand and gravel which had proved so fatiguing in the
morning, and after a while made them hear my shouts.
When I reached them, it was six o'clock; and though
at this height (12,200 feet) there was still good twilight,
Aralykh and the ruins of Artaxata below lay already
shrouded in gloom. Twenty-five minutes' more walking brought us to the place where the Kurds and the
other Cossacks had bivouacked; and here, when it
was already so dark that we could barely recognize
one another a few yards off, my friend came forward
and met me. He had spent most of the day near the
spot where we parted, coming down eventually to
this point, which was a little lower, had seen the Kurd
return, but of course could get no tidings from him of
me, had slept about a good deal among shady places
in the rocks, making up for the vigils of the last week,
and had latterly, as the evening deepened, wandered

round, keeping a sharp look-out on the slopes above.
We examined the provisions, and found that nothing
but a lump of bread, a mere scrap of meat, two eggs,
and a thimbleful of cold tea were left. Happily neither
of us had much appetite; the sun had kept hunger at
bay for him, and meat lozenges had done the same for
me; so our frugal evening meal was soon despatched.
A little hot tea would have been welcome—four weeks
under the sceptre of the Czar had made us perfect
slaves to tea; but as there was neither fuel, nor
water, nor a vessel to boil it in, the hope was no
sooner formed than abandoned. Accordingly, about
half-past seven, we lay down on the hillside, my
friend valiantly on the top of the ridge, I a yard
or two below him on the eastern side, the Cossacks
and Kurds all round where they severally pleased,
and we courted sleep. They, to judge by the sounds
that broke the mountain silence, courted not in vain,
but we two, although rather tired, found the position
too novel, and lay half conscious in a drowsy reverie;
dropping off at last to wake with a start at midnight, when the moon's pale horn was just shewing
over the Median mountains. Fortunately there had
been little wind. Though the air was sharp, and my
friend rose in a fit of shivering which at first alarmed
us, I do not think the temperature can have fallen
to freezing-point, and should have guessed it to be
about from 36° to 40° Fahrenheit, no great cold for an
exposed point about 11,500 feet above the sea. Unhappily we had no thermometer; it had been necessary to restrict our baggage to the lightest and most

indispensable articles. Even the aneroid which had come with us from Tiflis I had been forced by its weight to leave behind in the tent at Sardarbulakh.

After packing our scanty stock of camping gear as well as we could in the darkness, and counting the bundles on the Kurds' backs, we set off down the dark ridges and darker valleys, stumbling about over huge rocks under the feebly glimmering moon, losing often our companions, and sometimes the way itself. How we got safe down was a marvel to us at the time ; but one frequently has the same cause for wonder in night walks. Perhaps the muscles and sinews, knowing what depends upon them, acquire a sort of preternatural elasticity and readiness, which enables them to adapt themselves to an emergency, and carry one safely through innumerable risks. There was no track, but the Kurds seemed to have an idea where they were going. Many were the halts which the Cossacks made, stretching themselves on the grass to laugh and talk ; nor was it now worth while to hurry them. Now and then we tried to get a nap during these delays, but though scarcely able to walk for drowsiness, as soon as we lay down and shut our eyes, we became bolt awake. At length the morning star rose in unearthly brightness, and not long after we came to a sweet little grassy plain, where two or three Kurds, whose flocks were pasturing hard by, had lit a fire of withered bushes, to which our Kurds led us up in a friendly way, bidding us (as we guessed) warm ourselves. The Cossacks had nearly all gone on out of sight, and we were (as it afterwards struck us) entirely at the mercy of these wild, swarthy fellows, on whose glittering daggers and matchlocks the firelight played. However, they had no thought of mischief; perhaps, if it had occurred to them, the sense of hospitality, which is proverbially strong in the East, would have restrained them from harming those with whom they had eaten. Then between four and five o'clock another glorious dawn began; and just before sunrise we reached the tent at Sardarbulakh, much to the relief of Jaafar's mind, and flung ourselves down on the tent floor to sleep the sleep of the weary.

Roused again at eight or nine o'clock—both the watches had stopped, so we could only guess at the time of day—we ought clearly to have gone up Little Ararat, and obtained from his top a fuller notion of his great brother's structure. Provisions, however, ran short, and the Cossacks were anxious to return to Aralykh, taking back with them their comrades whom we had found in the two tents, as the post was to be withdrawn for the season. Accordingly the tents were struck, everything packed on the baggage horses, the Kurds paid for their day's and night's service on the hill. Then, before starting, the Cossacks gathered in a ring in front of the spot where the tents had stood, and began singing Russian songs. The words we, of course, could not follow—I believe they were mostly camp songs, some commemorating military exploits, some farewells to departing comrades—but the airs, usually lively, but occasionally tender and plaintive, dwelt long in our memory. One stood in the middle and led, firing off a gun at intervals, the others sometimes singing with him, sometimes merely joining in the refrain or chorus. The voices were good, and the time perfect.

In an English daily newspaper of July 27, 1877, I found the following passage :—"Utterly remorseless, the Cossack falls upon a hostile country like a demon of destruction. There is no getting away from his thirsty lance, no assuaging his fierce fury, no appeasing that innate devilry which makes him regard cruelty to his fellow-creatures as a delightful pastime. Mercy to the conquered is not a part of the Cossack creed. The savage does not expect it, does not give it. He is content to carry his life in his hand, for those to take who can ; but while it remains with him, he intends to make it pleasant, according to his lights, by miscellaneous pillage and slaughter."

Now I cannot say what the Cossack may be in war time, for I saw him only in peace. In all men the brute comes out at the taste of blood ; and no doubt in him also. What I can venture to say is that, comparing him in time of peace with the soldiers of other countries, I have never seen any so apparently gentle, so unlikely to prove, even in war, "utterly remorseless demons of destruction." These sons of harmony were the merriest, simplest, most good-natured fellows we could have wished to ramble over the hills with. The countenance after all cannot wholly belie the character ; and among the hundreds of Cossacks we met in the Caucasian provinces, there were fewer hard or

X

fierce faces than we had ever seen in as many fighting men before. "Wanton cruelty," "innate devilry," and so forth, are not passions that can be wholly repressed even in peace time; yet I never heard from either the Armenians or the Germans, who are keen critics of everything Russian, a word of complaint as to the behaviour of these irregulars among the people. No doubt the Cossack has a keen scent for supplies on a campaign, and helps himself pretty freely, without paying for what he takes. But there is not a particle of evidence to show that he has of late years ever done anything more cruel in war than all troops do,[1] the French, the German, or our own. Compare him with the Austrian Pandurs of last century, or the Bashi-Bazouks of to-day, and he seems almost white against such foul blackness. Of course I do not suppose that the writer of this article had anything particular in his eye. He wanted to write tellingly: and the article was telling. But is it not pitiful that at this time of day able writers should be content to stir up hatred between nations for the sake of a little literary effect?

Before noon we bid a regretful farewell to Sardar-bulakh, and rode down into the plain, this time taking a track outside of the buttress of Takjaltu, instead of behind it, and thence across the arid slopes to Aralykh, which we reached about four o'clock without further incident, though once during the way an alarm was given that there were strange people about, and

[1] We can all remember the false stories that were industriously circulated about the excesses of the Germans in France in 1870, and of the Federal troops in the American Civil War; yet it is now generally admitted that no invading troops ever behaved so well.

Jaafar rode ahead to reconnoitre. Owing, I suppose, to the bracing quality of the keen dry air, we were much less fatigued than we had expected to be. Colonel Shipshef welcomed us with characteristic heartiness, and we spent a pleasant evening with him, lamenting more than ever that unhappy event at the tower of Babel which made our communications so limited. Next morning we mounted the tarantass once more, and drove off across the Araxes and through the dusty villages back into the furnace of Erivan.

Two days later I found myself at the Armenian monastery of Etchmiadzin, near the northern foot of Ararat, and was presented to the archimandrite who rules that illustrious house. It came out in conversation that we had been on the mountain, and the Armenian gentleman who was acting as interpreter turned to the archimandrite and said : "This Englishman says he has ascended to the top of Massis" (Ararat). The venerable man smiled sweetly. "No," he replied, "that cannot be. No one has ever been there. It is impossible."

CHAPTER VIII.

ETCHMIADZIN AND THE ARMENIAN PEOPLE.

AFTER returning to Erivan from Ararat, we made a hurried expedition to the famous monastery of Etchmiadzin, which claims to be the oldest monastic foundation in the world, and has for many centuries been the seat of the Armenian Patriarch or Katholikos, the spiritual head of all true Armenians, in whatsoever empire, Russian, Turkish, Persian, Austrian, or British, they may dwell. It is distant about thirteen miles, some two hours driving, from Erivan, and the journey gave us our first experience of that wonderful vehicle the Russian telega. Our faithful tarantass had suffered from the roads to Aralykh, and been obliged to go into hospital, so at the posthouse they produced to us this contrivance—a cart, or shallow lidless box, about six feet long by four wide, set upon wheels with no pretence of springs or anything in the nature of springs. A little hay was thrown in, among which we were told to squat. We put in a travelling bag, but soon found it impossible to sit upon that, or on the sides of the box itself, for the jolting knocked one about like a pea on a hot iron. While the team of three scraggy beasts walked, the shocks came slowly and were tolerable, but as soon as the pace was quickened they became so violent that we could only hold ourselves in the cart by grasping its sides, and a whisky flask which had been safely lodged in my companion's breast coat-pocket was shot out like a cannon ball, and flung to a distance in the road, where of course it broke into a hundred pieces. How people manage to travel for many continuous days in such vehicles without grievous bodily harm, it is hard to understand, but the thing is done. The road was no doubt very bad, so bad that it was a relief to get off it into the bed of a stream or on to the steppe, whose natural stoniness was less horrible than the artificial stoniness of the highway. But this road was not worse than all roads, except the main post *chaussée*, are in these countries.

The evening was serenely clear. Ararat to the south, and the dark mysterious mountains towards Kars in the far west, riveted our eyes, and there was something inexpressibly solemn in the great desolate plain that lay around us under the dying light—a plain in which Armenian tradition places the site of the Garden of Eden. The curse of the flaming sword might well be thought to have clung to it, for few spots on earth have seen more ruin and slaughter than this Araxes valley. It has been the highway through which the Eastern conquerors and marauders, from the days of the Sassanid kings Shapur and Chosroes Nushirvan, down through those of the Saracen and Turkish and Mongol and Persian invaders, have poured their hosts upon the fertile shores of the

Euxine.   Here the Romans strove with the Parthians ; here Alp Arslan overthrew the Armenian
kingdom of the middle ages ; here, down to our own
days, Turks and Persians and Russians have carried
on a scarcely interrupted strife.   From Kars to
Djulfa there is hardly a spot of ground that has
not been soaked with blood, hardly a village that
has not many times been laid in ruins.   Yet when the
storm is past, the patient peasant returns ; he draws
water again from the ancient canals whose network
covers the plain, and remembers these scourges of
mankind only in vague traditions, where the names
of Nimrod and Semiramis are mingled with those of
Tamerlane and Nadir Shah.

It was nearly dark when we reached the village of
Vagarshabad at seven o'clock, and as we had no
interpreter there was some difficulty in discovering the
officials to whom our letters of commendation were
addressed.   When their houses were found they turned
out to be absent, so we drove straight to the monastery, prowled for some time in the deepening night
round its lofty walls, much like those of a mediæval
fortress, and at last made out a gate, to which after
long hammering there came a porter.   When he
opened and saw that we were foreigners, he brought at
last a young Armenian gentleman from the Armenian
colony in Southern Russia, who was able to speak
French.   Our troubles were then at an end ; we were
received with much friendliness by the archimandrite,
and lodged in a guest-chamber overlooking the great
front quadrangle.   On our apologizing for intruding

on their religious seclusion at so late an hour, they answered that to entertain strangers was with them a duty as well as a pleasure; so that we might have claimed hospitality even had we come unrecommended.

Etchmiadzin is the ecclesiastical metropolis of the Armenian nation,[1] and has been so, though with a long intermission (A.D. 452–1441), since the year A.D. 302, when, according to tradition, the first Christian church in Armenia was founded here by St. Gregory the Illuminator, on the spot whereon the Saviour had descended in a ray of light. The place was then called, from some ancient king who had founded it, Vagarshabad, a name still retained by the neighbouring village. The word Etchmiadzin means in Armenian, "The only-begotten descended."

Tiridates, or Dertad, the reigning monarch whom Gregory then enlightened (Enlightenment is the technical Armenian term for conversion), was the first king who embraced Christianity along with his people, Constantine's so-called conversion not happening till either twelve or thirty-seven years later, according as one reckons to the battle of the Milvian Bridge or to his baptism. Armenia, therefore, is the first country to have enjoyed the privileges of an ecclesiastical

---

[1] The authority of the Patriarch of Etchmiadzin was for a long time disputed by a patriarch who resided at Akhtamar, an island in the Lake of Van, and is, I fancy, still disputed by a patriarch at Sis, among the mountains of Cilicia, where the warlike Armenian tribes maintain a sort of independence. However, this latter rival has now few subjects; Constantinople and all the Gregorian Armenians (= those not united to Rome and not Protestants) throughout the world recognize Etchmiadzin.

establishment, although the attacks of the Persian
fire-worshippers, and of various Mohammedan Khalifs,
Sultans, and Shahs in later times, gave it a very
troubled and precarious existence.   At first the
bishop of Etchmiadzin was a suffragan of the metropolitan of Caesarea in Cappadocia, by whom Gregory
had been consecrated ; but when the Persian kings
established their supremacy in the next century, they
broke this link between Armenia and the Roman
Empire.   Shortly afterwards came the Council of
Chalcedon, whose decrees the Armenian Church first
hesitated, and finally, in A.D. 491, refused to accept,
thereby severing herself from the Orthodox Eastern
Church.   So to this day she remains out of communion with the Greek patriarch of Constantinople,
as well as with the Church of Russia, and is held both
by them and by the Roman Church to be tainted
with the Monophysite heresy, which the fathers of
Chalcedon condemned.   Ever since those days, though
attempts at reconciliation were occasionally made, and
seemed for the moment to be successful, she has
remained a perfectly independent ecclesiastical body,
owning no superior above her own Patriarch or
Katholikos, who is, in fact, a sort of administrative
Pope, but of course without infallibility.   He is chosen
by the whole body of Armenian bishops throughout
the world, who meet here for the purpose, and is then
confirmed by the Czar, who protects him and enforces
his authority.   Those Armenian Christians, a minority
dating from the time of the Crusades, who are in communion with the Latin Church, although allowed to

retain their own rite, of course do not recognise the prelate of Etchmiadzin, but have a patriarch of their own, who resides at Constantinople, and owns allegiance to Rome. There has lately been a schism among these so-called United Armenians, some refusing obedience to the Pope, while others cling to him. Small as the matter may appear to us at this distance, it excites great interest in the Roman Curia, for whose zeal or ambition nothing is too small or too great. And a desire to have the authority of the United patriarch who adheres to Rome supported by the Porte, against the other United patriarch who is disobedient, has been conjectured, not without probability, to be one chief motive which has induced Pope Pius IX. to extend his moral support to Turkey in her struggle with Russia.[1]

The monastery of Etchmiadzin (here, as in Russia, it is at monasteries that episcopal seats are fixed ; every Russian prelate lives in one) has been frequently destroyed or injured by the numerous invaders that have swept over the country, and as often restored.

---

[1] The schism began in 1869, when the Pope issued the bull *Reversuris*, by which he asserted his right to choose one out of three candidates presented to him for every bishopric, or to reject all three if he pleased, and also to have all the accounts and dealings of the Armenian Church and Patriarch laid before him. As no such right had (so said my informants) been previously exercised by him, a large body of the United Armenians in Constantinople, including the richest and best educated, refused to submit to this bull, and deposed the patriarch Hassun, appointing another pledged to resist Rome. The Porte, under the influence of Germany (as is supposed), recognized this rival ; and the Pope's object is believed to be to induce the Porte to withdraw that recognition, and enforce the claims of Hassun, who is faithful to him.

The present church is supposed to contain some bits
of wall as old as the fourth century, the main body of
it being ascribed to the seventh or eighth ; but I found
it impossible to get any information on the spot which
could be relied on, and the architectural style in these
countries varies so little from one century to another
that only a practised and skilful archæologist could
undertake to pronounce on the date of a building from
examining it.   Like nearly all the older churches of
Russia, as well as of the East, it is small—small, that is
to say, compared with its fame or importance—perhaps
a little larger than the Temple Church in London.
It is cruciform, with exceedingly short transepts and
a short apse—in fact, you might call it a square with
four shallow recesses—the interior rather dark, with
an air of heaviness which is scarcely redeemed by the
frescos on the walls, drawn and coloured in the usual
style of Persian arabesque, with birds, flowers, and
various conventional ornaments. However, any cheerful decorations of this kind are welcome after the
revolting pictures of hell and judgment that adorn
the walls of so many Russian and Greek churches.
There are two patriarchal thrones, one on each side
of the apse, and a tabernacle over the central altar
under the dome marks the spot on which the Saviour
descended.   Here a slab of marble covers the hole
through which St. Gregory drove into the earth all
the devils that in his day infested Armenia, and gave
false oracles in the heathen temples.   On this very
spot there had stood a shrine and image of the god-
dess Anahit, just as the hill of Monte Casino was

crowned, when St. Benedict first went there, by a temple of Apollo. Between the apse and the body of the church is a sort of screen, somewhat similar to the *ikonostas* of Russian churches, but it is only a small part of the Armenian service that goes on behind this screen. On the whole, the interior is impressive, with a certain sombre dignity, and an air of hoar antiquity about everything : its pictures, some of them portraits of sainted patriarchs, and other decorations, have little artistic merit, but they are less offensive to the Protestant eye than the black Madonnas incrusted with precious stones which are the glory of Russian or other Orthodox places of worship. Externally the church has little that is distinctive about it. The tall central cupola rises into an octagonal spire, or rather conical tower, of the usual Armenian type, and is said to date from the seventh century, though I cannot believe it to be anything like so old. So, too, the four smaller open towers at the four extremities, the windows and doors, with their mouldings (the elegantly carved porch at the west end is especially handsome), are all in the regular style of Armenian building, and probably all modern, the towers of the seventeenth century, the porch of the eighteenth. A learned ecclesiological writer (Dr. Neale), however, insists that the ground plan of the church is rather Byzantine than Armenian, and his reasons, so far as I can judge of such a matter, seem to be sound. Of true Armenian architecture the finest and most characteristic specimens are to be found in the ruined city of Ani, some thirty miles from here, towards Kars, and just within the Turkish border.

The other monastic buildings, only a small part of which consists of the dwellings of the brethren, are of no great architectural merit. What struck me as the oldest and most interesting are the two refectories, one of which, used in summer, a long, low vaulted room, with one narrow table running down the midst between stone benches, a throne under a canopy for the patriarch, and a sort of pulpit, whence reading goes on during meals, appears from its style to be not later than the twelfth century. However, there is a tradition assigning a much later origin to it. Old also is the library, to which we had come with great expectations, hearing of its treasures in the way of ancient manuscripts. Unfortunately there was no one on the spot who could tell us much about them, and I doubt if there is any one who knows much. The stock of printed books is quite small, not reaching 2000, and of course the great majority are in Armenian, most of the newer ones in Russian. There seems to be little ground for hoping that any Greek or Latin manuscripts, unless, possibly, of late ecclesiastical writers, remain to be discovered here ; it is rather to Orientalists that researches into the libraries of the Armenian monasteries are to be recommended. The treasury, or, as we should say, the sacristy, in which the holy relics that constitute the great glory of Etchmiadzin are kept, is a new building at the east end of the church. Unhappily we could not gain admittance, owing to a cause which might seem to

cast a painful light on the want of security, or at
least of confidence, among even the respectable ecclesiastics of this country. There is but one key to the
treasury, and that key is kept by the patriarch, who
carries it with him wherever he goes. He was then
in a cool mountain retreat some miles away on the
slopes of Ala Göz, and we were therefore obliged to
forego the hope of seeing the head of the holy spear
wherewith the Roman soldier pierced the side of
Christ. It is asserted to have been brought to Armenia by Thaddeus the Apostle, and has therefore a
far more respectable pedigree, so to speak, than the
rival " holy lance " which the Crusaders discovered at
Antioch with such magnificent results, or than that
which Sir John Maundeville tells us he saw at Constantinople in the possession of the Eastern Emperor, not to speak of other claimants. In this treasure-house there is also a fragment of Noah's Ark,
obtained, according to the legend stated in an earlier
chapter, by the monk St. Jacob ; and, what is the
most curious of all, a withered mummy hand inclosed
in a casing of silver, which purports to be the very
hand of St. Gregory the Illuminator. This hand is
actually used to this day in the consecration of every
patriarch, who being touched by it receives the grace,
as it were, direct from the founder of the Armenian
Church. It is an instance of the carrying out, on its
physical side, of the doctrine (I will not say of apos-
tolic succession, but) of the transmission through
earthen vessels of spiritual gifts, and their communication by physical means, which one is startled to find

still in full force in an important and respectable
branch of the Christian Church. In the middle
ages nothing would have seemed more natural or impressive ; in the nineteenth century it looks a little
different.

Within the lofty and battlemented wall that incloses
the monastery, which has in its day repelled many a
band of Tatar or Persian marauders, and may perhaps
even have stood sieges before the days of cannon—it
was repaired in the last century, but of its first erection
there seems to be no record—there lies a great mass
of buildings of different kinds, as well as some gardens
and open spaces. Besides the cells of the monks,
who number from twenty to thirty, there are, on the
west side of the great square, apartments for the patriarch and for the archbishops, bishops, and archiman-
drites from other monasteries, who are frequently to
be found here, consulting him on the affairs of their
churches, or attending the general and supreme synod,
which sits, almost in permanence, under his presi-
dency. There are many subsidiary buildings, and
among them a sort of bazaar, where some trade is
done, chiefly in hay and corn produced by the monastic
lands; in fact one has almost a little town within the
walls of this fortress convent, a mile in circuit. Finally
there is the seminary, a sort of school or college for
the education of young Armenians chiefly, but not
exclusively, with a view to their entering the priestly
office. The school is supported by the monastic
revenues, which, as they are said to amount to nearly
£10,000 a year, arising partly from landed property

here and in Georgia, but mainly from the contributions of the loyal Armenian churches throughout the world, can well afford this charge, in addition to that of a sum paid to the patriarch and the maintenance of the monks and their establishment.

We were received at the seminary, which occupies a new and fairly commodious building to the east of the cathedral, by the Armenian archbishop of Tiflis, who is at present acting as its director. This able and accomplished prelate, who has lived long in the West, chiefly at Venice, and speaks French fluently, told us a good deal that was interesting about the school and the prospects of education in the country generally. There were about eighty boys or young men then attending, who are of course lodged in the monastery, and for the most part remain in it from the beginning to the end of their education, coming often from great distances. Among those present in the dining-hall some were from the heart of Persia, others from Cilicia, others from all sorts of places scattered through Asia Minor. The well-marked national type of countenance, the dark eyes and straight, black hair, came out strongly; and the quick intelligence of many of the faces was no less characteristic. The school labours under serious disadvantages from the difficulty of procuring competent teachers, and the state of blank ignorance in which so many pupils come; it is however making manful efforts to extend and raise its instruction, and the very fact that funds formerly spent in selfish indulgence should now be voluntarily devoted to this public purpose testifies to

an awakened life and hopefulness in the Armenian
Church and people.

A magazine called 'Ararat' has recently been
established ; it is printed at the monastery, and of
course in Armenian ; nor is the press of Etchmiadzin
idle in producing educational manuals, the class of
books which are (strange as a British parent may
think it) at present most scarce among the Armenians of these countries. Doubtless the seminary
will do considerable good, both as a teaching insti-
tution and by acting as a centre of light and influence
to the Armenian population scattered through the
Turkish and Persian empires, some of whose children
already resort hither to be trained. In fact the
same sort of connection between a prelate living
under a Christian monarch and his flock scattered
through non-Christian lands is thus re-established
which the Persian kings broke in the fifth century,
when they cut off the Armenian bishops from their
dependence on a metropolitan who was the subject
of the Roman emperor.

A separate quadrangle, one side of which is formed
by the southern outer wall, and which is graced by a
fountain and pond in the centre, contains the rooms
appropriated to guests, and in one of them on the
first floor, opening off a small wooden gallery, we were
lodged. It was a Friday, but they made no difficulty
about giving us a substantial meat supper, some one
probably knowing that the English do not regard
those church fasts which are so prodigiously important
in these countries. It is really quite a new light to a

Western to find that the chief difference, in the
wilder places, between Christians, pagans, and Ma-
hommedans, consists in the times or rules of fasting.
We stayed the night in our chamber, suffering a
good deal from the heat, and next morning were
honoured by the apparition of an official, who
seemed to be something between a mayor and a
superintendent of police : his uniform was handsome
enough for anything. He followed us round everywhere with the greatest punctiliousness, doing the
honours of the monastery in rivalry with the archimandrite, and ultimately, when we started for Erivan,
sent with us, as a guard of honour, a brace of ragged
but fully armed tchapars, who galloped behind our
telega along the road, and added very much to our
sense of dignity, if not of security. There seemed to
be very few other guests in the convent at the time
of our visit. Probably it was the dead season ; the
heat was oppressive ; there were fevers about ; the
Patriarch, to confer with whom most of the ecclesiastical visitors come, was absent in the mountains.
He is named Kevork (George). At other times there
are usually several archbishops, bishops, and abbots in
attendance, though I fear they no longer work in the
garden, as it is related that they once did. " Forty-
seven archbishops," says Gibbon, " each of whom may
claim the obedience of four or five suffragans, are consecrated by the hands of the patriarch of Ekmiasin,
but the greater part are only titular prelates, who
dignify with their presence and service the simplicity
of his court. As soon as they have performed the

Y

liturgy, they cultivate the garden : and our bishops will learn with surprise that the austerity of their life increases in just proportion to the elevation of their rank."

Formerly Etchmiadzin was the resort of immense numbers of pilgrims, both from the surrounding country and from the Armenians scattered through Asia ; but now, like almost all the great old shrines, like Santiago, Einsiedeln, St. David's, Loretto, it has lost this source of wealth, and has also lost the visitors who halted at it as they passed along what was once the great trade route from Trebizond by Erzerum and Erivan to Tavriz and Northern Persia. The trade from Persia to the Black Sea now goes entirely through Turkish territory, I suppose in order to avoid Russian custom-houses, by way of Bayazid on the south-western side of Ararat. The village of Vagarshabad, lying a few hundred paces from the monastic fortress, is quite an insignificant place, with scarcely any trace of its former greatness. Only one mass of ancient brick building marks the place where there once stood, according to Armenian historians, 20,000 houses, the place where Tiridates reigned, at the time of his conversion, over a powerful kingdom. These Oriental cities, being mostly built of unburnt brick, and without great public structures, perish very swiftly, and leave little trace behind. Usually only the churches remain ; and so here, near the convent, there stand two churches, probably more ancient than the cathedral itself, those of St. Rhipsime and St. Caiana, who were martyred in the time of Tiridates.

Rhipsime was a virgin of exquisite beauty. Accompanied by a band of maidens, she had fled from Rome to escape the addresses of the reigning emperor, whom, as a pagan, she could not espouse. Tiridates was equally smitten by her charms, and when she refused him for the same reason, he put her to death with hideous tortures, and killed at the same time her nurse Caiana.

The other sights of the place I have described as fully as a modern reader's patience is likely to bear, and will therefore say nothing of the cuneiform inscription, nor of the bell which bears, in Tibetan, the Buddhist formula *ôm ôm hrum*, nor of the famous fruit garden. The most really interesting thing in the convent is the library, mean as its appearance is; but people ignorant as we were of Armenian and other Eastern tongues could of course make nothing of it. I cannot but hope that, with the progress of education, there may arise native Armenian scholars who will examine its treasures more thoroughly than any one appears to have as yet done.

The present condition of the monks leaves much to be desired, as far as knowledge and education goes, but in general their monastic life will fairly bear a comparison with that of most Western as well as Russian foundations. It is not squalid; nor is it, according to monastic ideas, rigid, for though they fast a good deal, they do not mortify the flesh otherwise, and have quite shocked Roman Catholic travellers by enforcing no rule of silence. It is enlivened by the visits of prelates and pilgrims from a distance, and now by the existence of the school, which might justify to a reforming eye the retention of the monastic estates, though it is happily needless to fear reforming eyes or hands in these lands of long repose. As no one seemed to speak any tongue but Armenian and Tatar, or in some few cases Russian, our communications with them were very limited. Their dress is becoming: it consists of a long black robe of a thin serge or tissue, not so thin as crape, and a peaked cap, from which a sort of veil of the same material falls back over the neck and shoulders. On the whole they impress a traveller perhaps more favourably than the inmates of convents generally do; inferior as they are in learning and polish to the brethren of that famous Western foundation, the mother of all Western monastic houses and the home of their founder, which is perhaps the chief rival of Etchmiadzin in antiquity and historical fame—the great Benedictine abbey of Monte Casino.

Unfortunately the situation of Etchimiadzin is by no means healthy, placed as it is in an excessively hot plain, on the banks of a stream which, being diverted into a number of channels for the purpose of irrigation, loses itself in fever-producing marshes. Except in the large convent garden just outside the walls, which borders the magnificent stone-faced fishpond, or reservoir, formed by a late patriarch, there are no trees anywhere near; the landscape is bare and open all the way from the glens of Ala Göz and the brown mountains of the Karabagh in the east to the hills of Kars, far on the western horizon.

The glory of the place is its view of Ararat, which rises full in front in indescribable majesty, covered on this side with snow for a good way down. We could not take our eyes off it all the time we remained. Doubtless the neighbourhood of the holy mountain adds sensibly to the veneration which the oldest seat of their faith and the storehouse of so many relics commands from all pious or patriotic Armenians.

The Armenians are an extraordinary people, with a tenacity of natural life scarcely inferior to that of the Jews, and perhaps more remarkable, since it has not been forced upon them by such unremitting persecution. They have been a nation known by their present name ever since the days of Herodotus[1] at least, and probably a good deal earlier.[2] Under the Persian empire they seem to have retained their own princes, merely paying tribute to the Great King, and marching in his armies, as they did under Xerxes against Greece. That the same sort of arrangement lasted on in the days of the Seleucid kings may be conjectured from the fact that Artaxias and Zadriates, under whom Armenia recovered her independence, are described as being not only descendants of the

---

[1] Herodotus speaks of them as living on the Upper Euphrates, but conceives of the Saspeires as occupying the eastern part of what we should call Armenia, placing the latter between the Medes and the Colchians. Perhaps his Saspeires are the Iberians.

[2] The kingdoms of Ararat, Minni, and Ashchenaz of the Bible, the Armenian kingdom of Xenophon's Tigranes, the lover of Panthea, were probably within the compass of what we call Armenia, though the former cannot be placed there with absolute certainty, and we never know how far anything in the 'Cyropaedia' can be taken as historical.

royal house but also generals or lieutenants of Antiochus the Great.　Not very long afterwards Digran,
whom the Greek and Roman writers call Tigranes,
threw off the suzerainty of the Parthian Arsacidæ,
who had become the chief power of Western Asia,
and made Armenia the centre of an empire which
stretched from the Orontes to the Caspian.　As he had
supported his father-in-law, Mithridates of Pontus,
against the Romans, he was attacked and his power
shattered by Lucullus, who penetrated to the capital
of Artaxata, at the north-east foot of Ararat.　None
of his successors was able to raise the kingdom to
the same pitch ; they maintained, however, a sort of
unstable independence, playing off first the Parthians
and then the Persian Sassanids against the Romans,
and the Romans against the Parthians and Persians.
From the time of Nero, who placed a native sovereign
of the Arsacid family on the throne, they had generally rather leant on their Western neighbours.　Shapur, the second of the Sassanid kings, conquered
Armenia at the time when he defeated and took
prisoner the unfortunate Emperor Valerian.　Under
Diocletian it was recovered for Rome, and Tiridates
the Great (of course not the Tiridates[1] for whose
fears Horace did not care, who was a Parthian, three
centuries earlier) returned to the throne of his ancestors.　The conversion of this Tiridates by his cousin,
St. Gregory the Enlightener, whom he had confined

---

[1] Horace, Od. i. 26, 5.　One can fancy Roman quidnuncs talking
about the alarms of Tiridates much as ours do about the Khan of Khiva
or Yakub Beg of Kashgar.

for fourteen years in a dry well, is the turning-point in the history of the nation.

From that day Armenia became the bulwark of Christianity in Asia. Overrun and ravaged by the Persian fire-worshippers, the first race or faith that set the example of religious intolerance and persecution, who at last extinguished the Arsacid kingdom about the year 440 A.D.; then, after the fall of the Persian power, by the Mohammedan khalifs of Bagdad; sometimes supported, sometimes abandoned by the Byzantine emperors, and torn all the while by internal dissensions and revolutions, she rose in the ninth century to be again a state of some importance in the world. The first flood of Arab conquest had subsided; the Roman emperors had even recovered lost territory; the Abbasside sovereigns had seen their dominions seized by a swarm of local potentates. Armenia was now ruled by the dynasty of the Bagratians, a family who claim to be descended from King David the Psalmist, and who may very possibly be really of Hebrew origin. Their capital was Ani, between Etchmiadzin and Kars, the magnificent ruins of whose churches and palaces remain to attest the transitory splendour and wealth of the kingdom they ruled. This Bagratid race gave a line of kings to Georgia, while some of its branches established themselves in Mingrelia and Imeritia. The family still exists, and ranks high among the nobility of Russia; one of them was the Prince Bagration, who was killed at Borodino in the Napoleonic campaign of 1812.

This mediæval Christian kingdom had bloomed in the lull of Muslim invasion caused by the decay of the great Bagdad khalifate. The storm that followed proved more fatal. The aggressive movement of Islam passed into the hands of a lately converted and fiercer race, the Turks, who were pressing in from the steppes of the Oxus. In the eleventh century the great Seljukian sultan Toghrul Beg conquered Persia, and became the master of Bagdad and the protector of the impotent khalif. His successor, Alp Arslan (the valiant lion), overran Armenia and Georgia in 1066 (the year of another famous conquest) ; the Romans of Constantinople, on whom Armenia had leaned, regarding with comparative indifference the miseries of Monophysite heretics.[1] Malek Shah, the successor of Alp Arslan, completed the conquest ; Ani was sacked, and the Christian throne of Armenia finally overturned in 1075 ;[2] while the Turkish arms were carried as far as the Caucasus and the Euxine.

In the repeated invasions and devastations of their country which occupied these weary years, a great part of the Armenian people were driven from it, and scattered over the adjoining lands, especially through Asia Minor, where their descendants still constitute a large element, probably nearly one-

---

[1] The Emperor Roman Diogenes, however, advanced against Alp Arslan into Southern Armenia, but was defeated and made prisoner in a great battle near the Lake of Van.

[2] Others give the date as 1079 or 1046. There is much confusion in the Armenian chronology ; the conversion of Tiridates, for instance, is by some assigned to A.D. 286. The Armenians have an era of their own, which begins in A.D. 551.

fourth, of the entire population; while the void which they left was partially, but only partially, filled up by the immigration of half nomad Mohammedan Tatars or Turkmans, whose villages now lie scattered through Russian and Turkish Armenia. The existence of Armenia as an independent state was at an end;[1] and her later history, which I have neither the knowledge nor the time to describe, is little more than a dreary record first of warfare between the Byzantine emperors and the Seljukian Turks, then of devastations by the Mongols and the hosts of Timur, still later of a long and indecisive contest between the Ottoman sultans and Persia for the possession of these once flourishing provinces. But the Armenian people survived. They clung to their religion with a zeal all the more desperate that it was now all that their patriotism had to cling to. Though a certain number must no doubt have embraced Islam, as the conquered have everywhere done, the bulk of the race remained true to a faith which was no doubt deeply corrupted by ignorance and superstition, but which was their very life-blood, and through many weary centuries of oppression turned to the sacred walls of Etchmiadzin as to an ark alone visible amid the rising flood of

[1] The Christian kingdom of Lesser Armenia, in the south-east corner of Asia Minor, of which we hear occasionally in the twelfth, thirteenth, and fourteenth centuries, lay towards Cilicia and the north-east corner of the Levant, and was quite distinct from Old Armenia. It was founded by Armenian fugitives from Ani under a Bagratid prince. Its last sovereign, Leo VI., a Latin of the family of Lusignan, died at Paris in 1393. Otto of Brunswick, an ancestor of the house of Hanover, was once crowned king of this Armenia. There are still in the wild Cilician mountains some Armenian tribes practically independent of Turkey.

Mohammedan dominion. At last help began to appear from the north. Russia, even before she had established herself in Georgia, had begun to interfere for the protection of the Armenian Christians, and, when she was planted south of the Caucasus, could do so with more effect. The famous patriarch Narses, who was elected in 1843, being then seventy-three years of age, and had been the foremost man in the nation for many years, always maintained that the true policy of the Armenians was to look to and aid the advance of Russia, whether she were selfish or not in her designs, since the rest of Christendom was indifferent, and anything was better than Turkish and Persian tyranny. The event justified his anticipations. In 1827 the Czar Nicholas went to war with Persia, and wrested from her the whole upper valley of the Araxes, including Etchmiadzin itself. War with Turkey followed in 1828: the invaders under Paskievitch penetrated as far as Erzerum, and when they retired on the conclusion of peace in 1829, a multitude of Armenian subjects of Turkey followed them across the border and settled in Russian territory, where, unsatisfactory as we may think their condition, they are infinitely better off than they were under the Sultan or the Shah. I do not say that the Armenians love Russia, but neither do they hate her: she has, at any rate, given them security for the honour of their families and the enjoyment of the crops they raise. The reviving sentiment of nationality, the generally diffused belief that the Ottoman power is sickening towards death, the spread of education, the easier intercourse with the West, the prosperity of individual Armenians in the foreign countries where they have established themselves as merchants, have all of them stimulated the hopes and aspirations of the more instructed classes, so that one even begins to hear of schemes for the erection of an Armenian state. Russia, of course, frowns upon such schemes, nor can any one think them easy of accomplishment. For the native Armenians are not only poor and unarmed, but cowed by long submission, while there is no European people that has shown any interest in them, or even any sense of the important position they occupy, and the services which they may one day render.

At present Armenia is a mere geographical expression, a name which has come down to us from the ancient world, and has been used at different times with different territorial extensions. The country, if one can call it a country, has no political limits, for it lies mainly in the dominions of Turkey, but partly also in those of Russia and Persia. It has no ethnographical limits, for it is inhabited by Tatars, Persians, Kurds, and the mixed race whom we call Turks or Ottomans, as well as by the Armenians proper. It has no natural boundaries in rivers or mountain chains, lying, as it does, in the upper valleys of the Euphrates, Tigris, Aras, and Kur. Of the numbers of the Armenian nation, or rather of Armenian Christians—for the nation and the church are practically synonymous—no precise estimate can be formed: it is commonly taken at 4,000,000 under Turkish rule,

800,000 under Russian, and 600,000 under Persian;
but some think that there are no more than 3,000,000
in Turkey. Others are scattered abroad in all sorts
of places—India, Southern Russia, Kabul, Hungary,
Abyssinia, Manchester. Wherever they go, they
retain their faith, their peculiar physiognomy, their
wonderful aptitude for trade.

In Constantinople and most parts of Asia Minor,
as well as in Transcaucasia, commerce is to a great
extent in their hands ; and they are usually found
more than a match for either Jews or Greeks. Here,
in their own country, however, they are chiefly peaceable, stay-at-home peasants, living in low, mud-built
cottages, or sometimes in underground dwellings,
tilling the soil just as their ancestors may have done
thirty centuries ago, very ignorant, poor, and unambi-
tious, scarcely distinguishable in dress and in some of
their habits, except, of course, so far as religion comes
in, from the Tatars who are interspersed among but
never intermingled with them. Here, in Russian
territory, the women go about unveiled, just as in
Europe ; but I fancy it is otherwise in Turkey and
Persia, where, of course, not merely prejudice, but prudence, suggests the concealment of what may attract
the notice of some brutal official. There seems, however, to have been a curious old national custom
which required women to remain not only secluded
but silent for some years after their marriage. According to Baron Haxthausen, an able German who
travelled here thirty years ago, the young wife is for
a year permitted to speak to no one save her hus-

band, and to him only when they are alone ; she may
then talk to her baby, and after an interval to her
mother-in-law, then to her sister-in-law, next to her
sister, last of all to other women, but always in a
whisper. After six years, however, though obliged to
go out veiled, she enjoys much power and consideration in the household, and if her husband dies, she
reigns in his stead. The worthy German approves
highly of this practice, not only as tending to increase
conjugal devotion, but as rendering possible a system
under which the married sons and daughters of a
family continue to reside in one household.

"Imagine," says he, "five or six young married
women (be it said with all due respect) living together in the same house, should we not anticipate
continual quarrels and disturbance and the loss of
all authority in the head of the family ? No such
thing ; this danger is removed. Women's quarrels
generally arise from the use of women's tongues ; and
it is not easy to quarrel for any length of time in
pantomime, whilst the amusement of the spectators
tends to allay (?) any angry feelings. Even afterwards, when freedom of speech is restored, this being
carried on in a whisper is unfavourable to quarrelling.
In short, to any one who has to manage a large
household containing several young women, I could
give no better advice than to introduce this Armenian
custom." However ancient and laudable this custom
may be, it is fast disappearing, and, so far as I learn,
now subsists only to this extent, that a bride may not
speak to her sisters-in-law for six months after mar-

riage, to her mother-in-law for nine months, and to her father-in-law for eighteen.

It is rather remarkable that whereas serfdom prevailed in Georgia and Mingrelia for many centuries, down till the recent emancipation by Alexander II., there is no trace of its existence in Armenia. Domestic slavery of course there was, as everywhere under Persian and Turkish rule ; but all Armenians not slaves were equal : there was neither serf on the one hand nor any noble caste on the other. While every second Georgian you meet calls himself a prince, no Armenian seems now to claim any title of rank (when they used one, it was *ishan* = prince), or has (so far as I know) accepted any from the Czar—an example worthy of imitation in more civilized countries. Some families of course enjoy special respect from their ancient or honourable pedigree ; and of these there were a few which in Persian times were exempt from taxation, and were hereditary heads of their villages, responsible to the Shah's viceroy, or to the Armenian Melik of Erivan. This personage was the head of one of these old families, and a sort of national chief or judge, enjoying as much power as the Shah or Sardar for the time being chose to allow him, and often appealed to by his humbler countrymen to compose their differences, or shield them from the tyranny of some Mohammedan official. The Tatars had a Khan at Erivan who corresponded in a measure to this Melik, and was probably a representative of some ancient princely house. All this was, of course, swept away by the Russian conquest : here, as elsewhere, the centralized bureaucracy of governors and judges appointed by the government is now in full swing.

Physically the Armenians are middle-sized, with a swarthy, yellowish complexion, less yellow, however, than that of the Persians, who are said to be (linguistically) their nearest relatives, black, straight hair, a forehead rather wide than high, and a large nose. The women are often handsome, with an erect carriage, regular features, and fine dark eyes. The language they now speak differs widely from that in which their ancient literature, dating from the fourth century, is preserved, and in which their worship is still conducted. They call it, and themselves, Haik, claiming to be descended from an eponymous hero Haik, who was the brother of Karthlos, ancestor of the Georgians, and the son of Thorgamos or Thogarmah, who was the son of Gomer the son of Japhet. It belongs to the Iranian group of the Indo-European family, and is said to be copious and strong, though certainly not melodious. Besides the ecclesiastical writings of the earlier middle age, the best known of which is the history of Moses of Chorene, there exist in the old tongue some ancient ballads, several of them containing versions of the Persian legends of Zal and Rustum. The earliest inscriptions found in the country are in a cuneiform character; somewhat later, in Græco-Roman times, the Greek alphabet was used by the Western, the Syriac by the Eastern Armenians, until, in the beginning of the fifth century, St. Mesrop invented the present Armenian character, and thereby, it has been thought, gave a considerable

impetus to the independent national feeling of the
people. He wrote in it his Armenian translation of
the Gospels, now accounted the model of the old
tongue in its purity, but barely intelligible to one who
knows only the modern vernacular, the origin of
which, or rather the disuse of the ancient language
in literary composition, is commonly assigned to the
fourteenth century, when the Turkish and Mongol
invasions had destroyed what little learning or wealth
had been left in the country. There exist a certain
number of recent ballads, sung to national airs, and
some of these airs have considerable sweetness, unlike
the church music, which is singularly harsh and un-
melodious.

In the southern and western parts of Asia Minor,
the Armenians generally speak either Turkish or
dialects of their own tongue much corrupted by
Turkish; but the establishment of schools among
them is calling Armenian back into use, and notably
strengthening their national sentiment. These schools
and the funds of the churches are in each community
managed by a local council, elected by universal
suffrage. The Armenians whom I saw boasted that
in no church was the lay element stronger than in
theirs; even the election of the local priest is entirely
in the hands of the people. In points of doctrine
and ritual the Armenian Church is extremely conser-
vative, and has been wise or fortunate enough to
avoid defining her faith with the particularity which
has produced so many schisms farther west. She
has never committed herself to Monophysite views,

although, chiefly owing to a national jealousy of
Constantinople, she refused to accept the decrees of
Chalcedon ; she has not formally expressed herself on
the subject of purgatory or the invocation of saints,
although the latter is of course practised ; she has
avoided the use of any word corresponding to the
term transubstantiation, so that practically a considerable diversity of opinion regarding the Eucharist
might prevail among her members.

The vigorous life which still dwells in the Armenian
race, and makes one expect more from it than from
any other of the Transcaucasian peoples, has chiefly
expressed itself in practical directions, most of all (as
has been said already) in money-making. Many
Armenians, however, have entered the civil or military
service of Russia, as well as that of Turkey (where,
unhappily, their reputation as officials is not very
creditable ; it is an old remark that the faults of a
subject race come out worst when they are put in
power over their fellows), and some have risen to posts
of high dignity. For instance, the commander of the
invading Russian army in Asia at this moment,
General Loris Melikoff, is an Armenian, as is the
present governor of Daghestan. Their family, properly Melikian [1] (ian is a patronymic in Armenian,
like Mac or Ap), is one of the oldest and most re-

---

[1] Melik is of course the old Semitic word for king, which appears in the
Melchi Zedek of Genesis. It is the same as Malek, or Melek (Adram
Melech, Abi Melech), and has now come to mean prince or merely land-
owner in the Eastern countries. (See a learned and interesting essay
by Sir E. Colebrooke on imperial and other titles in East and West,
reprinted from the 'Transactions of the Asiatic Society,' 1877.)

Z

spectable in Armenia.   There are, I believe, thirty
other Armenian generals in the service of the Czar.[1]
Russia is wise not only in turning Armenian ability to
account, but in thus giving an open career to ambition, which might otherwise find a vent in intrigues or
disaffection.

There is a considerable stirring of intellectual, even
of literary activity, among the Armenians, both here
and in Constantinople.   They see that the time has
come to make their voice heard in the world, and to
claim (however little prospect there seems to be of
their obtaining it) for their unhappy co-religionists
in the Asiatic provinces of Turkey some share in
Western sympathy.   Nothing can be more pitiable
than the condition of these poor people.   They are
not only (like the Rayahs of Bosnia and Bulgaria)
plundered and outraged by rapacious tax gatherers
and zaptiehs, they are also constantly exposed to the
robberies of the marauding Kurds, who live among
them, roving over the mountains in summer, and in
winter descending to quarter themselves upon the
Christian villagers, where they slay and pillage to
their heart's content.   The Ottoman Porte has not
the power, even if it had the will, to interfere.   In
fact, the sheep-dogs are little better than the wolves :
the burning and plunder of the bazaar at Van, last
winter, was the work, according to the uncontra-
dicted narrative that reached this country, not so
much of Kurds as of Turkish soldiers.   Why, it
may be asked, do the Armenians not rise in rebel-

[1] Generals Tergukasof and Lazaref are said to be also Armenians.

lion against these outrages, as their forefathers did
against the Seleucids or the Parthians? Partly
because they are unarmed, partly because the population is thin, with Tatars, Kurds, and Ottomans
scattered among them, but mainly because ages
of slavery have broken the spirit of the nation,
because there is no one to lead them, no means of
combined action, no such prospect of sympathy or
support from European powers as even the people of
Herzegovina or Bulgaria might have looked for. The
same causes, it will be argued, unfit them for independence or self-government. True enough; none of
the subject races of Turkey is now fit for self-government. But the question is not so much whether they
are fit as rather whether any sort of self-government, however bad, must not be better than the kind
of tyranny from which they now suffer, and whose
bitterness is in a measure intensified by comparison
with the peace and security enjoyed by their countrymen under the rule of Russia. The alternative to
some sort of independence for the Turkish Armenians
is absorption by Russia, who already uses her position as sovereign and defender of the Patriarch to
claim a sort of protectorship over the whole Church.
Without being actually discontented, however, the Armenian subjects of Russia are not devoted or zealous
subjects, while those who live under Turkey look on
her just as the Bulgarians do. Better the Czar than the
Sultan, is the feeling of both; but better any sort of
local independence than either Czar or Sultan. Their
remote geographical position renders it difficult for

any Western power to help them, and seems even to have made us comparatively callous to their wrongs, though why European Slavs should be really any juster objects of sympathy than Asiatic Armenians, it would be hard to say. For the present, help and deliverance seem to be far away from the Armenians of Turkey. But whoever considers their history, and marks the signs of awakening life they now show, cannot but believe that better days are in store for them. A race that has endured so stedfastly must have bone and sinew in it. Whether it will develop a civilization of its own no one can predict; but, when once the dying tyranny that has cursed it is dead, it may fairly hope, with its industry, frugality, and quick intelligence, to restore prosperity to countries which war and oppression have made almost a desert.

CHAPTER IX.

FROM ERIVAN TO THE BLACK SEA.

BEFORE taking leave of Armenia, I wish to say a few
words about the Kurds, who dwell scattered among
the other inhabitants through nearly the whole of its
area, and have recently won for themselves a horrible
fame by the massacres which they are using their
service under the Sultan's banner to perpetrate.
They are a remarkable race : indeed, of all that we
saw on our journey, their encampment on Ararat
interested me most. For there is something very
striking in coming for the first time upon that nomad
life which still prevails over so large a part of our
globe, and once prevailed even more widely. The
Kurds are only one, though perhaps the most important, of a great diversity of wild tribes who occupy
Western Asia, and dwell interspersed among settled
agricultural peoples, all through the upper parts of
Asia Minor and the border lands of Turkey and Persia.
From Ala Göz, whose pastures mark their northern
limit, their encampments may be occasionally found
as far south as the neighbourhood of Bagdad and
Aleppo ; a friend tells me he has even seen them
among the temples of Baalbec. To the east they go
as far as Urumia ; to the west, as Sivas and Kaisariyeh

in Anatolia. Though a part of this wide area is called Kurdistan upon our maps, they are nowhere its sole inhabitants. Tatars, or Osmanli Turks, or Persians, or Armenians, always occupy the valleys and towns, while they cling to the heights, seldom or never taking to agriculture, but living on the milk and flesh of their flocks. Their number has been guessed at a million ; of course there are no means of ascertaining it. In person they are mostly rather stout and strongly built than tall, with splendid chests and arms, swarthy complexions, small deep-set eyes of blue or grey, black hair, and a large mouth. The women, who are freer and more independent than those of Persia and Turkey, and are even said to have separate property, do most of the work ; robbery is the favourite pursuit of the men, whose dark faces and fierce restless glance give them a menacing appearance that does not belie their character. Nevertheless, those who know them best believe them to be a race of great natural gifts, apter to learn than Tatars and more vigorous in action than Persians. They are certainly much less fanatical : indeed, many (not to speak of those Nestorian Christians who are said to belong to this race, nor of the Yezidis, or so-called devil worshippers) have the reputation of being very indifferent Muslims. It is a proverb among their neighbours that no saint will ever come out of Kurdistan.[1] In fact, the

---

[1] During the great Mohammedan fast of Ramazan, when everyone is bound to abstain from all kinds of nourishment or stimulant from sunrise to sunset, the Kurds allow themselves to smoke in the day-time, alleging that tobacco was unknown in the Prophet's day, and therefore cannot have been forbidden by him.

theology of many consists chiefly in a belief in
Jinn, Peris, and Sheyts (devils).   It is not from
religious hatred, but simply in the exercise of their
profession of robbers, that they are the scourge
of the Armenian peasantry, whose villages they often
attack and plunder.   Some of those of higher rank
learn Arabic in order to read the Koran ; they have, I
fancy, no literature of their own, except wild songs ;
but their national airs are described as being not only
melodious, but full of a pathetic melancholy.   Their
tongue, of which there are many widely diverse dialects, is, so far as I can ascertain, a distinct branch
of the Iranian family, though it has adopted a good
many Persian words ; so probably there is no basis for
the belief that they are a primitive Turanian people,
representing those so-called Accadian races with whom
the early Assyrians came in contact, and from whom
Nineveh seems to have learnt its magic and a good
deal of its religion.

The first authentic mention of them seems to be that
which we find in the Anabasis of Xenophon, who describes the furious resistance offered to the passage
of the Ten Thousand Greeks by the Karduchi of the
Upper Tigris, about 150 miles south of Ararat.   They
were then quite independent of the Great King,
and carried on constant war with their neighbours,
especially the satrap or prince of Armenia.   Nor does
it appear that they were ever really subdued by any
succeeding potentate, Macedonian or Parthian, Arab
or Turk.   Later writers call them Gordyeni or Kor-
dueni ; a word which appears also in the Hebrew name

Qardu for the country north-east of Mosul, referred
to in a preceding chapter. Their name for themselves is
said to be Kart or Kartman. At present they profess
a sort of loose allegiance to the Sultan, but are practi-
tically their own masters, paying little or no tribute,
and divided into small clans, each of which obeys its
own chief. Individually valiant fighters, they have too
little idea of discipline or concerted action to be valuable in war ; and though news comes (June 1877) that
they are gathering to attack the Russian armies in
Armenia, it will be surprising if their alliance proves
of any real service to the Turks. Those who now dwell
in Russian territory, and who number about 10,000,
live pretty peaceably, and occasionally, like our friend
Jaafar, take service with the stranger, just as the
great Saladin, the only world-famous man whom
the Kurdish race has produced, did in the armies
of the Seljukian princes. One likes to fancy that
among the effete races of Asia some future may yet
be in store for these vigorous mountaineers, who have
never bowed to a foreign conqueror.

Of our journey back from Erivan to Tiflis, there is
little to tell that is worth the telling ; for we were
obliged, having the tarantass as a loan from a friend
at Tiflis, to travel with it along a reasonably good
road, and the only such road was the one we had
come by. Else we should have preferred to cross the
mountains on horseback, by a track which passes
over the skirts of Ala Göz, or to take, going still
farther west, the route through Alexandropol and the
valley of the upper Kur, by which the Russians send

most of their troops to operate in Armenia. As it was, we traversed for the second time the dreary uplands that lie north of Erivan and the stern, silent shores of the Goktcha lake. Only this was gained, that we were now able to see something of one of the prettiest bits of scenery on the whole route ; I mean the lovely wooded glen which leads from the pass down to the village of Delijan, and which in coming we had passed through at night. As this glen is a famous place for robbers, my experiences there may be worth mentioning. Descending it in the dusk, I had walked on alone before the tarantass, and was taking short cuts from one angle of the winding road to another, when the vehicle with my companions in it passed me, and went on ahead, leaving me ten miles to walk. Night fell before I had got far, and with night there appeared an unexpected annoyance in the shape of fierce dogs, which darted out when I passed a dwelling. Every woodman or peasant keeps several of these creatures, of a ferocity that has been famous since the time of Strabo, who says they were able to pull down a lion. Something of this strength they have certainly lost in the eighteen centuries since then, but it was not without difficulty that I could keep them at bay by volleys of stones. They can hardly have taken me for a robber, because the robbers are on excellent terms with the peasantry. I reached Delijan at last, pretty well exhausted, for I was suffering from a violent headache, but at any rate satisfied that the roads of Transcaucasia were safe as far as human enemies were concerned, since here was

a solitary traveller on foot, evidently a stranger, passing unmolested through a solitary wooded glen, whose
reputation for robberies was, as every one after our
arrival told us, specially bad.　This was on Saturday.
What was our surprise to hear on the following Monday forenoon that there had been that morning an
outrageous robbery in this very glen of two Tiflis
merchants, who were seized by a band, and stripped
of everything they possessed.　Was it true?　We
could never make out; but it was reported in all the
Tiflis newspapers, and everybody believed it.

The same Monday night, having driven all day
down the exquisite valley of the Akstafa river, and
over the barren steppe of the Kur, we crossed the
Red Bridge just after sunset, and at the next station
were of course met by the usual tales of brigands.
There had been a band about here lately, and several
travellers had been stopped.　Only yesterday somebody coming this way from Tiflis had seen one or two
armed horsemen peering round a hillside, and had
escaped them only by galloping to the station, which
luckily was near.　After this, it was urged by the
postmaster, to go on at night would be downright
folly.　Such is the perversity of human nature that
the more these stories were told, the less we believed
them ; and probably we should have disbelieved them
altogether could the usual innkeeper's motive have
been discovered.　But a Russian postmaster is not
an innkeeper : he supplies you with nothing but the
indispensable *samovar* (urn) to boil water for your tea.
We listened to these narratives while consuming tea

and our last hard-boiled egg ; and the food, such as it was, was all our own, for the postmaster had none to give us. If you lie down on the post-house floor, you do not pay for the accommodation, but may go on lying there gratis till he chooses to find horses, which, of course, he is usually reluctant to do. In this instance he did not pretend that there was a scarcity of horses, and, as I now on reflection believe, may really have thought we were running some risk. We persisted, however, and he eased his mind by sending a *tchapar* with us as an escort. Next station the same drama was acted over again. The same stories reappeared ; the same advice was even more solemnly tendered. However, it was now near midnight, Tiflis was only two hours away, and our impatience to rest in a civilized bed instead of on a post-house floor made us ready to face dangers more substantial than these seemed to be. " No," we answered ; " you may say what you like, but we shall go on ; to-night shall see us either murdered or in Tiflis. But if it is any satisfaction to you, or protection to us, give us two or three tchapars to ride beside the tarantass." To this the postmaster demurred, and, after beating about the bush for a good while, at last muttered, " We are more afraid of our own people for you than of the Tatars." After this there was no more to be said ; we called for horses, and drove off alone, amid many warnings, first that we would be brought back stripped and wounded, and, secondly, that even if we escaped the band, some stray marauder would certainly climb on to the carriage as we entered Tiflis,

and cut away the portmanteau which was tied behind.   Nothing, however, happened, except that once
or twice in the darkness, for it was as black as a wolf's
mouth, with thunderstorms growling in the distance,
we ran into Tatar carts making for the city, and were
nearly capsized.   At 2 A.M. we entered Tiflis, and
took possession of our old quarters there.

Three days spent in the capital, which seemed more
of an oven than ever, made us not unwilling to set
our faces homewards, since it appeared that the expedition through Daghestan we had meditated would
occupy a fortnight at least, more time than my friend
could spare.   There are but two ways of getting from
Tiflis to Europe, the one that we had followed in
coming, across the Dariel Pass and by railway to the
Sea of Azof, the other by rail to Poti on the Black Sea.
This latter line, opened in 1872, is the only railway
in Transcaucasia ; and now that Russia has, by going
to war, debarred herself for some time to come from
projects of internal improvement, it is likely long to
remain so.   Three other lines, however, have been
projected which would mightily open up the country.
One of these is across the mountains from Tiflis to
Vladikavkaz, avoiding the top of the Dariel Pass by
a tunnel a little to the east of the present road.   A
second is from Tiflis to the Persian frontier, near
Tavriz, passing through Erivan.   This would give a
stimulus to the trade with Persia, and would not be
difficult of construction except in one section, that
over the mountains north of the Goktcha lake.   The
third is from Tiflis to Baku on the Caspian.   This is

the necessary completion of the Black Sea line, and is much the most likely to be carried out, especially as it runs over a level country, where bridging the rivers is the only difficulty. It would greatly strengthen Russia's military position, as well as increase her Caspian trade, and would indeed leave Persia pretty much at her mercy. However, Persia is that already ; if the Russians are foolish enough to wish to annex in that direction, they may do so when they please.

Desiring to see something of the coast of Asia Minor, and especially of Batum and Trebizond, we chose the route by Poti, and on the 22nd of September took our seats in the train for the Black Sea. There is but one in the day, which leaves at 9.30 A.M., and is due at Poti about 11 P.M., the distance being 191 miles. The station at Tiflis lies a good bit out of the town, beyond the German colony, but the houses are creeping out towards it. There may have been, besides soldiers, some forty passengers, few of whom, however, were going through. Running up the valley of the Kur, we soon passed Mtzkhet, the ancient capital of Georgia, with its ruins scattered over the promontory between the Kur and the Aragva, in the midst of which rise two stately old churches, one of them the patriarchal cathedral of old Georgia. For Mtzkhet is admittedly the oldest city in the country. It was founded by Mtzkhetos, son of Karthlos, the eponymous hero of the Georgian race, who was fourth in descent from Noah through Japhet, Gomer, and Thogarmah, and brother of Haik, the ancestor of the Armenians. The Georgian annals present a long string of monarchs from these patriarchs downwards, which after all are just as authentic as George Buchanan's early kings of Scotland, or the dynasties of the Odin-descended Ynglings in Scandinavia, or most noble pedigrees in our own country. Anyhow, whether Mtzkhet is really the oldest city in the world or not, it is a place of vast antiquity, having unquestionably existed long before Tiflis, which sprang up in the fourth century A.D., was heard of. Tradition fixes it as the spot where Karthlos was buried, where stood a great image of Ormazd, whose worship had been introduced from Persia, and where St. Nina, whose cross of vine sticks was long preserved in the cathedral, converted the Iberian king and people to Christianity. In the cliff of soft rock which borders the river, innumerable caves have been hollowed out, evidently by hand, and were probably inhabited before any buildings rose on the flat above. Similar rock-dwellings appear at intervals all the way up the valley of the Kur, not mere scattered hermits' nests, but mostly crowded together to form a sort of troglodyte village.

Above Mtzkhet the railway, keeping along the southern bank of the river, enters a long defile between hills, which are sometimes wooded to their base, sometimes descend to the narrow bottom of the valley in precipices from forty to one hundred feet high. The scenery is pretty without being grand. What most strikes one is the great strength of the gorge in a military point of view. Fearing no enemy here, the Russians have not thought it worth their while to fortify, but even a small force could hold a much

larger one in check in this valley, which effectually
separates the upper basin of the Kur from the low-
lands stretching from Tiflis to the Caspian. After a
good many miles of this narrow glen, the hills recede
a little, and the town of Gori appears lying in a small
plain at the foot of a castellated rock, where a broad
shallow stream comes down from the Caucasus to
mingle its sparkling waters with the muddy Kur.
Here, a little before one o'clock, we left the train,
meaning to catch the corresponding one next day,
drove into the town which is half a mile away, found
quarters at a humble inn lately set up by an Armenian,
and after a while went round to present ourselves to
the German apothecary, Mr. Schoff, to whom, as the
representative of learning and culture in the place,
we had brought a letter of introduction from Tiflis.
Much to our pleasure, we found not only the Herr
Apotheker himself, who belonged to one of the " colonial families " of Tiflis, but a hearty welcome from his
wife, a Franco-German lady, who spoke excellent
English. Mr. Schoff led us through the modest
bazaar to visit the one sight of Gori, its castle perched
on a rock that rises abruptly out of a plain so flat
that you cannot help supposing it to have been a lake
bed, drained off when the ravine through which the
Kur forces its downward way was formed. From the
top of the rock, nearly 200 feet above this plain, there
is a magnificent view over the Caucasus to the north,
most of the great peaks between Elbruz and Kazbek
being visible. We, however, were in ill-luck here,
as we had been at Pjätigorsk, on the other side of

the chain. There was, as there often is in this valley, a violent gale blowing from the west, but the mountains were covered with such thick low-lying clouds that the snows could not be seen, only a long line of forest-covered heights. The position is so strong and commanding that a fortress may well be believed to have existed here from the remotest times; but it is impossible to say what date ought to be ascribed to the existing walls. In the midst of them stands a small and very ancient church, now used as a powder magazine by the Russian garrison. The natives call it the Golden Hill, saying that here the emperor Heraclius kept his treasures in the great war he waged with Persia.

The town below is a poor place, with a bazaar consisting of two or three arcades, and but slight traces of its former greatness in several old churches, one of which shows a sacred picture presented by Justinian. Its population, which is under 4000, consists mainly of Armenians, who abound in the country places as well as in the towns all up this part of the Kur valley, and keep themselves distinct from the Georgians. The climate is much cooler than that of Tiflis, and the environs prettier, so that people have often regretted that Gori was not made the capital of Transcaucasia when the Russians crossed the mountains, especially as Tiflis had been shortly before reduced to ruins by the Persian invaders of 1795. Now that so many public buildings have been erected at Tiflis, it is too late to make a change.

The evening was pleasantly spent in discourse with

our host and his wife.   He was evidently one of the
chief people in the town, having been appointed to his
place of state apothecary by the government, which,
I suppose, considers the supply of medicines a matter
of public interest ; and he possessed a good knowledge of natural history.   At 6.30 A.M. next morning
we started in his company for the place we had halted
at Gori to see, the **Petra of the** Caucasus, the rock-city
of Uphlis Tzikhé.   It lies about five miles off to the
east-south-east, **a distance** which it took our **vehicle**
nearly two hours to traverse, so rough was the **track**
along the hillside.   This telega was the most primitive form of cart we had met with, consisting of a
simple flat board upon wheels, with neither sides nor
seats.   We sat on the edge, letting our legs dangle
over, an arrangement which had the advantage of
enabling us to drop off readily when the way became
more than usually hilly or rocky.   Except for the
name of the thing, we should have gone faster on
our own legs, and the air was so fresh up here that
the morning sun need not have harmed us.   However,
gentility before everything is the rule in the Caucasus
as elsewhere, even when gentility consists in riding
in a cart.   Much of the land in this valley seems to
be left untilled ; what we crossed was mostly open
brown steppe, like that of the hills round Tiflis, on
which the withered stems of the weeds that cover it
were rattling in the wind.   There was not a house the
whole way till we came to a tiny cluster of huts, surrounding a rude old church, above which, to the east,
rose a ridge of broken crags running down towards

the Kur, which flowed along the valley to the south.
Here the Armenian priest of the place, living in a
slightly superior hut, which boasted two rooms and
a picture of the Virgin, received us, and gave us, as
guides, his assistant and the head of the village, an
intelligent old peasant. They led us up the face of
the crags by a steep winding path, partly built up
of stones, partly cut out of the cliff, to the top, where
we found ourselves suddenly in the midst of the city,
a city with streets, palaces, shops, private houses, all
hewn in the solid rock without a fragment of masonry
or a piece of timber anywhere through it. The sloping
side of a hill, or what might rather be called a broad
tongue of rocks projecting from the ridge behind,
and descending southwards towards the Kur pretty
steeply (though much less steeply than the western
face of this tongue up which we had climbed), has
been honeycombed with grottoes large and small,
some mere holes, like those in the cliffs at Mtzkhet,
but many of them regular houses, with large and
handsome chambers, and smaller rooms opening off
these. Two in particular struck me, not more by their
size than by their architectural style and the finish of
their ornament. One was a hall 28 feet long by
26 feet wide, and about 20 feet high, in the centre of
which there had stood two columns, the ornamental
bases of which, and a piece at the top adhering to the
ceiling, were all that remained, the middle part having
been broken away. Along the ceiling, both here and
in several other dwellings, there run beams of stone,
that is to say, the rock has been carved into the shape

of beams, obviously for ornament, and in imitation of the beams of a wooden house. These beams are crossed at right angles by rafters hewn in the rock, the workmanship very fine and true, though simple. This apartment is open in front towards the east : at the back a short flight of steps leads up to a sort of gallery under three arches, from one end of which there is a passage into two smaller rooms of equal height, with windows looking down the western cliff. The other house, which faces to the south, commanding a noble view of the Kur valley, is somewhat smaller than the last, and about 20 feet high : its ceiling is vaulted into a dome, and adorned with deep octagonal mouldings, not unlike those of the Pantheon at Rome, while the arch which forms the entrance is surmounted by a pointed gable, running back to the solid rock behind. Between the top lines of this gable front and the arch there were pilastres hewn and other bits of ornament, which the weather has destroyed. There was nothing to indicate how the front of these chambers was closed, whether by long wooden doors, or by walls of rock or of loose stone, which may have been since destroyed. These two are only the largest and most perfect out of a mass of dwellings, standing close to one another all over the slope, the roofs of the lower forming the streets in front of the higher, just as in the modern Georgian and Osset villages which one sees built on the steep declivity of a hill. Channels to carry off the rain water run along the streets or beside the flights of steps which connect a lower street with one above it. About halfway down the hillside one finds a long, winding, subterranean passage cut through the rock, which leads down to the river flowing at the bottom, and which was no doubt so constructed for the sake of defence. By it the inhabitants could supply themselves with water from the river, while in time of war it might be closed, or at least defended more easily than an open way. Steps were cut all the way down this tunnel, but in many places they have disappeared. This was the only approach from below, as the path we climbed by on the west side of the cliff is quite modern. On that side the place presented escarpments which made attack impossible; it was probably protected by walls on the north and east. The rock is a comparatively recent sandstone, whose strata dip to the south (i.e. away from the Caucasian axis) at an angle of about 20 degrees. It is mostly fine-grained, but occasionally coarse, passing into a kind of conglomerate with pebbles of quartz imbedded.

The city is not large, covering, perhaps, only some six or eight acres of ground, but every part of its area is covered with these dwellings, nor is there one of them, except a small brick church, which shews any trace of masonry. The church is, therefore, probably later in date than the other edifices, though it is obviously very ancient; and this favours the idea that the city itself must be assigned to pre-Christian times, that is to say, to some time before the fourth century of our era, when the Georgian kings embraced Christianity. So far as I know, there is absolutely nothing else on which a conjecture as to its age can be based. The Georgian annals ascribe its foundation to a mythical king Uphlos (*uphlos* means " lord " in Georgian, and *tzikhé* " fortress "), who was the son of Mtzkhetos, the son of Karthlos, the eponymous patriarch of the Georgian nation ; and then, making a leap, they tell us that it was a fortress of note in the third century B.C., when they bring Alexander the Great into these countries.[1] The resemblance which the style of decoration bears to that of Georgian and Armenian buildings of the tenth and succeeding centuries would lead one to believe that it belonged to that time, when Georgia was a tolerably civilized country, rather than to the savage ages, when men dwelt in caves like those in the cliff at Mtzkhet, or like the rude grottoes which line the banks of the Upper Kur at Vardsi, on the borders of Armenia.[2] The absence of a church might be explained by supposing that in some of the numerous invasions which have wasted this country it has been destroyed, as many of the edifices of Uphlis Tzikhé certainly

[1] I need hardly say that Alexander never was here ; the only Caucasus he saw was the so-called Indian Caucasus or Hindoo Koosh of Afghanistan, which is supposed to have been then called Caucasus by his flatterers, wishing to parallel his exploits with those of Hercules, who went to the Caucasus to liberate Prometheus.

[2] One of these grottoes at Vardsi is a chapel, adorned with rude frescoes, and attributed to Queen Tamara ; but of course it may be later than the other caves, which were probably used in her time by hermits as a sort of rock monastery like those of the Thebaid. In Russian Armenia, among the mountains east of Erivan, there are some remarkable little churches and tombs hewn in the rock. Probably the habit of constructing grottoes was a general one in these countries, clung to even when a knowledge of architecture was considerably advanced.

have. One thing is at least clear. The people who lived here were no mere brutish troglodytes, but a cultivated race, with an appreciation of architectural beauty, and workmen capable of executing fine designs with truth and grace. They were evidently familiar with large wooden houses—witness the beams in the ceilings—with the column, and even with the arch. Was it then fashion, or adherence to ancient custom, or the needs of defence, that led them to create a city of caves like this; not in a woodless land such as that which lies round Idumaean Petra, but within sight of the sumptuous forests of the Caucasus?

Returning to Gori, we took the mid-day train, the same which had brought us from Tiflis yesterday, for the west. We had very nearly missed it, for the ticket for the luggage we had left at the station had been lost; and we were obliged to find an interpreter, and through him make a piteous appeal to the railway officials to let us have the goods despite the want of the ticket. Such an appeal would have failed in France or Germany; but with these good-natured people it ultimately succeeded, and they even kept the train, the one train of the day, full of officers and troops, waiting for fifteen minutes while this difficulty of ours was adjusted; an instance of indulgence to unpopular England which a little surprised us.

The line follows the Kur through an open, bare, flat-bottomed valley up to a place where a road runs off southward to Borjom, the summer residence of the Grand Duke, and most fashionable of all the Cauca-

sian hill-stations.   Up beyond it, on the way to
Armenia, the government has planted another "odd
lot" of Russian Dissenters, somewhat similar to our
Molokan friends, called the Duchobortz.   Here a
large part of the passengers, and most of the soldiers,
left the train, and here, unhappily, rain came on,
which destroyed our chance of seeing the snowy
range to the north. A little farther, about three o'clock,
we reached Suram, an ancient town with an ancient
castle, standing at the foot of the ridge which divides
the basin of the Kur, whose waters seek the Caspian,
from those of the Rion flowing towards the Black Sea.
It connects the Caucasus on the north with the great
mountain system of Taurus and Armenia to the
south.   As has been remarked in an earlier chapter,
this ridge has also a great meteorological importance,
for on the one side it obstructs the cold dry winds
from the inner continent of Asia, and on the other
side arrests the rain clouds coming up from the
Black Sea, thus increasing the warmth and humidity
of Imeritia and Mingrelia on its western side, while
it leaves to Georgia and the steppes towards the
Caspian an arid soil and a climate of extremes,
hotter in summer than the Euxine coast, and far
colder in winter. This ridge was the great difficulty
encountered by the Poti-Tiflis railroad.   The English
engineers who made the line proposed to tunnel
through it, but the Russians shrank from the cost,
and characteristically preferred the plan of carrying
the line over the top, which is likely to involve far
more expense in the long run. Every year the

winter snows and spring storms do mischief which interrupts the traffic and requires large repairs ; while the risk of a mishap on the steep incline was declared by the engineers themselves to be serious. This incline is one of the steepest, if not the steepest (excluding, of course, the Rigi line), in the Old World : 1 in 20. The train is pulled up by a Fairlie engine, of course at a slow pace, and descends also very slowly and cautiously. No bad accident has happened yet ; I suppose more people are killed at Preston station, which is generally accounted the worst in England, in a month than on the Trans-caucasian railway in a year.

This ridge, though of so much consequence both in a climatic and an engineering point of view, is not very high, not 1000 feet above the village of Suram, and only 3600 feet above the sea. Its upper part is covered with beech woods, which are especially tall and luxuriant on the western side, where the railway de-scends with terrific steepness into the deep valleys of Imeritia. Nothing can be more beautiful, or less like the scenery round Tiflis, than the long, narrow, winding glens, hemmed in by bold cliffs of sandstone and lime-stone, through which the line finds its way, crossing and recrossing the foaming stream, to the wider vale of the Kvirilla, the principal affluent of the Rion or Phasis. Ruined castles stand out upon nodding crags, which are draped with wood and tufts of luxuriant fern, while up the gorges one has glimpses of forest-covered mountains rising behind, and now and then a snowy peak appearing far to the north. It is a country

the little steamer that lay in the river to cross the shallow bar, so that we were prisoners here till the sea fell, and perhaps for a fortnight. For the steamers which run from Poti to Constantinople and Odessa leave only once a week, and, as they can neither enter the so-called harbour of Poti nor wait outside in the open sea, are forced to lie, the one at Batum, thirty miles to the south, the other at Sukhum Kaleh, twice as far to the north, whither passengers are conveyed by tenders drawing only four feet of water. Each steamer gives thirty-six hours of grace, and, if the tender does not appear by that time, sails on her watery way, leaving the luckless passengers to sicken of fever at Poti before the next one comes. This was cheering. But there was no mistake about the facts. We walked to a point on the artificially raised bank of the river, the only elevated spot in Poti, which is so flat that you literally cannot see where you are, and watched the lordly breakers foaming on the beach half a mile off. We saw the tender lying in the stream, without even a fire in her furnace, and were told by the captain that he could not think of trying the bar. We asked every French- or German-speaking creature we could find whether there was anything that could be done, and were told that nothing could be done except to wait, and that at this time of year, when the weather once broke, it usually continued to blow and rain for days, possibly weeks, together, so that it was likely enough that we might not get out to even the next following steamer, which was due a week from now. We watched the wind swaying the tops of the melancholy poplars, and vainly tried to persuade ourselves that it was going down. We enquired whether a smack could not be hired to carry us to Batum or Trebizond, but it was agreed that no smack would venture out. Besides, there were none. We thought of getting horses to ride along the coast to Batum—that very coast where the Russian troops have lately been checked in several bloody fights by the Turks—but it turned out that there was no road across the frontier, only hills and pathless swamps. So at last we settled down to the conclusion that, if the bar continued impracticable to-morrow, there was nothing for it but to retrace our steps to Tiflis, and go home over the Dariel Pass, and by railway from Vladikavkaz to Odessa, a circuit of about eleven hundred miles. This seemed too absurd to be true ; but those to whom we turned for advice agreed that it was the only alternative. Having at last, then, reached a conclusion, and seeing that there was nothing for British energy to do, we thought of Mark Tapley in the swamps of Eden, which must have been rather like Poti, only pleasanter, and set ourselves to see the sights of the place.

Sights, however, there were none. There is a wretched sort of market, consisting of some booths set down in an ocean of mud, where ill-flavoured grapes and rotting plums are exposed for sale among crockery and hardware even coarser than one generally finds in Russia. Some languid Mingrelians were lounging about, but nobody seemed to have anything to do ; nothing, except a little fruit, was bought or

sold. Every street, if these roads with wooden shanties placed here and there along them could be called
streets, was as wretched as the last, and when the
squalls of rain drove us into the inn again, even its
bare walls and empty rooms seemed better than the
melancholy folk who are so thoroughly in harmony
with their dwelling-place. My friend, who is as near
perfection as a human creature can be, has but one
fault. He is a determined optimist, and has many a
time disheartened his companions by attempts to put
the best face on things when there was no good face
to be put on them. But Poti was too much for him.
We both relapsed into a moody silence, and not a
word more was said about the bar.

The river, white with the mud of Caucasian glaciers,
is as wide as the Thames at Kingston, with, of course,
far more water, but somewhat sluggish for the last
thirty or forty miles of its course through the flats. It
used to fall into the sea south of the site of the present
town, at a place where there is still a big lagoon called
Palaeostom (old mouth), whose borders are said to be,
if possible, more pestilential than the town itself. An
ingenious friend of mine who has been at Poti insists
that the Dragon[1] in the Argonautic tale symbolizes
the poisonous marshes of the neighbourhood, and that
Jason was really a skilful Greek engineer who drained
them, and whom King Aeëtes, like many Oriental
princes since his day, refused to pay for the work, so

---

[1] It certainly is true that this very common legend of the dragon who
infests the neighbourhood of a city, and is killed by a young hero, is
generally found in places where there are swamps which formerly bred
disease.

that he was obliged to pay himself and decamp with his navvies. If this be so, I can only say that things are ripe for another Jason.

The houses are one-storied and nearly all of wood. Ponds have established themselves in permanence along the sides of the streets and roads, soaking through from the river, which is above their level ; in fact, the town stands in water and out of water ; marshes around it for many miles each way, and west winds bestowing upon it 62 inches of rain in the year. It is the paradise of frogs, whose croak is heard all day and all night ; and wild boars find themselves at home in the swamps, where they are rarely disturbed. In such an atmosphere, everything falls to pieces ; so it is perhaps not so wonderful that in this town, which has been a town ever since the time when Medea eloped from it with Jason, where the Greeks trafficked with the Colchian kings, and the Romans had a fortress (called Phasis, whence the name Poti), and the Genoese a factory, there should be now only one relic of antiquity, the ruined gate of a Turkish fort captured and dismantled by the Russians in 1829. Up till that time, though the Czar had been established in Imeritia since 1810,[1] the Mingrelian coast had been retained by Turkey, who, however, made no use of it except for the purposes of the brisk slave trade she kept up with the Abhasians and the Tcherkesses.

We returned more dejected than ever from our

[1] An Imeritian king ceded his realm to Russia in 1804 ; subsequently one of his family rebelled ; the revolt was suppressed and the country finally occupied in 1810.

ramble along the melancholy banks of the Phasis.
Some little comfort, however, was at hand.   All the
great moralists are agreed in holding that the highest
pleasure is to be found in doing good to others.   Well,
a thrill of this pleasure was ours when, on going to
the house of the British vice-consul, we found there
a young Englishman, left alone to represent a commercial house and protect British interests, to whom
the sight of two fellow-countrymen was evidently as
great a joy as his exhausted frame could support.   He
had had the fever so often as to have lost count of the
times, and was reduced by the general dismalness and
monotony of Poti to that state of reckless indifference which the articles of the Church of England call
wretchlessness.   Nothing to do, for trade was languid,
nowhere to go to, not a soul to speak to, except a
Russian police officer.   If our detention in Poti had
the effect of brightening one day in this melancholy
life, then, we felt, we had come to Poti not wholly in
vain.   He was a pleasant, hospitable fellow, and we
spent the rest of the afternoon with him, listening to
his accounts of the Mingrelians and Russians, and the
difficulty of doing business in a country where you
could not trust any one's word, nor get a stroke of
work done when your back was turned.   On his floor
we found a whole sheaf of lately arrived English newspapers, among them the reports of the September indignation meetings, which were then at their height,
and of which, of course, we had not heard a word
before.   The last *Times* contained Mr. Gladstone's
speech to a mass meeting at Greenwich ; what a vivid

impression of the life and movement of the West it gave after the unspeakable stagnancy of these countries.

Business is never very brisk at Poti, our young friend told us, because the Russian tariff strangles import trade, while as for exports—they are chiefly ornamental woods, some dye stuffs, and a little silk and grain—the uncertainty whether a contract to deliver goods will be fulfilled at the time fixed, or rather the certainty that it will not, constitutes a serious difficulty. It is also always uncertain how long your goods may have to lie before they can be shipped ; for no vessel drawing more than four feet of water can cross the bar, and the anchorage is very bad outside. There is no port, though some futile attempts have been made to erect a pier and break-water on the north, or opposite, side of the river ; there is only the stream itself with this fatal bar. Everybody now agrees that the Russian government ought not to have made Poti the terminus of the Black Sea railway, but rather Sukhum Kaleh, at the foot of the Caucasus, eighty miles off, where there is a fair road-stead. Everybody throws the blame of the mistake on somebody else, and accusations of corruption are freely bandied about. All the evil comes from an unlucky mistake that was made after the treaty of Adrianople was drawn up in 1829. Russia insisted on, and Turkey yielded, the cession of her territory as far as the river Tchorok (the ancient Acampsis), which falls into the sea a little to the west of Batum. But when the treaty had been drawn up and signed, and the ratifications exchanged, it was discovered that the

name actually written in it was not Tchorok, but
Tcholok; the Tcholok being a small river on this, the
north-east, side of Batum.   Thus Batum was left to
Turkey, and Russia lost the much desired and indeed
indispensable outlet for the trade of her Transcaucasian provinces.   Had such an error happened in a
contract between two private persons in England,
the Court of Chancery would, upon sufficient proof
of the intention of the parties, have ordered the
deed to be reformed.   But happening between nations,
there was no remedy; and Russia had to make
the best of the seabord that was left to her.   In the
interests of the world as much as her own, it is to
be hoped she may now acquire Batum.   The Turks,
of course, make no use of it, and she may.

However, Russia's loss was Poti's gain.   The place
rose from being a mere cluster of huts under the
Turkish fort to a town of five or six thousand people,
mostly Mingrelians, but with an admixture of Armenians, Turks (i.e. natives of the Ottoman empire),
Gurians from the neighbouring mountains, and Russians.   I doubt if it will grow much more, for nothing
will ever be made of the attempted port, since the
waves carry away the breakwater as fast as it is
built, and the Mingrelians of the plain are incurably
sluggish.   Gifted by nature with splendid frames and
a wonderfully rich country, they live in a state of
wretchedness and ignorance that passes that of any of
their Christian or Mohammedan neighbours, except,
perhaps, the Abhasians.   It seemed odd to have come
"*Phasidos ad fluctus et fines Aeëtaeos,*" and to find

2 B

nothing but poverty where the oldest traditions place
a treasure-house of riches—the Colchis of King Aeëtes
and the Golden Fleece, the spot where lay the isle of
Aeëtes' sister, the luxurious enchantress Circe.[1]   But
these countries have been singularly unfortunate in
their history.   They have been battled for by hostile
empires, none of which was strong enough to retain
them ; and they have, ever since the fall of the Genoese
Black Sea trade, lain out of the track of commerce
and civilization.   Mingrelia here belonged partly to
the all-benumbing Turks, partly to a dynasty of local
princes called Dadian, owning allegiance first to
Turkey, then to Russia, who kept the peasantry in
the most abject serfage.   With their emancipation by
the present Czar in 1866 a better day has dawned
on them ; though the only use they seem so far to
have made of their liberty has been to break out in
agrarian riots, which had been quelled just before our
visit.[2]

Next morning brought a sudden change in the
weather.   The sky was perfectly clear, the strong sun
was raising a cloud of steam from the wet soil through
the still chilly air, and on rushing up to the river bank
to see whether there were signs of movement on the
steamer, we were astonished to discover both to north

[1] Mr. Gladstone has shewn in the chapters on Homeric geography
of his ' Homer and the Homeric Age' that the Aeaean isle is probably
conceived of by the poet as lying in the extreme east rather than in the
west.

[2] The imagination of Constantinople had turned these riots into a
general insurrection of the Caucasian tribes, which was duly telegraphed
to Vienna, and figured in the English papers toward the beginning of
August 1876.

and south long lines of snowy mountains. There had been a heavy snow-fall in the storm of the last two days, and not only the whole chain of the Caucasus to the north down to a height of 7000 feet, but the mountains of Guria and Lazistan, on the borders of Turkey, were covered with a thick white mantle. Already on the bank at which the steamer lay—there was no wharf, only the clay bank—a crowd of intending passengers had encamped, who turned out to be Turkman and Persian pilgrims to Mecca, who were journeying thither by way of Constantinople and the Red Sea. Having nowhere else to stay, they had squatted down here beside the little vessel, so that there might be no risk of her escaping them. Pictures of patience they looked, each with his carpet bundle beside him, immovable as Egyptian gods, and with no more expression on their faces.

There was, unhappily, much more risk that the steamer would not escape at all. Though the wind had fallen, the sea was still high on the bar. We questioned the captain, but he looked at the great breakers coming in with a steady roll—you can just see them from the town over the bushes that line the river—and shook his head more solemnly every time he looked. We packed up, breakfasted, and had everything conveyed on board, with a sort of vague notion that we should thereby add to the chances of a start. At first they promised to try at ten o'clock; then, when ten o'clock came, at noon. Noon came, the hour of departure was postponed till one; one arrived, and though everybody was now on board,

the captain hesitated still. As it was admitted that
the large steamer for Constantinople, which was waiting for us at Batum, would wait no longer than eight
o'clock that night, things looked serious, and we began
again to enquire about the trains back to Tiflis. Perhaps the tender would have never got away, had
there not been another tender in the same plight,
that one, namely, which had to carry the passengers
for Odessa to Sukhum Kaleh, where the Odessa
steamer lay awaiting them. Her more daring skipper
got up his steam, and soon after one o'clock dropped
down the river to try the bar. Then we took heart
of grace and followed, our decks crowded fore and aft
with the pilgrim throng. The Odessa boat plunged
in among the breakers, and in ten minutes was safe
through, rising and falling on the long rollers of the
smooth open sea as she turned her prow to the north,
and steamed away to the Caucasian coast. With this
encouragement, we paused, collected our strength, and
made a rush at the bar. The water certainly was
very shallow, so shallow that one could make out the
sandbanks under the fretting foam that broke over
them, but by good luck we hit the right channel, and
almost before we had ceased to hold our breath, the
foam was behind us, and the bright blue sea all round.
Of Poti, whose houses are not as high as the low trees
that fringe the shore and the stream, we no longer
saw anything except the lighthouse, and heartily
hoped we should never see it again. The conduct
of Medea might have been more leniently judged
if her critics had known what sort of a place it

was she escaped from. A less attractive hero than Jason would have done to tempt a lady away from such a den. But the countless bards who have sung of the Argonauts do not seem to have been strong in local knowledge. From Apollonius Rhodius to Mr. William Morris, nobody says anything about the bar at the Phasis mouth, though it must have given a vessel so large as the Argo some trouble to cross it at short notice, when Medea came on board by moonlight. To be sure, she was a sorceress, and may have known how to lay the breakers or deepen the channel.

Soon after the war between Russia and Turkey broke out, a telegram reached this country which caused the liveliest joy to all who have ever been at Poti, a telegram stating that the town had been completely destroyed by the Turkish ironclads. Like other telegrams from Turkish sources, however, this one turned out to be in excess of the truth. Two ironclads had appeared off Poti, and no doubt might easily have destroyed it, had they come near enough. But the water was, or they thought it was, too shallow to let them do so, and it is doubtful if any of their shot reached the town. However, the inhabitants fled in a panic, so Poti now remains in the possession of its frogs only, who may very likely have ensconced themselves in the deserted houses. Long may they retain it.

From the deck of the steamer this wonderfully bright evening we enjoyed what was the finest panorama of mountains that either of us had ever seen. All

along the north and north-west horizon, the Caucasus
was visible through an arc of 250 miles from the
neighbourhood of Suram, till it sank beneath the sea
far beyond Sukhum and Pitzunda, a line of innumerable snowy peaks that stood glittering against the
clear sky, each perfectly distinct at this vast distance.
In the extreme east there was a gap, where the ridge
of Suram lies, for it is not high enough to be visible
one hundred miles off; and thence, from east-south-
east to south-west, the eye travelled along the bold
and rugged ranges that lie south of Imeritia and Mingrelia, lower indeed than their northern rivals, but
deeply snowed in parts, and reaching 9000 or 10,000
feet above the sea. Highest and boldest among these
rose the serrated group of Lazistan, between Batum
and Trebizond, descending with splendid steepness
into the deep waters. In front of this majestic amphi-
theatre of mountains lay a stretch of low and wooded
land, with a white sandy beach surrounding the eastern-
most bay of the Euxine, whose coast can be traced
trending off on either hand, to north-west and south-
west, in a magnificent sweep. Just behind Poti the
marshy plain stretched far inland; but farther south,
near the boundary line of the two empires, the
hills come down to the shore, and we saw that very
piece of rocky woody ground where the strongly
posted Turks have lately repulsed several Russian
attempts to advance upon Batum. Imagine this vast
landscape bathed in that marvellously clear, still,
luminous air which in these countries succeeds a storm,
the glassy waters round the vessel heaving softly as

they reflected the delicious hues of evening, the line of snows that encircles two-thirds of the horizon gleaming with rose and violet against the last rays of the level sun ; historic cities set like gems round the ample bay from Trebizond in the south-west to the famous Greek shrine of Pitzunda on the north, and you have a picture to which the whole Euxine and Mediterranean can scarcely supply an equal. It is the end of the great line of inland seas that stretches from here to the Straits of Gibraltar, a noble limit to the farthest voyages of the ancient world.

CHAPTER X.

FROM POTI TO CONSTANTINOPLE BY THE BLACK SEA.

IT is little more than thirty-five miles from Poti to Batum; but our vessel was so slow and heavily laden that it was nearly dark when we entered the bay of Batum, and slipped under the side of the larger steamer, formerly a man-of-war, but now belonging to the Russian Steam Navigation Company, which was to carry us to Constantinople. There is no proper harbour; only a semicircular bay formed by a promontory which runs out sufficiently to protect the anchorage ground from westerly winds. Towards the north and north-east there is, therefore, no shelter, and when a gale rises from that quarter, ships have to run out to sea. Nevertheless, Batum is the best port along the whole south-eastern coast of the Euxine, and has been a place of some note from the earliest times. The Greeks called it $\beta \acute{a} \theta v s$ $\lambda \acute{\iota} \mu \eta \nu$ (the deep haven), whence the modern name. At present, however, it has but little trade: the town is small, and I saw but few vessels lying off it. There is no cart-road either inland or along the shore into Mingrelia, so that neither exports nor imports need be expected. In the hands of the Turks it is useless, while, if the Russians acquire it, they will make it the terminus of the railway to Tiflis, and the outlet for all the Transcaucasian trade.   Its transfer to them would, therefore, be really a gain to the world at large as well as to the conquerors, and whatever results the present war may have, it is difficult, especially when one has just come from Poti, not to hope that such a transfer may be one of them. The ground rises steeply behind towards the mountains, which cannot be less than 8000 feet in height, thickly wooded below, rugged and rocky above ; in fact, a most difficult piece of country for an army to operate upon.[1]   These hills run all along the coast, rising farther west to a height of nearly 10,000 feet, and the Tchorok, a strong and rapid stream, seems to come down through them in a deep valley.   I suppose it must be in the delta at its mouth, to the west of the promontory whereon the town stands, that the fevers which infest Batum are bred.   All this coast suffers from these intermittent fevers or agues, wherever there is a bit of swampy land, and sometimes even where none such can be discerned.   But no place is half so unhealthy as Poti.

We passed during the night the magnificent cape where the highlands of Lazistan run down into the sea, and at sunrise Trebizond lay glittering before us, its white houses rising from the bay among cypress groves and orchards.   The steamer anchored to take in cargo at eight o'clock, more than a mile from the shore, and we had plenty of time to see this famous

---

[1] The town, so far as I could make out, was not then fortified, though there was an old castle standing just above the beach. However, the water is so deep that those who control the sea could make the place untenable for an enemy by the fire of their ironclads.

city, which has been a famous city ever since the days
when adventurous Milesians first made their way from
Ionia, coasting along in open galleys, into these strange
seas where races dwelt whose very names have been
forgotten.

It stands on a steepish hill, washed on two sides,
the north and the east, by the sea. Eastward lies
the bay, which is not a safe harbour, being open to
the north and north-east, but affords deep water
and a good bottom for anchoring. At the northern
horn of the bay is the castle, whose ancient walls are
built on a bold projecting cliff. Here, probably, stood
the first Greek settlement, which needed a strong
position to hold its own against the fierce natives.
The mediæval fortress whither the Byzantine emperors sometimes fled from their capital, and where,
indeed, a Christian empire lasted on for eight years
after Constantinople fell before the Ottomans, is a
little way back from the sea, and occupies a flat-
topped, rocky hill between two deep ravines. The
mouldering walls and towers still stand along the
edges of the cliff, festooned with climbing plants, but
the buildings within are gone. Except these walls,
three small Byzantine churches, two of them turned
into mosques, and a few bits of marble covered with
old Greek ornament, built here and there into more
recent edifices, there are scarce any traces of antiquity
to meet the eye.[1] The better houses stand scattered in

---

[1] Mr. Biliotti, the British consul, and a skilful archæologist, informed
me that hardly any relics of Greek art have been found in or near Trebizond. It is always so, he says, in places which have been the seats of
Byzantine power.

their own enclosures or gardens; they are sometimes
two or three stories high, brightly painted, the roofs
red-tiled, and the windows often covered with wooden
lattices. As in most Eastern towns, you frequently
come upon a space either vacant or strewed with the
remains of deserted houses, and fancy you have got
to an abandoned suburb, when a little farther the
habitations begin again. The bazaar is not a series of
covered arcades, as in Constantinople or Cairo, but a
maze of steep, narrow, winding lanes, where a donkey
could scarcely pass, between open booths in which men
sell or work. Except for fruit and for bread, which
is commonly made in twisted rolls or large thin pan-
cakes, there seemed to be no buyers. Most of the
dealers were Armenians, a few Greeks, hardly any
Turks, though fully half the population of the town,
and more than half, they say, of the adjoining district,
is Mohammedan.

There had been some alarms of massacre just before
our visit, the fanaticism of the Muslims having suddenly risen at the entry of a body of volunteers, proceeding from Lazistan (where the people are said to
be wholly Muslim and exceptionally fierce) to fight
against Servia and Montenegro. As these wild fellows
paraded the streets, the Christians fled to their
houses, while a considerable number of Mohammedans
were inspired to join the ranks. Nothing happened
at the moment, but the Greeks and Armenians continued to think that a volcano was ready to burst
out beneath them, and told us with terror that the
governor had not regular troops or police enough

to resist an outbreak, in which Muslim volunteers and
irregulars would no doubt be the foremost. Meantime
all seemed quiet. The presence of the European
consuls does something to reassure the Christians ;
but there are hardly any other Franks in the place,
only one or two agents of the steamboat companies
(the Austrian Lloyd's and French Messageries), whose
vessels call. The trade, most of which is in Armenian
hands, is mainly with Persia through Erzerum (to
which two roads lead) and Bayazid. A certain quantity of British goods, especially cotton stuffs and
hardware, is imported, and finds its way through the
adjoining parts of Asia Minor, but the exports (except from Persia) are trifling. There is little local
industry, and whatever is made is very rough and
poor in workmanship. We looked in vain through
the bazaar for any pretty things to carry away ; even
the modern silver work is coarse, much inferior to that
of Georgia. Turkish is the language commonly spoken,
even by the Greeks, although an old Greek dialect
holds its ground, a dialect which is said to differ widely
from the modern Greek of Constantinople, and to
have preserved the ancient pronunciation in some
sounds. For instance, the first syllable of αὐτος is
pronounced as a sort of diphthong, not *avtos*, as in
modern Greek. The climate, whose heat is moderated
by constant sea-breezes, would be delightful were it
not for the wet mists which, during the whole year,
except two months of autumn, come up from the
sea and produce rheumatic attacks from which new-
comers suffer severely. Snow never lies ; but in

winter there are terrible storms from the north-east,
with showers of sleet and snow, and a short, high sea
that makes navigation dangerous on these exposed
and harbourless shores.

Trebizond dwells in my memory as a sort of en-
chanted city. Perhaps a place seems more out of the
common range of things if, instead of entering it along
dusty roads, you come and depart gliding slowly over
dark blue waters. Its situation is wonderfully beautiful, with the serrated range of Lazistan on the one
side, a group of snowy peaks plunging into a deep sea,
and on the other the bold, bluff cape on whose top
tradition places the encampment of the Ten Thousand
Greeks. Then how picturesque is the interior: the
grand old walls of the fortress rising out of glens of
green ; solemn cypress groves standing all round and
sheltering the tombs of the dead ; glimpses down the
dark and narrow streets, or through arches of trellised
vine, of an intensely blue sea basking in the sunlight.
Such a strange, silent sea it seems, without a sail to
spot its surface : as the city too is silent, for though
there are some few people moving about the streets
that lead up from the landing-place, and sitting in
the bazaar, there is nowhere any bustle, but rather a
dreamful sense of hush and languor which agrees well
with that air of departed greatness that seems to
brood over the place.

Embarking in the afternoon, and indeed barely
catching our steamer, which started earlier than had
been expected, we got from the deck a good idea
of the structure of the coast. Immediately behind

the town there rises a bold hill of igneous rock,
the flat tabular top of which may have been the origin
of its name (Trapezus, from τράπεζα) ; and beyond it
are mountains from 2000 to 3000 feet high. Still
farther back, some eight or ten miles inland, a second
range, parallel to the coast, and thickly wooded,
attains a height of 6000 feet. Over its passes, paths
lead to the lofty table-lands which form the centre of
Asia Minor, and which are mostly bare and dry, rich
in soil and minerals, but very sparsely peopled. All
along to the west for 400 miles the coast has much
the same character. It is everywhere bold, with
scarcely a scrap of flat land except at the deltas of
the two great rivers, descending to the water occasionally in cliffs, but more frequently in steep slopes,
which are often clothed with park-like wood. Behind
the hills that front the sea there is usually a gentler
acclivity ; then a second range of woody mountains,
and through the gaps in these, peeps of much loftier
summits far inland, some spotted with snow, and little
short of 10,000 feet in height. The steamer generally
keeps two or three miles from the shore ; but in this
clear air and sunny weather, it is easy, even at that
distance, to enjoy the exquisite and perpetually varying beauty of its rocky headlands round which the
white wave surges, and sweet little bays into which
streamlets descend through thickets of oak and hazel.
The greenness of everything was most refreshing to
eyes wearied with the bare dryness of Georgian and
Armenian landscapes. It is a strangely solitary
country. Now and again you see houses dotted about

in twos and threes, but villages are rare, and of towns
there are but three or four all the way from Batum
to the Bosphorus.

Next night, the second of the voyage, brought us
to Kerasun, the Cerasus of the Greeks, whence cherries
are said to take their name, as pheasants do from
the Phasis. There we lay several hours, taking in
a cargo of nuts, and by the bright moonlight saw a
picturesque little town lying along the west side of a
high rocky promontory. At daybreak we called again
at Ordu, a smaller and even more picturesque seaport,
where white houses with red-tiled roofs lie scattered
among their corn-fields, vines, and orchards all up the
slope of a high woody hill. The cargo we took in, consisting of beans, was brought out a mile or so in open
boats, and as there were but few of these for the work,
they had to go and return several times. With them
other boats came, bringing grapes, plums, peaches,
pears, and melons, all of which found a ready market
on board. Wild, simple-looking fellows the boatmen
were, wearing a fez with a gay-coloured handkerchief
tied round it, a short open jacket of scarlet or blue,
short trousers, and a purple sash bound round the
waist. Turks and Greeks seem to dress much alike,
nor could we distinguish them by their faces. By
the help of one of these boats it was possible to get a
swim in the waters of the Euxine, which were deli-
ciously warm, yet fresh, and perceptibly less salt than
those of the ocean.

Our third night was spent in lying at anchor off
Samsun, which is the most considerable port in this

whole stretch of shore, though it has nothing better
than an open and rather shallow bay. It is unhealthy,
perhaps because it lies between two great deltas,
thrusting long tongues of flat, marshy, bush-covered
land into the sea, those of the Iris and Halys (Yeshil
Ermak and Kizil Ermak), that Halys which Croesus
crossed under the encouragement of the Delphic god,
who told him that, if he did so, he would destroy
a great empire, but omitted to add that the empire
was his own. Samsun is the emporium of the tobacco trade of these parts, and the terminus of the
road which runs up to Sivas, the capital of a large province. It is a rambling, tumble-down sort of place,
much less handsome and elegant-looking than Trebizond. I went on shore with a Hungarian gentleman,
who had joined the steamer at Kerasun. A long, irregular street, sometimes wide and sometimes narrow,
runs along the shore, but we could find no proper
bazaar, indeed no sight whatever except the remains
of a fine old Genoese castle with mouldering yellow
walls, dating from the fourteenth century. At that
time the enterprising countrymen of Columbus had
the whole trade of the Euxine in their hands, and
owned many a factory and fortress along these shores
as far as the Crimea. There was something of an
Italian look about the courtyard, with its gallery of
slightly pointed arches, supported on columns, running all round ; and in the street a pretty little marble
fountain seemed to tell us that some hand more delicate than a Turk's had set it up. Tobacco fields and
olive yards bordered the road to Sivas, which mounts

the hill behind; in the distance we saw the bold mountains, between which the Halys descends in a swift, unnavigable stream from the table-lands within.

The night following was the fourth of this slow voyage, in which we lay-to during nearly as much time as we steamed ahead. The bright moonlight enabled me to make out, as we passed it, the lofty square promontory, crowned by a lighthouse—rare sight in the dominions of the Sultan—under the shadow of which Sinope lies, immortal as the birth-place of Diogenes, and as the cause, by the bombardment it suffered, of the Crimean War. Its harbour is the best, indeed the only one in all this part of the coast; but we did not call, having no cargo to take in.[1] Apparently it has now but little trade. The last two nights we had been lying at anchor; so I had found it possible to sleep in the tiny cabin. But to-night, when the vessel was in motion, the screw proved too much for me, its shaft bumping and quivering immediately under my pillow in the extreme stem; so stretching out on the deck a Kurdish rug and the skin of an Armenian bear, I slept there *à la belle étoile*, and enjoyed the novelty of the situation. But for the wretchedness of the cabin accommodation, the voyage was delightful; we felt quite sorry to think that only another day and night lay between us and Constantinople. It was not only that such a succession of exquisite land- and sea-scapes unrolled themselves

---

[1] Dr. Radde has noted the interesting fact that the flora of the eastern half of this coast of Asia Minor is of the Central European type, while that of the western half, from the neighbourhood of Sinope W., belongs rather to the Mediterranean type.

before our eyes as we glided slowly along, that every
morning brought a stoppage off some picturesque
village, a swarm of boats full of wild, bright-eyed
fellows round the ship, a plunge in the delicious brine.
The vessel itself was a little moving world, full of
variety and interest. To the passengers received
from Poti, there had now been added half as many
more, picked up at the different ports on the way; and
taken together, they made a kind of Eastern mena-
gerie we were never tired of examining. Towards the
bow of the steamer, in front of the captain's cabin,
which forms a small house on the deck, was a nest
of Persians on their way from Teheran and Tavriz to
Constantinople, some to buy goods there, others to
proceed thence to Mecca. One of the latter was sick,
and tenderly nursed by his companions. They wear
long green or red-brown robes, baggy linen trousers,
and tall, conical hats of black Bokhara lambswool,
with a linen or cotton coloured skull-cap underneath,
and colour their beards, and sometimes their eyebrows, as well as their toe and finger nails, with
some yellowish-brown dye, let us say henna. Here
they sat all day long upon their carpets, frequently
making tea over a small charcoal brazier, and drinking it very weak, out of tiny glasses like those with
which children furnish a doll's house. Sometimes
they slipped noiselessly along to the cabin—two or
three of the richer sort had berths in that vile little
den, and, though perfectly still and unobtrusive, were
not very agreeable inmates when they took to shaking
out their bundles. Sometimes they read out of dimi-

nutive books, but generally they **sat cross-legged**, talking eagerly to one another, and never taking any notice
of the other passengers, much less of the scenery.
There is something interesting in their finely cut faces,
a look, if not of refinement, at least of ancient culture.
Just abaft of them, between the captain's deck-house
and the funnel, were planted their hereditary enemies,
the Turkmans, of whom we were carrying quite a **horde**,
all pilgrims to **Mecca, from** the south-east shores of
the Caspian, **perhaps from** Khiva or Bokhara. **For-**
midable-looking fellows they are, **tall and robust**, with
short, blunt noses, and small, fierce eyes, a complexion
brown rather than dark, and a look which, though
stolid and grave, has in it a latent ferocity like that of
a caged panther. It is better, one reflects, **to meet**
them here than in their native steppes, **where they**
make a slave of every one whom they do not murder.
They sat or lay through the livelong day silent **in**
the same spot, overshadowed by their brown sheepskin caps, seldom, **except at supper, addressing** one
another, and hardly moving, **save to perform** their
devotions, which **they do** most regularly, **standing in**
two rows, and prostrating themselves on **the** deck
towards Mecca at the proper intervals. (The Persians
seemed much less devout.) At sunset **they** wrapped
themselves in their large sheepskin **coats,** having
worn during the day, if it was fine, only a linen under-
cloak, and dirty linen or cotton trousers, and lay down
all together in a tangled heap, one man's head **over**
his neighbour's **legs**. Their arms had been taken
from them, to be restored at the end of the voyage ;

2 C 2

only a knife was left to each to cut his bread withal. It was Ramazan, the month when Mohammedans fast from sunrise to sunset; so they took but one meal, which generally consisted of a sort of gruel. They had no flesh to eat, but some of them refreshed themselves with tea. These pilgrims are conveyed all the way from Poti to Mecca for about £2 5s. each; and their number is increasing every year. Indeed here in the East, as well as in France, the facilities which steam gives for travelling have made the habit of pilgrimage much more general, and pilgrimage has a sensible effect in strengthening religious animosities. He who returns from Mecca is something of a hero and a saint at home, his saintship showing itself chiefly in a fiercer hatred of the infidel. The perceptible increase during the last twenty years of Mohammedan fanaticism is due in no small measure to the stimulus which Mecca, with its sacred sights and furious crowds, supplies. When these Turkmans should have reached Stamboul, they were to be transferred to another steamer of the same Russian company plying to the East Indies, and be carried by it through the Suez Canal and down the Red Sea. A long way round, to be sure, from the southern extremity of the Caspian; but over and above the superior ease of a sea journey, they could thus avoid passing through the territory of their Persian foes. For the Turkmans are devout and orthodox Sunni Muslims, and abominate the schismatic Shiahs on the other side of the captain's cabin.

Still further towards the stern the stray Greeks and

Armenians whom we have gathered up on our way
have planted themselves, together with some so-called
Ottoman Turks, bearing no resemblance to the Turkmans.   Except a few turbaned Ottomans, all, both
Christians and Turks, wear the red fez, and the
poorer ones their brilliant crimson sash, with more or
less of picturesque variety in jackets.   The richer
Turks, who come to dinner in the cabin, are in European coats and trousers, according to the French style,
which now prevails everywhere in these countries.
These cabin Mohammedans seem to care very little
about the Ramazan fast, and one of them partakes
freely of the excellent Crimean wine which the
steward provides; and otherwise, too, gives no sign
of remembering the existence of the Prophet of Mecca.
I fancy there is a good deal of laxity among the better
class of Turks, just as there is among Russians of
the same class about observing the fasts which the
Orthodox Church so strenuously inculcates.   Several
of these Turks have their wives and children with
them, who are made to encamp in a corner of the
deck at the stern, where a little movable railing is
set up to divide them from the other passengers.
Here, with a maid or two, they sit and lie, some with
their faces only veiled, some enveloped in an ample
blue-checked cloak, which covers head and body too,
not stirring from the spot through the whole voyage.
They seem to be unvisited and unregarded by their
husbands, and get their meals in a wretched sort of
way off platters brought to them from the cook-shop.
The children are pretty: one sweet little creature,

with yellow hair and eyes of dark hazel, runs about the deck: the rest lie dozing among their mothers and nurses.

Nothing strikes a Western with more disgust than the way he sees women treated in Mohammedan countries. It is not so much the enforced seclusion that revolts you as the tacit assumption that women are inferior creatures altogether, unfit to be companions for men, but rather to be reckoned a link between him and the brutes, and treated with little more regard than the latter. That they acquiesce uncomplainingly in this view, and assert their power in hidden and crooked ways, does not make the sight less offensive, or the result less mischievous. Although the Christians sometimes adopt the policy of seclusion, and defend it as the only safeguard they have against the lust of tyrannical officials, they treat their womankind in quite another spirit, and feel the contrast in the position of woman to be the most fundamental difference that separates them from the Muslims. Probably it is this which, more than anything else, makes them progressive, while the others remain stagnant. These Muslim women are almost mindless : what then can they do for their children ?

Besides the three main groups of Asiatics (Persians, Turkmans, and Turkish subjects) which I have mentianed, and one or two stray Georgians and Russians, there was a little knot of Franks, mostly gathered at the stern, consisting of an Italian from Trieste (acting somewhere as vice-consul of Russia), a Hungarian

engineer, who had fought in the Polish insurrection
of 1862, a Frenchman, a German, and ourselves.   We
were the only travellers for pleasure, and, being very
curious about the country and its inhabitants, were
made the receptacles of a great many interesting
facts, which we tested as well as we could by cross-
examination.   French was of course the medium of
conversation, as it has now, superseding Italian, become in many parts of Turkey ; but German, Italian,
and English were also heard.   Reckoning in all the
tongues, there were at least eight constantly and
regularly spoken on board ; Russian being the language of the ship herself, though several of the officers
knew some English.   This beats for variety even
the South American steamer from Bordeaux, where
French, German, English, Italian, Spanish, and Portu-
guese may all be heard every minute on the deck.
The mixture of races and tongues is the phenomenon
that at first strikes one with most surprise in the
East ; but, after a little, one comes to consider it as
natural, and the dominance of three or four great
languages in Europe, and of one language in each
several country, as being rather the exception.   With
a curiosity which was certainly not Oriental, and
perhaps scarcely polite, we spent hours in rambling
through this little world of nationalities (one group
excepted, from which everybody was of course
bound to keep his eyes averted), and reflected what
an admirable mirror it was of the larger world
which is formed by these borderlands of Asia and
Europe.

On the fifth day of the voyage we made our last
call, off a charming little village called Ineboli,
nestling at the foot of a steep and wooded hill, where
coal, they say, has been found. Unhappily, the shore
is exposed, with no harbour near. From this point
the line of coast trends inwards, forming the great
shallow bay of Bithynia, in the middle of which is
Eregli, where there are extensive coal beds, as yet
little worked, but worked sufficiently to supply the
Turkish navy. Holding on a straight course for the
Bosphorus, we saw the land recede farther and farther,
till at sunset the beauties of bay and glen and
promontory were lost in the haze of distance, and
nothing remained but a line of grey serrated mountains, bearing dark patches of forest on their middle
slopes.

I despair of conveying the impression of melancholy which this coast of Asia Minor makes upon the
traveller, whatever be his political or religious pre-
possessions. Here is a country blessed with every gift
of nature, a fertile soil, possessing every variety of
exposure and situation, a mild and equable climate,
mines of iron, copper, silver, and coal in the mountains, a land of exquisite beauty, which was once
studded with flourishing cities and filled by an industrious population. And now from the Euphrates to the
Bosphorus all is silence, poverty, despair. There is
hardly a sail on the sea, hardly a village on the shores,
hardly a road by which commerce can pass into the
interior. You ask the cause, and receive from every
one the same answer. Misgovernment, or rather no

government ; the existence **of a power which does**
nothing for its subjects, but stands in the way when
there is a chance of their doing something for them-
selves. The mines, for instance, cannot be worked without a concession from Constantinople ; and to get this
concession, you have to spend months **in** intriguing
and bribing only to find, when you are just beginning
to work the vein, **that** the local governor, **who** can
stop everything, is changed, or that some other official
turns up who must also be bribed, so that **the whole**
process has to **begin** *de novo*. Our friend the **Hun-**
garian engineer, who was on his way back from Kara
Hissar, a town **far up among the mountains behind**
Kerasun, where he had been "prospecting" for minerals, and who, like his countrymen generally, sympa-
thized strongly with Turkey against Russia, assured
us that there was no question as to the existence of
valuable mines all along these ranges, some of which
had been worked by the ancients, but that the difficulties of getting any contract you could rely on were
such that every project had been or was being abandoned. Of course, there is no capital in the country, all
must come from Constantinople or Western Europe.
The account he gave of the condition of the people
near Kara Hissar was **truly** pitiable. **The** exactions
of those who farm the **taxes**, and go about with armed
men squeezing pretty **nearly** what **they** please out of
the helpless peasants, discourage every effort to improve agriculture, and make **it** scarcely worth while to
carry on agriculture at all. Lands are everywhere

falling out of cultivation. Villages are being deserted.[1]
Round Trebizond, as we were told there, even the
better families are selling their old jewels, and sinking
into beggary. There are no manufactures, except of
just so much coarse pottery and woollen stuffs as each
village needs. Owing to the want of roads, it does not
pay to bring corn from the interior for shipment save
when prices rise very high ; and if the crops fail in
any district, a famine follows, because food cannot be
carried to it from other places. Nothing is raised or
shipped from the few seaports except such raw pro-
ducts as nuts,[2] beans, wool, and wax, with sometimes
a little grain. Of course, nobody has any motive to
save money, for it would be taken from him as soon
as he was known to have it. If he does save, his only
security is to continue to go ragged. The police are
few and unorganized (a trustworthy informant told me
that in the large province of Trebizond there are only
fifty policemen to 800,000 people) ; and, indeed, there
is so little security for life and property that the
wonder is that robberies and massacres are not more
common. A sort of traditional awe still surrounds
the government in the eyes of all but the Kurds, who
are practically independent, and wander about as far

---

[1] Even in the larger towns the population seems to be diminishing.
Trebizond was estimated towards the close of last century to contain
80,000, and Sinope 50,000 inhabitants : now the former city has but
30,000, and the latter, I believe, about 6000.

[2] The nuts are mostly exported to Taganrog, on the Sea of Azof.
They go from Kerasun in the country boats in spring, when navigation
becomes safe after the winter storms.

west as **Sivas,** plundering **and** murdering **to their** heart's content.

All this oppression and misery falls upon the Mohammedan population equally with the Christian. In fact, along the coast the Christians are so far better off that they **have** the English, Russian, and French consuls to appeal to, whereas the Mussulmans have nobody. But in the interior, where there **are no** consuls, the Christians are doubtless worse off, since, being unarmed, and without any means of legal **re-**dress (for their testimony may be, and usually **is,** rejected in the courts of justice), they are practically **at** the mercy of a neighbour who covets their vineyard, or an official who carries off their daughters. What cruelties and oppression go on in these almost un-explored regions, which few travellers have crossed, nobody knows ; even the consuls of the coast towns tell you that they can only guess, for though all sorts of stories come down, the details can never be relied on, certain as it may be that some outrage has been perpetrated. **As to** the likelihood of a general mas-sacre of Christians, opinions vary. It would be easy enough, for the government have no troops to check a Mussulman rising, while **the** Christians are timid and unarmed. On the other hand, the richer Mohammed-**ans** would do their utmost to prevent **it,** for it would become the signal for general pillage and confusion, **in** which they too would suffer. **There** seems **to** be **no** doubt that the feeling of Mohammedan hatred towards Christians is now sensibly more bitter than it was at the time of the **Crimean War.** Many causes have been assigned for this. I believe one of them to be a dim feeling that the Ottoman power is dying, and a sense of helpless rage at perceiving that the Christian population, whose numbers do not diminish so fast as those of the Muslims, are secretly looking forward to their emancipation.

On the morning of our sixth day from Poti, the bluff hill appeared which marks the entrance to the Bosphorus, and beyond it the rocky coast of Thrace, trending away west-north-west towards the Balkans. Asia Minor is flatter here than round Sinope or Ineboli, but some miles back a long line of low limestone mountains, covered with wood, seems to run parallel to the shore. Nearing the Bosphorus, we discover the two Symplegades, or Wandering Isles, which no longer inspire the least fear that they will dash together and crush the passing vessel, for they lie fully three miles apart, each being a mass of bare black rocks, close, the one to the Asiatic, the other to the European shore, and quite outside the mouth of the straits. There was a great stir and bustle on board when it was known we were within two hours of Stamboul. The Persians made up their bundles, tying braziers and tea-cups inside their carpets; the Turkmans strutted about in the glory of their re-covered arms; even the Turkish husband condes-cended a word or two of directions to his wife in her sheep-pen at the poop. Stamboul, as the stronghold of Islam, and the burial-place of divers Muslim saints and conquerors, is almost as sacred in Mohammedan eyes as it is, for another set of reasons, in those of

Eastern Christians, and, for a third set, in those of the curious traveller. After all that has been written and printed about it since the days of Herodotus,[1] it would be absurd for me to attempt a regular description either of the city or of the magnificent avenue which leads to it. I shall only remark on a few salient points which a reader may be willing to have recalled to his mind.

The northern or upper end of the Bosphorus is bare and stern. Sharp black rocks rise on either side, backed, on the Asiatic, by steep hills, nearly 1000 feet high, and covered with thick low woods, while the European shore is bare and brown. The sea frets in foam upon these cliffs, for however calm it may be elsewhere, a breeze or swell is rarely wanting here. Sailing down the current, which runs pretty swiftly out of the Black Sea—it is so strong at one point that boats have to be tugged up along the shore by ropes[2]—the breadth gradually diminishes from two miles to about one mile, when we heave-to under the guns of a small recently strengthened battery, and send ashore an officer with our papers. Lower down we halt again off the town of Buyukdere, on the European side, and are

[1] Herodotus tells us of a Persian satrap named Megabazus, who was taken to the Bosphorus, and shewn Chalcedon on the one side and Byzantium on the other. When they told him that Chalcedon was the older town, he remarked simply, " These Chalcedonians must have been blind."

[2] It is now ascertained that this current, due to the overflow from the Black Sea of its lighter, less saline water, is partly compensated for by an under-current running the other way from the Aegean to the Black Sea, and which apparently consists of the heavier, more saline water. The existence of such an under-current was conjectured as long ago as the time of Procopius, but has only recently been proved.

met by a boat from a Russian frigate lying here off the
summer villa of the Russian Embassy, to which we
deliver despatches from Tiflis.   General Ignatieff, they
tell us, is away in Russia ; so every one knows that
nothing decisive can happen just yet.   A little farther
we pass, still on the European side, the village of The-
rapia, where stands that terrestrial paradise in which
Sir Henry Elliot is watching over British interests.
A lofty pile of buildings, with a cool marble gallery
running from end to end, rises from the edge of the
deep, brilliantly clear green water ; behind, a garden,
full of choice shrubs and shadowy walks, covers the
hill slope, while in front one looks right up the winding strait into the Euxine, whose broad expanse can
just be seen, crisped with white waves.   Then we
double the promontory where the mighty fortress
stands in which Mohammed II. entrenched himself
before the last siege of Constantinople, lofty walls
built in the shape of the name of Allah, with three
stupendous towers ; then, as the channel narrows, the
current flows stronger, and we glide more swiftly
between gay villages that grow more frequent, and
at last melt into a continuous town.   The landscape
softens as woods and gardens begin to clothe the steep
hills and embower the white-walled villas, steamers
thronged with people meet us, and light caïques flit
over the glassy floor of this unrivalled street, which
is at once a river and a sea, till at last an amphi-
theatre of hills appears crowned with white houses,
tall black cypresses, the huge domes of mosques and
a forest of slender minarets, with a crowd of vessels

lying below, and the Sea of Marmora glittering in a
wide sheet of silver beyond.

Constantinople is one of those few places in the
world which surpasses all expectations.   It is more
beautiful, more unique, more commanding than any
description has prepared you to find it.   As everybody knows, it consists of three parts : firstly, Stamboul
proper, the city of Constantine, standing on the site of
old Byzantium between the Sea of Marmora and the
Golden Horn (a long narrow inlet off the Bosphorus) ;
secondly, Galata, a town which grew up in the later
middle ages, also in Europe, but on the opposite or
north-east side of the Golden Horn, and Pera, an extension of Galata up the steep hill which rises behind it ;
and finally, on the other or Asiatic side of the Bosphorus, the towns of Scutari and Kadikeui (Chalcedon),
with their far-stretching suburbs.   This immense mass
of houses covering the three shores, and running far up
along the margin of the Bosphorus in a continuous
street, gives the impression of a vast population, far
larger than the 800,000 at which the inhabitants are
commonly estimated.   I do not suppose that Paris,
with its million and a half of people, spreads over a
wider area.   But then, though the streets of Constantinople are narrow, there are huge empty spaces
scattered through it, covered by ruined houses, or
gardens, or graveyards, so that great part of the surface is not really occupied by the living at all.   However, this sense of a teeming multitude round you
adds to the grandeur of the view.   Nobody knows the
proportions which the various elements of this popu-

lation bear to one another. The Armenians reckon themselves at 200,000, the Greeks are nearly as numerous, the Mohammedans more numerous, probably 350,000 ; the balance consists of Bulgarians and Franks. Stamboul proper and Scutari are the Muslim quarters *par excellence* (though there are some Christians in Stamboul too), Pera and Galata the Christian. On the top of Pera hill stand the winter palaces of the ambassadors—tremendous piles, among which our own and that of the German envoy are the largest, and have occupied the finest sites. Their conspicuous position towering among the houses of the Franks over against the decaying palaces and offices of the Sublime Porte on the crest of Stamboul aptly typifies the sort of protectorate which the powers of Europe have assumed over the Sultan, and the independent jurisdiction their representatives claim in this strange town. Constantinople indeed is not a city, but several cities, distinct communities dwelling together, but not mingling, since they have neither feelings nor interests to unite them. Or, rather, it is a huge caravanserai, where men of all nations meet for business or pleasure, and abide for days or years without feeling it a home. It has no corporate existence for them, nor can they have any local pride in it. What sort of municipal feeling can be looked for in a town where one-half the inhabitants call the other half dogs, and that other half is constantly expecting to be set upon and massacred ?[1]

---

[1] I was told in the end of September that there had been several panics among the Christians ; but, so far as a passing traveller could

It is pleasanter to return for a moment to the external aspect of the place. Constantinople has two glories— the glory of the mountains, and the glory of the sea. In every landscape the background is formed by the bold heights of Scutari and the more distant Mysian Olympus, with its snowy summit cutting the clear air like mother-of-pearl. In the city itself there is scarcely a yard of level ground. Old Stamboul is built on a long ridge rising some two hundred feet above the waters that lave it on either hand, a ridge whose top, indented by hollows and crowned by massive mosques and graceful white minarets, with here and there a pile of ancient ruin, offers a sky-line always changing as the beholder moves, but always beautiful. Then no city has such a sea—a sea deep to its very margin, intensely clear, intensely blue, penetrating everywhere, till you can hardly recognize its arms ; a sea that narrows to a river in the Golden Horn and Bosphorus, and spreads into a shoreless expanse in the broad Propontis, studded with shining isles. The central

judge, their fears, however real, were not quite justified by anything the Mohammedans had yet said or done. An atmosphere of terror and wonder grows up in such a place at such a time—indeed it always exists in the East—in which unreasonable fears are entertained. I was warned that it was dangerous to pass alone through Stamboul by day, and wandered into it at night without experiencing any difficulty except from the want of lamps and the abundance of sleeping dogs. I was forced to take the *cavass* of the Sublime Porte (a sort of soldier porter who is sent with strangers, and receives a heavy fee) with me to St. Sophia, being told that a Christian entering it unprotected might be torn to pieces ; and next day happening to pass it again, and having a sudden longing for another glimpse of Justinian's church, I procured an entrance by the simple means of tendering a medjidi (a coin worth 4s. 6d.) to the doorkeeper, and saw the Mohammedan worship proceeding to my heart's content.

spot of every view is the spot where these three waters meet, Seraglio Point, where the first Greek colonists built their Byzantium, where afterwards stood the palace of the Eastern Caesars, and where now stand the ruins of the fortress palace of the Ottoman Sultans; a wilderness of broken walls and towers, with cypress groves between, and the dome of St. Sophia rising behind. No spot on earth has seen so much history and so much crime as this, where dynasties of tyrants have reigned for sixteen weary centuries.

It has become a commonplace to say that the traveller ought to admire Constantinople from the sea, and then depart without landing, lest the spell be broken. A more foolish commonplace it would be hard to find. Constantinople is just as wonderful within as it is from outside. No doubt there is much to disgust and repel a stranger; much dirt, neglect, vice, and even ugliness. But there is far more to excite his curiosity and touch his imagination. Its mosques, its tombs, its crooked, rugged streets, with their crumbling houses of every tint, interrupted here by a spreading plane tree, there by a grand old Byzantine arch or cistern; its bridge of boats, over which a many-tongued crowd streams incessantly; its Fields of the Dead shaded by gloomy cypresses; its gardens green with vines and ruddy with pomegranates; above all, those majestic walls and towers, that have stood untouched since the fatal day of Mohammed the Second's conquest—all these and many more details of its inner form and life are as picturesque, as full of endless

interest and charm, as the view from the bosom of the
sea is noble and imposing.   Modern improvement has
not yet laid its destroying finger on this accumulated
wealth of beauty, the gift of many ages and races, as
it too surely will when the Turkish dominion ends.
If ever a war is undertaken on behalf of Constantinople, let us understand that it is not for the sake of
the Turks, but for aesthetic reasons only : to preserve
the loveliness of a city that is unique in the world
and could never be replaced.

CHAPTER XI.

SOME POLITICAL REFLECTIONS.

THOUGH I have not written this book with any political purpose, I am unwilling to lose the opportunity of stating the conclusions to which, as it seems to me, any unprejudiced observer must be led by travelling through Russia and Asiatic Turkey. Seeing is like nothing else. I do not mean that it necessarily gives one new ideas ; indeed, the largest and most careful study of these countries could hardly enable a man to develop any views absolutely new on a question which has been so thoroughly thrashed out during the last few years. But seeing with one's own eyes and hearing people on the spot talk—people who are, so to speak, themselves part of the problem—brings home to one certain facts and principles with a force and clearness which no amount of reading can give. One seems to perceive better what are the main and essential, what the secondary and accidental, factors in the problem. I will therefore try to state, as shortly as possible, the main impressions which this journey gave me as to the condition and prospects of Transcaucasia and the adjoining provinces of Turkey, the attitude of Russia, and the interests of England, premising only that I went with a mind which, so far as it was prejudiced, was prejudiced against Russia, which I had learnt from childhood to look upon as the enemy of freedom, the power which oppressed Poland, and had enabled Austria to crush Hungary.

Respecting Transcaucasia, I have little to add to what has been said in an earlier chapter. It is not a prosperous country, yet signs of improvement may be discovered, and it is infinitely better off now than formerly under its own princes, or under the rule of Sultan and Shah. Life and property are secure. One railway has been made, and others are projected ; commerce and industry are backward, yet not absolutely stagnant. Antagonisms of race and religion are far less fierce than in Turkey, Mohammedan races living contentedly under a Christian government. European ideas and inventions are beginning to be known, and may in time lay hold of the still sluggish minds of the people. The two great obstacles to moral and material progress are the want of schools, which the government is just beginning to establish more generally, and the co-existence—I can hardly say mixture—in the population of so many diverse and mutually repellent elements. Each race, Georgians, Armenians, Tatars, Persians, Lesghians, Mingrelians, Russians, Germans, is too weak numerically to absorb the rest, and too distinct in religion, language, and habits to blend on equal terms with any of the others. This is a phenomenon that constantly meets one in Eastern countries, and deserves more attention than it has received, as being not only a consequence, but a cause, of their unprogressive state.

For while in civilized Europe a small nation, if it be self-governing, is quite as likely to thrive as a large one, it is otherwise in regions so poor, so ill-governed, and so much exposed to the attacks of their neighbours as these are. Every great Oriental state has certainly shown itself bad enough, but to a large and powerful people there are always given chances which a small people cannot have.

The difficulty of fusing these races, or even of uniting them under a common system of law and administration, lies in the fact that the one force which controls them, the one channel in which most of their life flows, is religion. They have no patriotism, in our sense of the word, for they have neither a historical past (being mostly too ignorant for that conception) nor a country they can call exclusively their own. Religion is everything, since it includes their laws, their literature, and their customs, as well as their relation to the unseen world ; and religion is not a fusing but a separating, alienating, repellent power. In ancient times there were in Western Asia and Europe pretty nearly as many religions as there were races, but these religions were not mutually exclusive, and required from their believers no hostility to other deities. Hence the ease with which the Roman empire drew so many diverse nations into its bosom, and formed out of them a sort of new imperial nationality. The rise of Christianity altered all this, since it claimed to be a world religion, which could own and brook no rival. Mohammedanism repeats the same claim, with a fierceness which the comparative barbarism of its professors has in the course of time rather intensified than diminished, while Christianity has learnt to look with more tenderness or apathy on forms of error. The different sects of Eastern Christians, though united in their aversion to Islam, from which they have suffered so much, have quite enough mutual jealousy to prevent any cordial political union. Greeks, Russians, Armenians, Bulgarians, would each and all of them prefer a Mohammedan government to that of any of the others, if such a government were a less detestable tyranny than that of the Sublime Porte now is. The problem is one far more difficult than Western or Central Europe had to deal with in the Dark Ages, when so many different races lay weltering together on the same territories, for then the omnipresent, all-pervading power of the Church was a unifying and assimilating power, which formed new nations by linking men of different blood and speech in the bond of a common faith. Here the force of religion is a centrifugal force : its lessons are fear and hatred.

To return from this digression to Transcaucasia, it may be said that the process of fusion which cannot but be supposed indispensable to its ultimate well-being has scarcely begun, and will necessarily be a very slow one. But in the mean time Russia, though her government is mainly military, is not altogether neglecting her duties to the people. She has emancipated the serfs, and substituted regular local courts for the old feudal jurisdictions which were even less pure and certainly more oppressive. She has exerted herself to foster various branches of industry with more zeal than success, and, by creating security, has made it possible for foreign capital and enterprise to flow into the country. No doubt there is a good deal of corruption, a good deal of over-government and bureaucratic pedantry. But the laws are mild and equal for all subjects; and as there is no disaffection, I do not think there can be much oppression. Even in religious matters, while certain advantages are accorded to the dominant church, the worst evil a Roman Catholic or Protestant suffers is that he is forbidden to proselytize, and, if he marries a wife of a different persuasion, must suffer his children to be brought up in the Orthodox Eastern faith. Hardships, no doubt, these are, but hardships trifling compared to those which we were recently inflicting on Roman Catholics in Ireland. The Russian Church has never been theologically intolerant, but religion and loyalty or patriotism— words which mean much the same thing to a Russian —are so closely intertwined that one must not expect the lesson of religious liberty to be learnt in a day.

Russia's difficulties in the Caucasian countries, as in her other Asiatic provinces, arise from the want of two things, men and money. She has not got men to spare for colonization, seeing that, in addition to Siberia, Turkestan, and her newly acquired vast and fertile territories on the river Amur, she has far more land at home than there are people to cultivate it. When he can have a rich farm on the Don or Lower Volga for next to nothing, the peasant is not likely to cross the Caucasus or the deserts of Central Asia. Of all the states of Europe, there is none that has so little

motive to conquer or annex as Russia, for she has
already far wider territories than she can turn to account for centuries to come. Then she wants money.
In old Russia itself there is a vast deal still to do, and
the money to do it is not in the country, but, like
that which made the railways, must enter from the
West. Every annexation costs her far more than
it brings in. The process of buying land with money
raised on mortgage is one that cannot go on long when
you are paying seven per cent. for the money and
getting next to nothing from the land. In fact, Russia
has for the last twenty years or more been making
bold drafts on the future, which it is by no means
certain that the future will meet. She cannot continue indefinitely the practice of renewing these bills
at increasingly heavy rates ; and there are only three
possible courses open to her : repudiation and total
loss of credit, a disgrace which it is not to be supposed
she will ever bring herself to face ; heavier taxation,
which so poor a country as Russia still is could not
bear (it would at least make the government very
unpopular, and check the rising domestic industries) ;
and, thirdly, retrenchment. As Russian finance is practically out of the reach of criticism (though what
purport to be the public accounts are published every
year), no one can quite tell the present state of affairs,
but it is understood that the most which the ministers
claim is that they had very nearly or quite succeeded,
when the present war broke out, in escaping the deficit
of former years. The debt, as everybody knows, is
already very large, and most of it recent.

In these circumstances not only war, but conquest also, is obviously against Russia's interest. In fact, annexation is even more pernicious than war, since it involves a constant drain of money which lasts when the temporary excitement of war is over and the people are no longer willing to make sacrifices for a present and exciting object. She might have made all her railways with the money she spent in subduing the mountaineers of the Caucasus, but when once she had occupied the country on each side of the chain, that subjection became necessary to secure peace. In Central Asia a piece of work of the same kind, and probably no less costly, lies before her. All this is, of course, perfectly well known and foreseen by intelligent Russians, who cannot understand why foreigners should not credit them with perceiving what is so obvious. It is felt most strongly by the Emperor and his advisers, on whom a responsibility rests such as no statesman in a parliamentary country is ever required to face. It made them hang back from war when the popular excitement against the Turks, who had perpetrated the Bulgarian massacres and seemed on the point of crushing Servia and Montenegro, was blazing high over the whole country. They were ultimately unable to avoid war, because the other European powers did not join them in threatening Turkey with a joint attack, to which, of course, she must have yielded, while they had given pledges it was impossible to recede from. But wholly apart from any question as to Austrian susceptibilities about the Danube, or English susceptibilities about

the Dardanelles, their **domestic interests clearly pre-**
scribe a policy of abstinençe **from annexation. To**
add any large territory, **either in Asia** or Europe, to
their already overgrown empire, would be to undertake responsibilities which they are not equal to, and
under which their system might well break down.

Maps have a great dèal to answer **for in** clouding
men's minds. When a **boy** looks at a map, he fancies
that the country which covers the most space on it is
the most powerful. **It is** wonderful how many **of us**
remain boys in this regard. Because Russia's dominions stretch over a vast space **on the surface of the**
globe, an utterly fallacious notion of her resources has
been generally accepted in the **rest of** Europe. She
has undoubtedly the elements of **one day** becoming a
very powerful monarchy. **But for** modern warfare,
which is, above all things, **a matter** of money and
science, she is probably less strong than the weakest
of the three other great military states of the continent. And **for** the administration of semi-civilized
territories, **she is** still more unfitted, having no such
stock of able, vigorous men, with well trained minds,
as we send every **year** to India. The highly educated
Russians (i.e. the **true** Russians, **for I** except the
Germans) are often brilliant, but almost always super-
ficial ; the great mass are not **only** ignorant, but,
with all their natural cleverness, incapable of steady,
solid, intellectual work, even work of a very humble
kind, improvident, impatient. In European Russia,
Germans are promoted over their heads ; in Transcaucasia, they are considered inferior, as officials, to

the Armenians. They strike you, also, as wanting initiative, I mean that moral initiative which depends on a resolute and tenacious will, that does not fear responsibility. They are a bright people, a good-natured people, a likeable people, indeed a gifted and attractive people ; but somehow you do not feel them to be a strong people, whom a race like the English or the German need fear in the long run. The Russians, therefore, with all their versatility and quickness, are not yet, and will not for many years to come, be thoroughly civilized. Till they become so, they may govern, but they must remain unable not only to civilize the races on a lower level, but even to give to those races such an impulse towards material progress as will make them profitable subjects, a strength to the empire instead of a mere dead-weight impeding its onward march. Besides, Russia has problems at home more than sufficient to absorb the energies and tax the wisdom of her statesmen, land questions raised by the recent emancipation of the serfs; labour questions, which the socialist party, not yet numerous, but active, is bringing before the people ; religious questions ; constitutional questions, which the establishment of local assemblies has helped to pose, and which will certainly rise into greater importance. These facts are so well known and weighed by thoughtful men in Russia herself that they find it hard to understand why territorial aggression should be so constantly assumed to be the chief object of their national policy. It is easy to shew them that the steady advance of their frontier accounts for the existence of such a belief; easy, also, to remind them that there are plenty of people among themselves, and especially in the army, who still desire conquest. But the main facts remain, which I take to be indisputable: first, that Russia is far less powerful for attack than she is believed to be; secondly, that further conquests will only injure and weaken her. Either, therefore, she will abstain, or, if she does not, she will suffer for it, and be all the more likely to break up, all the less formidable in future to her neighbours.

These are considerations which must, I think, force themselves upon every one who travels in Russia, but perhaps most clearly on one who observes her government in her lately acquired Asiatic provinces. They ought to dictate, they must necessarily influence, her policy not only towards the Porte, but towards her Asiatic neighbours generally. Let me now try to state, with the same brevity, the impressions produced by what one sees and hears in Asiatic Turkey and Constantinople. I pass over the European provinces which I visited, because we have lately heard so much in England about European Turkey that no more is needed.

The first thing that strikes you—you have been told it a hundred times, and yet it strikes you fresh like a discovery—is that in Turkey there is one country, but many nations. The Turks, or (as we ought rather to say) the Mohammedans, are not Turkey any more than the Protestants beyond St. George's Channel are Ireland, and have no more claim to be considered as the representatives of the

people; in fact less, for they are not the most intelligent and industrious part of the population. They
are one out of several nations dwelling on the same
soil, but not intermarrying or otherwise mingling, and
having nothing in common except mutual hatred. It
is therefore a profound error to extend to them that
sympathy which is given to a people resisting foreign
invasion, even in an unjust cause, for the country they
defend is not theirs. In the present war they are quite
as much invaders as the Russians, and their expulsion,
not their triumph, would be the true "liberation of the
territory." This is so, not because they came as conquerors, for most parts of Europe are held by the
descendants of conquerors, but because they have
remained a conquering military caste, refusing equal
civil rights to their subjects, maltreating and oppress-
ing them in every conceivable way, and maintaining
their ascendancy neither by superior numbers nor
superior civilization, but by the power of the sword.
They are still, in fact, a hostile army encamped among
unarmed subjects who detest them, and are kept in
check partly by the want of arms and courage, partly
by their own intestine jealousies. This is most con-
spicuously the case in Europe and the islands, where
the Muslims are in a comparatively small minority;
but it is also true of Asia Minor and Syria, where
they are equal, or nearly equal, in numbers to the
Christians; and it only ceases to be true in the lower
valleys of the Tigris and Euphrates, where the Christians are comparatively few.

Of course I do not mean to ascribe this to the

national character of **the so-called Osmanli Turks as
an** intruding race from **the steppes of Turkestan ;**
for they are **not** really **Turks at all.** Very little
Turkman blood flows in the veins of the modern
Mohammedan population of Asia Minor and Europe ;
hardly more perhaps than **there is of** Frankish blood
in the modern French. **That** population is composed
mainly of the descendants of those subjects[1] of the
Eastern Roman **empire who** embraced Islam **as the**
tide of Seljukian and Ottoman conquest advanced
westward and northward, partly also of the mongrel
race which has sprung from the marriages of Osmanlis
with the Greek, Georgian, Circassian, and Slavonic
captives brought in by the perpetual slave trade ; **and**
of janizaries, the offspring of Christian parents seized
in childhood, and brought up as Mohammedans. How
little of the true Turk there is in the modern Ottoman may be seen by any one who will compare the
heavy languid faces and flabby figures of the Turkish
royal family, for instance, with their drooping eyelids, smooth foreheads, and sensual rounded outlines,
and the **firm, hard,** angular bony features, small, fierce,
restless eyes and well-knit frames of the **genuine**
Turkman or Tatar of the Aral or Caspian steppes.[2]

[1] Those Byzantine subjects were themselves a greatly mixed race,
consisting partly of the primitive inhabitants of Asia Minor and Thrace
Hellenized under Macedonian and Roman rule, partly of a heteroge-
neous slave population brought into the empire from all the surrounding
countries.

[2] There are still some Turkman tribes who wander about Asia Minor
with their flocks and herds, but they do not mix at all with the other
inhabitants. There are also several places in Asia Minor where you
may see a few genuine Turks still remaining, just as in the valleys of

It is not a matter of race, but of religion, which is far more serious. No Mohammedan race or dynasty has ever shewn itself able to govern well even subjects of its own religion; while to extend equal rights to subjects of a different creed is forbidden by the very law of its being.

The result is that, when foreign armies enter, whether it be Bulgaria or Armenia, they are welcomed as deliverers by the subject population; and when they retreat, it is upon those unhappy subjects that the inhuman vengeance of the Turkish soldiery is wreaked. In Armenia, at this moment, a timid and inoffensive people who have never meditated insurrection, who are not even accused of anything more than sympathy with the invaders, are being slaughtered by thousands in their blazing villages. I dare say the generals in command have not ordered or approved these massacres and torturings. That they are the spontaneous acts of irregular soldiers, perpetrated on their own unarmed fellow subjects, makes them an even more dreadful evidence of the condition of the Turkish empire.

The second fact, which comes home with unexpected force to the traveller who sees even a little of Asiatic Turkey, is, that the Turkish government is dying. It has been sick for a long time; and it may have yet a good many years to linger. But it is not the less certain that the sickness is incurable. It has no

the Asturias villages occur where the blue eyes and light hair of the people shew the permanence of a Gothic type; but these are rare exceptions.

money, and, having lost its credit, has no chance of
getting any more from the West. Little can be raised
by taxation, for the country is poor in quite a different
sense from that in which Russia is poor—the sense of
having absolutely no presently available resources :
a thin population, the best part of which has been
through large districts either massacred or drawn off
to perish in battle ; mines that have not been opened
for want of capital ; a soil only a small part of which
is now under cultivation ; a total want of roads and
railways. There are really no rich people, except a
few Greek and Armenian merchants in Constantinople,
and a knot of palace favourites who have fattened on
the spoils of the provinces ; and very few even moderately well off. Worse even than the want of money is
the want of capable and honest administrators, or of
any tolerable machinery of government. There is no
aristocracy either of birth[1] or wealth from which administrators or ministers could be drawn. Office has
for many years past been given to palace favourites,
who have climbed into power by the interest of their
female relatives, or by subservience to some already
established favourite. Among such men corruption
is so natural that it is not surprising to find it all but
universal ; so that even if a tolerable administrative
system were introduced, it could not be worked for
lack of diligent and upright officials. To suppose
that the men now in power would consent to have

---

[1] The old local aristocracy of the Beys is pretty nearly gone in most
places, and has been so entirely excluded from administrative functions
as to be unfit to assume them.

themselves ejected in favour of Franks is to suppose
them willing to save the state by sacrificing all that
the state means to them, all that makes it in their
eyes worth the saving. The fact is that the Turkish
empire would, like so many other Oriental monarchies,
have been broken to pieces long ago either by conquest from without, had not the jealousies of the
European powers maintained it, or by revolts within
(such as that of Mehemet Ali), had not the plan been
adopted of never leaving a governor more than two or
three years in the same spot, and did not the presence
of the Christians dispose all Muslims to see their
safety in sticking to the central government.

The Mohammedans of Turkey are not without
their good qualities ; and in point of sobriety, industry, and honesty, the peasantry of Asia Minor, at
least, may be favourably compared with those of some
far more civilized countries. Their courage in battle
it is unnecessary to praise. But take the race as a
whole, and consider them as they have shewn themselves in matters of government and war during the
last two centuries, and they appear hopelessly stupid,
apathetic, helpless. They have not within those two
centuries produced even a capable military leader ;
and, when they were at their best, in the great days
of Mohammed II. and Suleiman the Magnificent,
they never produced anything else ; no administrator,
no thinker or writer, no poet, no artist. To the
thought or to the wealth of the world they have never
made the smallest contribution. And now they are
obliged to go to foreign races even for their generals.

That the Turkish government **deserves to die is a** thesis I shall not argue, being content **simply to** point to the condition to which it has brought some of the finest countries on earth. It is really not so much a government, in our sense of the **word, as** no government. Some philosopher, impressed by the evils of bureaucratic centralization, has defined the perfect government as anarchy *plus* a street constable. Here you have anarchy *plus* the tax-gatherer. **In this** paradise of *laissez-faire* nothing is done for the people or by the people, while everything is done **to** prevent one-half of them from protecting themselves. **Government is a device** for squeezing, with enormous waste in the process, a certain sum of money out of **the** poorest class, to be spent, most of it on the Sultan's harem and palaces, and the rest on ironclads **and** rifles, **and for** permitting everybody with arms in his hands to seize his neighbour's fields and carry off his neighbour's daughter when he takes the fancy. What has been written about and from Constantinople during the last few months has enabled most people to judge of the character of the Ottoman ministers and their system at the centre of affairs. But things are quite as bad at the circumference as at the centre. The attention of **the** West was so much drawn towards Herzegovina and Bulgaria by the events **of** last summer there that the miseries of the Asiatic subjects of the Porte have been unreasonably forgotten or neglected. They are fully as great as those of the Slavs or Cretans ; and in so far worse that in Europe there exists no large body of tribes making murder and robbery its regular and daily occupation as the Kurds, and latterly the Circassians also, do in Armenia. If any one will take the trouble to read the complaints of oppression and cruelties presented to the Porte by the Armenian Patriarchate in 1872 (since reprinted in England), and some of the more recent statements printed by the Armenians in England on the same topic, he will see that the state of Turkish Asia presents as grave and pressing a problem as that of Bulgaria itself.

It is easy to draw an indictment against the Porte. Details of its weakness and the misdeeds of its officials could be given to any extent, but the theme is so familiar that everybody is by this time either convinced or resolved not to be convinced. Far less easy is it to say what remedy can be applied to these evils, or what sort of government can be substituted for the Turkish. Setting aside annexation to Russia, which would of course be a boon to the Armenians as compared with their present condition, but in itself not a good thing either for the annexed provinces or for Russia herself, the question appears to be whether it is possible to reform the Turkish government, or whether an effort ought rather to be made to do in Asia Minor what was suggested for Bulgaria, and has in large measure been done in the Lebanon, and establish a dependent but practically self-governing state. Such a state could only be Armenia, as the Armenians are by far the most industrious and energetic race in that region, and in some parts outnumber the Mohammedans. They have already a constitution, obtained about 1861, with small elected councils in every parish, which manage the schools and the ecclesiastical property, a representative assembly in each province, and a national assembly, also representative, of 160 members, which meets in Constantinople, and appoints permanent committees for civil and ecclesiastical business, communicating with the Porte through its president the Patriarch.[1] Although this organization is voluntary, that is, has no power of enforcing its will even on the Armenians, it has worked well, and done much to spread education among them, and to apply for the common good such funds as they can save from the rapacity of their enemies. Does the Armenian people then furnish materials for a new political community, or do the conditions exist which could give it a reasonable chance of success?

In the first place, though there are said to be over three millions, some say nearly four millions, of Armenians in Asiatic Turkey, many of them are scattered through the western and southern parts, especially in Cilicia (where some tribes have maintained their practical independence since the fourteenth century, when the kingdom of Lesser Armenia ended), so that in Armenia proper, the country

---

[1] This organization embraces only the so-called Gregorian Armenians, who acknowledge the Patriarch at Etchmiadzin as their spiritual head. They have a Patriarch at Constantinople who is, *quoad spiritualia*, under the jurisdiction of Etchmiadzin. The United, or Roman Catholic, Armenians, with their Patriarch (at present there are two rival claimants), and the Protestant Armenians (numbering about 25,000, and nearly all Presbyterians), remain outside of it. There used to be much ill-feeling between these three sets of Armenian Christians ; but latterly a more liberal and friendly tone has prevailed : the sentiment of nationality is softening down even the spirit of hostility to so-called schismatics.

round the Upper Euphrates and Tigris, there may
perhaps be no more than 1,700,000. There they live,
mixed with a considerable Muslim population of
Osmanli Turks, Tatars, Kurds, and other hill tribes.
No doubt, if an Armenian principality were erected
here, their co-religionists would flock in from other
parts, as they flocked into Russian Armenia from
Turkey after the war of 1829. But even so, their
numbers would remain small, while the untamed
Kurds and other Mohammedans would constitute an
element of difficulty. Moreover, the Armenians, laborious and intelligent as they are, with a capacity for
improvement of which their recent progress gives
ample proof, have been trodden down by the heel of
tyranny for so many centuries as to make it doubtful
how far they are fit for self-government or capable of
self-defence. They may in time recover, as their
awakened national feeling ripens and strengthens, the
courage and political self-confidence which would
enable them to hold their own ; as yet they have not
given such evidence of these sterner qualities as the
Greeks and Servians gave in winning their own
freedom. Besides, there can be little doubt that
Russia would strenuously oppose the creation of a
principality towards which her own Armenian population would gravitate, and whose existence would,
unless she could make its head her own creature,
deprive her of the influence she now exerts in Asia
as the protector of the Patriarch of Etchmiadzin and
of the Armenian nation in general.

In the view of these obstacles, patriotic Armenians

themselves, as well as intelligent Franks who know
the country, seem rather to incline towards the less
revolutionary, but perhaps not really easier, expedient
of attempting, even after so many failures, to improve
the Turkish administration. Respecting a certain
number of the reforms that are needed, there is a
general agreement. Christian evidence ought to be
made necessarily receivable in all courts, and placed
in all points on a level with that of Mussulmans.
The Mohammedan law, whether based on the
Koran or on the Traditions, ought to be declared
inapplicable to causes in which Christians are concerned ; or, in other words, jurisdiction over them
ought to be (as the Hatt i Humayun provided) confined to the so-called Nizam or civil courts, instead of
going to the Sheri or ecclesiastical Mohammedan
courts. They ought to be admitted or required to
serve in the army and the police ; and as it would
probably be found impossible to disarm the Muslim
population, it may, perhaps, be necessary to permit (as
has been done in the Lebanon) the Christians to carry
arms. After all, however, it is not so much changes
in the law that are wanted as more faithful administration of the reforming ordinances so often issued
by successive Sultans, and in practice so constantly
neglected or overridden. How to secure their proper
execution, how to check the corruption and partiality
of the judges and the extortions of the tax-gatherers,
is the real problem.

The plan most commonly proposed is to set up
side by side with the local governor an adjunct,

whether a European consul or some other trustworthy
Frank, who shall watch the governor, report upon his
proceedings, receive complaints from the district of
any oppressions practised there which the governor
may not have properly dealt with, and forward such
complaints, with his own comments, to Constantinople.
Some think such an adjunct ought also to have a veto
on the governor's proceedings, but as this might make
the whole thing unworkable, it would clearly be better
to limit him to the duty of watching and reporting.
But, then, what security is there that these reports
would be attended to at headquarters? The Armenian Assembly, through the Patriarch at Constantinople, makes frequent complaints of wrongs suffered
by their co-religionists; the European consuls sometimes set in motion their respective ambassadors, yet
how seldom and how tardily is redress granted. It
would seem necessary to supplement the local pro-
tectors of Christian subjects by a central commission
at the capital, which could bring a permanent and
effective pressure to bear upon the Porte. And what
what would this be but to put the Sultan's government into tutelage, and involve the European powers
in the dilemma either of themselves administering the
Turkish empire or of seeing their efforts baffled by a
policy of *non possumus* and perpetual delays?

Moreover, it is not merely, perhaps not so much, an
honest purpose and good laws that are wanting to
the Ottoman administration : it is force and power.
Except by sudden and spasmodic efforts, the government cannot make itself obeyed. The police are

inefficient, save for mischief; the irregulars cannot be kept in order; the **Kurds** systematically defy **all** authority, and, indeed, **though living** within the bounds of the empire, have never been properly its subjects. No amount of supervision and reporting will get over this fatal defect of **weakness.**

These are some **of** the difficulties which **will have** to be faced when terms of peace come to **be** discussed, for it is hardly to **be** supposed that things **can be** allowed to fall back to their old footing **without at** least an attempt to better the state of the Asiatic as well **as of** the European **Christians.** Although he would be a sanguine **dreamer who** should expect that any reforms can make Turkish rule satisfactory **or per-**manent, still it may be quite **possible to ensure such a** measure of security for person **and property as** would allow the inhabitants **of these** provinces to advance in numbers, in wealth, and **in** intelligence, and thereby make them ultimately fitter for self-government. **The** European powers effected this in the Lebanon, after the massacre of 1860, by substituting for the Turkish officials local Christian governors and mixed courts, **by** establishing **a local** police force of all races, and excluding the Turkish soldiery. That security would also render **possible another** beneficial influence which **one hears** occasionally discussed on the spot, **I mean** colonization from Europe. **There are, even close to** Constantinople, large tracts of fertile land suitable for the plough and for pasture, which are now lying untouched, tracts where industrious settlers ought to be welcome, and which they might probably have for a merely nominal payment. But it would be necessary for them to come in numbers sufficient to protect one another; roads would have to be made to give them access to the sea, and special arrangements must be made respecting taxation. Nothing would do so much for Asia Minor as an influx of such settlers; and any government but the Turkish would have long ago tried to attract them.

It remains to say a few words on those British interests in the re-settlement of the East of which we have heard so much. I pass by the question how far England would be justified in maintaining a reign of cruelty and oppression for the sake of avoiding certain possible but remote dangers to her own dominion, and at the cost of disgracing her own best traditions and of alienating from her the sentiments of the other peoples of Europe. I propose rather to look at the matter from the most purely sordid and selfish point of view. It does not often happen that the conscience of a nation prescribes one line of policy, and its interest (taking "interest" in the narrowest sense) another; and I think it will appear that this case shews no such divergence.

There are two spots in the possession of which by the Turks our advantage or security is supposed to be involved, firstly Constantinople and the Dardanelles, and secondly Armenia; and there are two modes in which it is supposed that the possession of those spots may affect us, first as regards our trade, secondly as regards our dominion in India. So far as trade is

concerned, it would undoubtedly be an injury to us if
Russia were to become mistress of the Bosphorus. At
present she has a rigidly protective tariff, and may possibly be misguided enough to cling to it for a good
while yet. Her customhouses could check our import
business with the southern shores of the Black Sea
and with Northern Persia, into which we send some
goods *via* Trebizond and Erzerum. However, the
total value of **this** trade is but small, for the bulk **of**
our Persian trade goes to Southern Persia by Bussorah,
and both **Persia and Asia Minor** are poor countries,
daily growing poorer. The utmost loss we could
suffer by its stoppage would not exceed, say, £150,000
a year;[1] and what part would that sum be of the cost
of fighting to protect it? So much for that branch of
our interests.

India, and the route to India, are far more serious
matters. True it is that we conquered India without
the aid of the Suez Canal, and re-conquered it, one
may almost say, twenty years ago, at a time when **we**
were doing our best to discourage the incipient canal
project. Still it will be generally admitted that **the**
freedom of the canal is important, even if far from
vital, to our military position in the East. But how
does Constantinople affect the **Suez Canal?** Simply
in this **way, that it** supplies **a strong,** perhaps an
impregnable position, **where a** fleet might **be** kept

[1] The total value of our imports into Asiatic Turkey during the **year**
1875 was (if I do not mistake, being unable to get at the figures **at** this
moment) not much **over £3,000,000.** Of course it is impossible to estimate exactly the **profit on this** trade, **but it cannot** amount to any very
large sum.

which, in the event of war, could sally out and
annoy us, or, if it could get so far, attack Port Saïd.
If Constantinople were in the hands of an active
naval power, we might have, in war time, to increase
our Mediterranean fleet by three or four ironclads,
and would be strongly tempted to occupy and fortify
a port in some island such as Crete or Cyprus. The
cost of those two operations would not in twenty
years amount to what we should spend in a single
campaign. That is literally all the difference that
the control of the Bosphorus by Russia could make
to India. It would leave her 1000 miles by sea
from Egypt, and a distance of two months' march
by land. How much simpler for her to contrive that
a couple of merchantmen should be sunk in the Suez
Canal. People say she could attack Syria, forgetting
that she is now, in Transcaucasia, nearer to Syria
than she would be at Constantinople. Add to this that
Russia has neither money to build a fleet, which is
now the most expensive engine of war a country can
attempt to use, nor sailors to man it—her Black Sea
fleet has always been notoriously bad, for the plain
reason that she has a wretched mercantile marine—
and the danger of her being able to drive the navy of
England from the sea must appear altogether vision-
ary. What would Nelson have said to such fears ?

It is also supposed that the annexation by Russia
of Turkish Armenia, and in particular (why, it is hard
to divine) of Erzerum, would imperil our hold upon
India. Armenia commands the Euphrates valley,
the Euphrates valley leads to the Persian Gulf, the

Persian Gulf to the Indian Ocean. All perfectly
true, but what are the distances? Why, it is as far
from Erzerum to the Persian Gulf as from Dover to
Belgrade, and there are neither roads nor railways
between. Here, again, the map has much to answer
for ; for, as some one has remarked, people study
these countries in a map on so small a scale that
they are quite misled as to the areas to be traversed
or annexed. Nor is it easy to see what ground
there is for the assumption that the possession of
Erzerum necessarily involves either the desire to seize
or the seizure of Bagdad or Damascus. Such advantages as Russia can require for moving towards the
Persian Gulf her position in Transcaucasia gives her
already. But for the respect which is due to some of
those who appear to have entertained it, the idea of a
Russian attack upon India might be pronounced the
merest chimera, or, as Lord Hardinge used to call it,
a political nightmare. For, even setting aside the prodigious difficulties of the route, we are, as the Russians
know, infinitely stronger as well as better placed for
defending than she for assailing. Supposing, however,
that she should wish to harass us by intrigues with the
frontier tribes, or even to meditate an invasion, she
has a far readier means of access than either by the
Euphrates valley or from Turkestan. Persia is a
country of great natural resources, with a splendid
geographical position between the Caspian and the
ocean, inhabited by a population less warlike and
fanatical than the Turkmans of the Oxus, a population industrious and settled, though reduced by

misgovernment to a point far below its natural level.
Without a fleet, and practically without an army, it
lies at Russia's mercy whenever she chooses to march
eight or ten regiments into it. Some one has suggested that she wishes to conquer Turkish Armenia
in order to attack Persia, as if she were not, with the
command of the Caspian and of the Araxes valley as
far as Djulfa, already admirably placed for that purpose. And from Persia she could menace India much
more effectually than from either Khiva, or Bagdad,
or Antioch.

Russia, however, has shewn no signs of desiring to
acquire Persia. Nor is there any reason to think she
covets the rest of Armenia, having got the most fertile
parts of the Araxes valley already. She certainly
wants Batum, and ought to have it, and may perhaps
take a slice of coast along with it, by way of satis-
fying the vulgar desire to see some tangible result for
a war, and for the sake of gaining an easier approach
from the sea to the Araxes valley. But having no
substantial motive for a large annexation in that
quarter, it is hard to believe that she will make one.
On the reasons above stated, I submit that nothing
which the Czar can do in or obtain by the present war
will make any substantial difference to the special
interests which England has as the mistress of India.
It is upon these special interests that stress has been
laid by the friends of the Porte ; and it is just there
that the case, when looked closely into, breaks down
most completely. The occupation of the Bosphorus
and Armenia would bring him not a day nearer to

Peshawur, nor put us a day farther from Bombay, than we are at this moment.

But it is perfectly true that the acquisition by Russia of Constantinople, or of any considerable territory in either Asia or Europe, would seriously affect the prestige, as it is called, of England in the Levant and Euxine countries, her influence and moral weight. It would also be a misfortune for those countries themselves. The Russian system is too stiff and repressive; Russian officials are too uneducated, too corrupt, too anxious to advance the interests of their own church; in fine, Russia is altogether too imperfectly civilized and enlightened to make the further extension of her power a benefit. For the moment, of course, it would be preferable to the misrule of the Porte; but in the long run it might prevent the growth of something better. Nor do the Christian subjects of Turkey, Greeks or Armenians, wish for her success, except as a means of coercing the Porte. Better the Czar, they say with one voice, than a continuance of present evils; but rather give us, if it be possible, a reformed Turkey, bitted, so to speak, and spurred by Western riders, with as large a measure as may be of local independence. The name of England is still great in these countries. She is regarded with a mixture of admiration and disappointment: admiration as the home of wealth, freedom, and invention; disappointment and surprise as the apparent friend and protector of Turkish oppression. Her interference on behalf of the subject peoples would be welcomed with far greater satisfaction than that of Russia, for it would not be suspected of being a cloak for the aggrandizement of her own church or empire. She is believed to be, if perhaps disposed to favour Mohammedanism, yet at least impartial between the rival Christian sects ; and this alone gives her a great advantage in lands where the jealousy of Greeks, Armenians, Bulgarians, and Roman Catholics is so keen and watchful.

If the fall of the Turkish dominion is only a question of a few years sooner or later, is it not folly to cling to the *status quo*, and make its maintenance the chief aim of our policy ? In the moral and political, as in the material world, there is in reality no such thing as a *status quo :* all is change and motion, if not from worse to better, then from better to worse. England may save the Sultan from foreign invaders, she may aid him to suppress internal revolts. But she will not thereby arrest that sure and steady process of decay which makes his government more and more powerless for anything but evil. She may delay, but she cannot prevent, the arrival, after another era of silent oppression, varied by insurrections and massacres, of a day when the Turkish empire will fall to pieces, and its spoils be shared by powerful neighbours or revengeful subjects.

A wise policy, foreseeing the inevitable, would endeavour to prepare for it, and would seek in the elevation of the native races the means of excluding those neighbours whose real or supposed ambition excites so much alarm. Degraded as they are, after ages of slavery and ignorance, the Christian populations nevertheless offer a more hopeful prospect than the Muslims; yet even the Muslims might, under a firmer and juster administration than they have yet enjoyed, an administration which should secure to every man the fruits of his industry, and give them the chance of learning from the West something more than its vices, become far more capable than they now seem of self-government and of a peaceful union, as equals instead of rulers, in a common state.

Both the power and the ambition of Russia have been grossly exaggerated in this country. Many of us have mistaken her vast area and large population for real strength: most of us have done less than justice to her sentiments and purposes, which, if not ideally disinterested, are probably no more selfish than those of the other great European powers. But supposing the interests of England to be really imperilled by her advance, our true course surely is to remove those grievances which make her influence powerful, and have obliged the Christians of Turkey to look to her for help. It is our supposed indifference to their sufferings that has justified Russia's interference, and has given her the sort of protectorate she claims, and which it is feared she will use to our detriment. And the strongest barrier that could be erected against her further advance would be found in the creation among the subjects of Turkey of communities which would be unwilling to exchange a state of tolerable prosperity and peace under local institutions and officials of their own faith, protected by the Western powers, for the pressure of the Russian bureaucracy and the Russian Church. Those who think worst of the Czars would then see both the pretext and the means of their aggression extinguished, and might regard with equanimity the approaching fall of Ottoman power. No observer of the present condition of Turkey will deny that the process of constructing such institutions will be difficult and its results uncertain. But it is essential to remember that only a choice of evils is offered, and that while the evils of the present state of things are intolerable and daily increasing, such a solution as that which has been mentioned gives at least a gleam of hope for the future, a foundation on which freedom and prosperity may be slowly built up. It is indeed not merely the most promising solution : it is the only solution. Everything else is at best postponement, and leads back, sooner or later, to the same *status quo*, whose fruits are insurrection, bankruptcy, massacre. Each former postponement has only aggravated the dangers and difficulties of the situation, far more grave now than they were in the days of the Crimean War. Further delay may make them insuperable, and may wreck the chance that yet remains of relieving these unhappy peoples from their load of misery, as well as of regaining and strengthening the legitimate influence of England in the East.

LONDON : PRINTED BY WILLIAM CLOWES AND SONS, STAMFORD STREET AND CHARING CROSS.